LIVES BEYOND BORDERS

SUNY series in Multiethnic Literatures

Mary Jo Bona, editor

LIVES BEYOND BORDERS

US Immigrant Women's Life Writing,
Nationality, and Social Justice

Ina C. Seethaler

Published by State University of New York Press, Albany

© 2021 State University of New York

All rights reserved

Printed in the United States of America

No part of this book may be used or reproduced in any manner without written permission. No part of this book may be stored in a retrieval system or transmitted in any form or by any means including electronic, electrostatic, magnetic tape, mechanical, photocopying, recording, or otherwise without the prior permission in writing of the publisher.

For information, contact State University of New York Press, Albany, NY
www.sunypress.edu

Library of Congress Cataloging-in-Publication Data

Name: Seethaler, Ina C., author
Title: Lives beyond borders : US immigrant women's life writing, nationality, and social justice
Description: Albany : State University of New York Press, [2021] |
  Series: SUNY series in multiethnic literatures | Includes bibliographical references and index.
Identifiers: ISBN 9781438486192 (hardcover : alk. paper) | ISBN 9781438486208 (pbk. : alk. paper) | ISBN 9781438486215 (ebook)
Further information is available at the Library of Congress.

10 9 8 7 6 5 4 3 2 1

Für Oma und Mama

CONTENTS

Acknowledgments — ix

Introduction: Reading Memoirs by Immigrant Women in the United States — 1

Chapter 1 A Genre for Justice: Life Writing and Undocumented Migration — 35

Chapter 2 Living Like an Alien: Blackness, Migration, and Depression — 59

Chapter 3 Transnational Adoptee Life Writing: Oppressed Voices and Genre Choices — 87

Chapter 4 (Re)Negotiating the Self: Collective Memoir and Border Crossings — 125

Chapter 5 Life Narratives and the Syrian Refugee Crisis — 147

Epilogue The Power and Future of Immigrant Women's Life Writing — 165

Notes — 171

Works Cited — 185

Index — 207

ACKNOWLEDGMENTS

I could not have completed this book without the support so many people graciously offered. First and foremost, I am grateful to my family, who nurtured my wish to become an immigrant, a state of being that made this project possible. And thank you to Mike Bezemek for our global adventures that gave me the energy to keep going.

It pains me to say that the person who first instilled in me the idea to pursue the topic for this manuscript, Georgia Johnson, is no longer with us. Getting her feedback on the final version would have meant everything. She largely shaped me into the scholar I am today. My initial writing and research also benefited tremendously from the insights and mentorship of Penny Weiss and Joya Uraizee at Saint Louis University.

Since our undergraduate studies, Pascale Cicolelli has believed in my ability to write a book. Our library days laid the foundation for this publication. Likewise, Anna Deters, Shannon Koropchak, and Amy Sattler have always offered companionship, sweets, and murder mysteries when needed. Becoming friends with Amanda Barton, Candis Bond, Michelle Parrinello-Cason, and Emily Tuttle in graduate school was one of the best things that ever happened to me. Our daily interactions, to this day, ease my anxieties and raise my self-confidence. At Coastal Carolina University, I have found my snake squad (do not ask, because I cannot explain)—Tara Craig, Franklin Ellis, Anne Ho, Jaime McCauley, Victoria Knudsen, Jenn Mokos, Jenny Schlosser, Douglas Weathers, Matt Wilkinson, and Lisa Winters—who welcomed me into their community. Kaitlin Sidorsky never refused to let me vent about finishing this project. And everyone at CCU's Center for Teaching Excellence and Learning, including all my colleagues who had to hear about my writing and revision process for years during Faculty Writing Circle sessions, deserves a trophy for their patience.

Crucially, I appreciate the faith that SUNY Press, the anonymous reviewers of my manuscript, and especially Rebecca Colesworthy and Mary Jo Bona have put into this book. Their expert feedback made these chapters immensely stronger.

An early version of chapter 1 appeared as "A Genre for Justice: Life Writing and Undocumented Immigration in Rosalina Rosay's *Journey of Hope*" in *Life Writing*, vol. 12, no. 3, 2015, pp. 309–324. © Taylor & Francis. Preliminary findings of chapter 3 were published as "Transnational Adoption and Life Writing: Adoptee Voices and Stylistic Choices in Jane Jeong Trenka's *The Language of Blood*" in *Meridians: Feminism, Race, Transnationalism*, vol. 13, no. 2, 2016, pp. 79–98. © Indiana University Press.

INTRODUCTION

READING MEMOIRS BY IMMIGRANT WOMEN IN THE UNITED STATES

> Monarchs migrate. This is different than species that emigrate. Species that emigrate only travel one way. Species that migrate travel back and forth between two different places. They have two homes.
>
> —Jane Jeong Trenka (*The Language of Blood* 37)

> Although love of country is required by the Prophet, / one should not live in misery / merely because one was born in a certain land
>
> —Sa'adi (qtd. in Sattareh Farman-Farmaian, *Daughter of Persia* 145)

In her memoir, *The Language of Blood* (2003), South Korean adoptee Jane Jeong Trenka frequently makes reference to monarch butterflies as symbols of her transnational existence. In the first of the epigraphs above, Trenka challenges the notion that immigration has a starting and an end point, instead using the notion of perpetual "two-worldliness." Born in South Korea, raised in Minnesota, and now living again in Seoul, her ongoing negotiation of a multiplicity of homes frames many immigrant women's life writing.[1] *Lives beyond Borders* is interested in how racialized and minoritized immigrant women's rootedness in multiple spaces grows life writing as a social justice instrument that establishes a communal and relational sense of self and offers crucial intersectional insights into varying forms of multilayered oppression.[2]

When Iranian writer Sattareh Farman-Farmaian references the medieval Persian poet Sa'adi in her memoir, *Daughter of Persia* (1992), as seen in the second epigraph above, she bravely declares that the Prophet Mohammed's demand for devotion to one's country of birth cannot justify having to live in "misery." When your place of birth cannot guarantee your well-being or even survival—due to poverty, gender discrimination, or other types of oppression—then, Sa'adi claims, it is a person's human right to migrate. I use both Trenka's insistence on the existence of a transnational self and Farman-Farmaian's appeal to a human right to migrate to develop a more inclusive analysis of immigrant women's life writing.

Due to its long history as a tool of resistance for minoritized communities, life writing provides a fruitful foundation for crucial discussions about migration, intersectionality, and social justice.[3] According to Gillian Whitlock, "autobiography is fundamental to the struggle for recognition among individuals and groups, to the constant creation of what it means to be human and the rights that fall from that, and to the ongoing negotiation of imaginary boundaries between ourselves and others" (*Soft Weapons* 10). To this humanizing effect, Eva Karpinski adds a special focus on immigrant women by stating that "writing as an immigrant woman in the genre of autobiography means writing both in a borrowed tongue and in a borrowed genre—grappling with a legacy of (or indebtedness to?) inherited models of androcentric or mainstream autobiographical representation" (*Borrowed* 2). Like Karpinski, I am intrigued by how "women have consistently attempted to rewrite and remake autobiography, by 'translating' the traditional project of autobiography into new forms and theories of self-representation" (*Borrowed* 13).

Lives beyond Borders seeks to establish that immigrant women's life writing not only modifies literary norms but also has the potential to change cultural and social perceptions that shape traditions, laws, and understandings of nationality and social justice. Such changes might be especially called for in a political climate that, in 2019, empowered the then President of the United States to admonish four female U.S. citizen lawmakers of color to "go back and help fix the totally broken and crime infested places from which they came" (Rogers and Fandos), and when an unprecedented number of arrests of nonviolent undocumented migrants were made under said president's administration (Gomez). In this light, life writing matters because, as Elsa Lechner optimistically asserts, "through life narrative . . . we might get closer to each other and build a common history of peace and respect, regardless of eventual and sometimes radical personal differences" (637).

This book employs Kay Schaffer and Sidonie Smith's definition of life writing as an "umbrella term that encompasses the extensive array and diverse modes of personal storytelling that takes experiential history as its starting point" (7–8). While autobiography is often considered the more sophisticated and literary subcategory of life writing, memoir has established itself as a popular format. According to Sidonie Smith and Julia Watson, memoir "directs attention more toward the lives and actions of others than to the narrator" (*Reading* 198). Whitlock calls it "a form of self-reflective writing that is personal, often conversational, and a meditation about the place of the self in history" (*Weapons* 20). And G. Thomas Couser adds that memoir "has been a threshold genre in which some previously silent populations have been given voice for the first time" (*Memoir* 12). It might not come as a surprise then that publication of memoirs has increased 400 percent between 2004 and 2008 and that, as Ben Yagoda surmises, memoir has become the "form of the culture: not only the ways stories are told, but the way arguments are put forth, etc." (7). Memoir's popularity and its more accessible, relational, and less stylized nature is conducive, I argue, to immigrant women's social justice advocacy.

My discussion of migration, gender, and memoir, is based on Steven Hunsacker's definition of nation as comprised of the "importance of territory, history, and some shared means of self-definition (whether linguistic, religious, or ancestral)" (2). In my understanding of how immigrant women negotiate their identity in their memoirs, the "trans" in transnational implies multiple crossings of places, boundaries, and times, but also captures the possibility of transgression, of "changing the nature of something" (Ong 4). It certainly does not merely capture a singular or binary geographical existence. According to Mae M. Ngai, "a focus on the transnational, with its emphasis on multiple sites and exchange, can potentially transform the figure of the 'other' from a representational construct to a social actor" (60). Representations of migration in a transnational vein establish understandings of a plural sense of self that challenges controlling images of immigrant women, redefines the link between nation and life writing, and demands social action. Considering this transnational focus, it might seem paradoxical that my study limits itself primarily to the writing of women who have migrated to the United States. Yet, I propose that a spotlight on the experiences of female U.S. migrants is instructional as the United States remains a highly desired destination for migrants globally and because the United States has the geopolitical power to shape perceptions of migrants as well as migration policies and patterns worldwide.[4]

My investigations explore the following questions and more: How do immigrant women work with and extend forms of resistant autobiographical writing by feminist and minoritized communities? How does their life writing—which challenges nationalism and established "Truths"—broaden our understanding of the genre as well as of immigrant experience, history, identity, national belonging, and literature? How is our perception of social justice—and its links to gender, nationhood, and artistic and literary engagements—altered when studying female migrants' narratives? My cross-cultural, comparative study of life writing by immigrant women in the United States extends the existing critical work on immigrant life-writing studies. Texts by immigrant women—through genre mixing, figures of a "doubled self," and the inclusion of unconventional elements like fairy tales and crossword puzzles—challenge fixed identities based on nationality, essentialisms, stereotypes, and patriarchal hierarchies to use memoir as a rhetoric of social justice. This book uncovers doubled constructions of identity and reevaluates the purpose and form of life writing for immigrant readers who might find themselves in these narratives as well as non-immigrant audiences who are encouraged to look at migration on a more personal and concrete level.

GENDER AND MIGRATION IN THE UNITED STATES AND WORLDWIDE

In 2017, 44.4 million people (13.6% of the population) had migrated to the United States in their own lifetime. Forty-five percent of them were naturalized citizens while 27 percent were permanent residents. About 23 percent were undocumented (Radford). Historically, the U.S. immigration system is built on family reunification, skills-based entry, diversity (through the so-called visa lottery), and protection of refugees ("How the United States Immigration System Works"). The current Immigration and Nationality Act provides for up to 675,000 annual visas, across all immigration categories, in addition to an unlimited number of visas for spouses, parents, or children under the age of twenty-one of U.S. citizens. The president, in consultation with Congress, sets a limit each year on the number of refugees allowed to resettle in the United States. In order to become a U.S. citizen, immigrants must live in the United States as lawful residents for five years (in some cases three years, such as for spouses of U.S. citizens).

While proposals in the past have pushed for a reform in immigration laws that would prioritize immigrants with higher educational or professional skills levels, the Trump administration linked green cards to education, age, and English language skills as well as prohibited immigrants it deemed likely to rely on public assistance from receiving permanent residency (Krogstad and Gonzalez-Barrera). When he became president, Trump also halted refugee resettlement and significantly lowered the numbers of resettled refugees; he further suggested that the diversity visa lottery should be abolished and announced that the Deferred Action for Childhood Arrivals Program (DACA) would be ended. Under the Trump-Pence administration, the issuance of H-1B visas for highly skilled workers decreased. Additionally, this administration decided to not renew Temporary Protected Status for 98% of about 320,000 people currently living in the United States due to war or natural disasters in their home countries (Krogstad and Gonzalez-Barrera). Last, a 2019 "Remain in Mexico" policy, also ironically known as "Migrant Protection Protocols"—which might be violating international law—is trapping thousands of people legally seeking asylum in the United States in Mexican detention camps, waiting for their court dates (Pitzer). Considering this multilayered attack on immigrant rights in the United States, many people find it crucial to share their stories to speak up for their communities, especially at the intersection of migrant and gender identities.

According to the 2017 United Nations International Migration Report, 48.4 percent of all migrants worldwide are women (15). *Lives beyond Borders* posits that whether they migrate voluntarily or desperately, whether they are trafficked or displaced, their stories matter as they can shape cultural, social, and political reactions to migration in productive ways. But while women are migrating in great numbers, including to the United States, their economic, creative, cultural, and other contributions are still inadequately acknowledged.[5] When immigrant women's existence receives recognition, especially in nonscholarly political and popular contexts, it often reduces them to their supposed hypersexuality and hyperfertility, which are seen as a "threat to racially grounded definitions of national identity" (Guzmán and Valdivia 223). Hence, as Donna Gabaccia illuminates, once more female migrants arrived in the United States, concerns were voiced that "immigrants were no longer the productive and ambitious contributors who had arrived in earlier migrations" (39), and the constant questioning of women's loyalties led to "intensive scrutiny both from other immigrants and from Americans" (xi). To push against such sexist and nativist portrayals, *Lives beyond Borders* makes an intervention in the presentation of women's transnational experiences through the genre of life writing. It builds on a powerful body of scholarly writing about women's life narratives and adds an essential comparative focus on migration, citizenship, and intersectionality. It revises dominant narratives of migration and life writing as immigrant women's life writing disrupts representations of migration and calls into question prevailing historical narratives of nationality and assimilation.

As I will show in the following chapters, innovative negotiations of assimilation forces in the works I study constitute a major divergence from traditional patterns. Much male and European immigrant life writing offers assimilation as a central trope. Nationalist narratives set a seamless assimilation as the ultimate goal of immigration. *The Promised Land* (1912) by Mary (originally Moshke) Antin, for example, describes her Russian self as dying after coming to the United States. Traditionally, the immigration process has been perceived as the loss of the immigrant's original culture, and new immigrants are discussed in terms of their adaptability to American culture and their eagerness to change their identity. They are expected to lose their birth identity as it is supposedly unsustainable in a new country. Only if assimilation occurs is migration seen as successful, and often immigrants are confronted with the burden of proving their Americanness by verifying they have given up their cultural heritage, whether that is a viable choice or not.

In contrast to fantasies of assimilation, female migrants remain at high risk of experiencing exclusion and violence not only because of their gender but also their nationality, migration status, race, ethnicity, class, language, religion, ability, sexuality, as well as possible lack of cultural knowledge and access to support networks. They show remarkable courage and perseverance to overcome structural hardships; their unexamined coping mechanisms differ in important ways from men's. Chapters on the works of authors who were born in Mexico, Ghana, South Korea, Iran, Vietnam, and Syria offer a broad geographical perspective and tackle important current justice issues, such as undocumented migration and the Syrian refugee crisis.

Paralleling immigrant women's social invisibility, many academic and scientific approaches to studying migration used to be male-centered or looked at women merely as dependents of migrating men.[6] According to Gabaccia, when she published *From the Other Side* in 1994, "most histories of immigrants in the United States begin with the experiences of migratory men disguised as genderless humans" (xi). Since the 1990s, feminist researchers have, in larger numbers, started to challenge approaches that ignore gender, and with a strong recent research focus on female migrants within the U.S. care industry, gender is becoming a more and more essential methodology in studies about global human movements (e.g., see Hondagneu-Sotelo). With this book, I follow Gabaccia's call to "write more monographs on immigrant women . . . [and] identify topics that beg for comparative study" (xiii).

While all migrants share some of the same risks and experiences, women's reasons for migrating, levels of bodily safety during migration, and life after migration can be vastly different. As Christiane Timmerman and colleagues clarify, "personal migration motives and decisions are influenced by gender roles and positions, which are highly dependent on the opportunities that men and women have to migrate. . . . Men and women have different migrant networks, which lead to divergent migration experiences; [and] the existence of a gender ideology that penetrates all spheres of society" affects people's opportunities differently (8). We can, thus, gain invaluable insight into migrant lives from focusing on women and, in particular, their life writing, an approach that the social sciences have mostly ignored. Because stories written by non-celebrity women-of-color only rarely receive support from publishers in the United States (Rak 133), the complex information that immigrant women's lives make available is often lost.

Lives beyond Borders follows Cynthia Huff's call to "foreground the existence and importance of women's writing traditions" with a specific focus on immigrant women (4). I analyze the memoirs of female migrants that build on a rich history of modifications that women and minoritized communities have made to traditional autobiographical techniques, which center authority, rationality, legitimacy, and universality in the white, male, heterosexual experience. Indeed, "deploying autobiographical practices that go against the grain, [a female author] may constitute an 'I' that becomes a place of creative and, by implication, political intervention" (Smith and Watson, "Introduction: De/Colonization" xix). The women whose works I discuss adapt practices to establish a communal authorial subject and a subjectivity dedicated to equity and survival that sensitizes the public toward social justice issues in their communities. They powerfully share immigrant women's pain and resilience.

RESEARCH QUESTIONS AND METHODOLOGY

In *Scattered Hegemonies* (1994), Inderpal Grewal and Caren Kaplan proclaim that effective transnational feminist analysis needs to be interdisciplinary, transnational, and intersectional in its comparison of cultural divides and must take cultural, social, economic, and other differences into consideration without relying on ethnocentrism. In this book, then, I accept Grewal and Kaplan's challenge to design a comparative project that is interdisciplinary (ranging from literature to Women's and Gender Studies to Political

Science to Social Work), intersectional (being conscious of connections between immigrant women's identity markers such as race, gender, ethnicity, nationality, class, and religion and how these intersections shape access to power and experiences of oppression), and transnational (following women's movements between Mexico, Ghana, South Korea, Iran, Vietnam and the United States, as well as between Syria and Turkey). In my application of intersectionality as an analytical framework, I am deeply indebted to the Combahee River Collective's 1977 "Black Feminist Statement," which declares the "multilayered texture of black women's lives" (328), as well as Kimberlé Crenshaw's seminal 1991 essay, "Mapping the Margins: Intersectionality, Identity Politics, and Violence against Women of Color," in which she conceptualizes intersectionality as "multilayered and routinized forms of domination that often converge in . . . women's lives, hindering their ability to create alternatives" (1245).

I began this manuscript as an international student from Germany on an F1, non-immigrant visa. Since then my status has changed to that of a permanent resident through a marriage-based green card. I, thus, write as a racially privileged, transnational subject myself, and my research is necessarily informed by my own moving between national spaces and cultures. I am acutely aware of the differences that separate authors, readers, and critics in this scholarly endeavor and attempt to read and analyze my case studies ethically and empathically. I certainly strive for a feminist methodology and epistemology. Leaning on Sandra Harding's approaches to establishing a feminist standpoint, I value women's diverse experiences and emotions as a powerful methodological tool. Much like the memoirists in this study, I perceive my writing, research focus, and methods as political.

In a 2018 special issue of *a/b: Auto/Biography Studies* on "Lives outside the Lines: Gender and Genre," Eva C. Karpinski and Ricia Anne Chansky specify that the intent of the collected articles is "not to ascribe gender to specific genres or to decide who performs gender in their chosen genre more successfully than others, but, rather, to explore the nuances of generic particulars in a manner that allows us to better grasp the means by which medium extends the potential for expressing gender in life narratives" (507). I emulate these objectives in this book. I view the structures that immigrant women resist and write against through feminist and postcolonial frameworks and, consequently, shift between autobiographical, feminist, and postcolonial theoretical lenses. I expose different ways of knowing and show how cultural and historical values, interests, and unexamined assumptions affect the production of these women's life writing and the nature of their experiences. I discuss power in the political and symbolic realms and systems of oppression at the intersection of gender, race, class, and citizenship.

My use of the concept of citizenship is shaped by Lisa Lowe's claim in *Immigrant Acts* (1991) that "although the law is perhaps the discourse that most literally governs citizenship, U.S. national culture—the collectively forged images, histories, and narratives that place, displace, and replace individuals in relation to the national polity—powerfully shapes who the citizenry is" (2). Rooted in a postcolonial perspective, I analyze how colonialist, imperialist, and neocolonialist practices and ideologies influence female migrants' identity formation processes as well as their practices of challenging master narratives and perceptions of citizenship and nationality. Through an interdisciplinary approach, I hope to answer, among others, the following questions: How and why do female immigrants adapt the norms of memoir? What identity formations and performances do they advocate? How do they use life writing as a political tool? Are they successful in challenging patriarchal constructions of knowledge?

Aware that "the 'I' of reference is constructed and situated, and not identical with its flesh-and-blood maker" (Smith and Watson, *Reading* 71), I contend that life writing offers a powerful and emancipatory site for the analysis of immigrant women's identity formation and their agenda of resistance. Aihwa Ong demands that studies of migration patterns take into consideration "everyday meanings and action . . . as a form of cultural politics embedded in specific power contents" (5). Life-writing texts, I propose, offer excellent access to these kinds of stories. Because memoirs tend to be concrete in their depictions of lived experiences, they can deliver nuanced insights and further our understanding of women's transnational lives.

The textual choices in this book reflect my wish to focus on texts, writers, demographic groups, and geographical regions that have not received enough academic attention. While only six core texts cannot capture the complexities and experiences of all immigrant women, I treat these memoirs as case studies that offer insights into prevalent *patterns* regarding the identity formations and political messages in immigrant women's writings. Much like the writers in *This Bridge Called My Back* (1981) employ life writing to acknowledge and celebrate differences and demonstrate their exclusion from systems designed by the white heteropatriarchy, the writers in *Lives beyond Borders* create a community across cultures, sexualities, and nations to demand social justice for minoritized peoples. All writers in this book are linked in their acknowledgment of mutual oppression based in forces of racism, sexism, capitalism, and colonization, which makes an intersectional approach to reading these women's life writing absolutely essential.

WOMEN'S LIFE WRITING AND THE RELATIONAL SELF

The "power to say 'I' and to be heard is not something everyone can take for granted" (Karpinski, *Borrowed* 225); but immigrant women rely on a long history of feminist life-writing techniques that made it possible for marginalized populations to voice their selves. The analysis of women's autobiographical writing became an established field, taking women's experiences into consideration in the early 1980s (Smith and Watson, "Introduction: Situating Subjectivity" 5). Essential texts on the characteristics of female life writing include, among many others, Domna Stanton's *The Female Autograph* (1984), Estelle Jelinek's *The Tradition of Women's Autobiography: From Antiquity to the Present* (1986), and Sidonie Smith's *A Poetics of Women's Autobiography: Marginality and the Fictions of Self-Representation* (1987). These critics revealed how women's life narratives push back against the traditional autobiographical subject that is marked as "male, white, propertied, . . . socially and politically enfranchised" as well as, I would add, able-bodied (Smith and Watson, *Reading* 116). Sidonie Smith and Julia Watson elaborate that conventional autobiography "entwines the definition of the human being in a web of privileged characteristics. Despite their myriad differences, of place, time, histories, economies, cultural identifications, all 'I's are rational, agentive, unitary. Thus the 'I' becomes 'Man,' putatively a marker of the universal human subject whose essence remains outside the vagaries of history" ("Introduction: De/Colonization" xvii). *Lives beyond Borders* builds on a strong foundation of scholarly insights into how women have manipulated the genre to represent their experiences that are not subsumed by a supposed male and privileged universality.

Critics have commented on memoir's "transgressiveness" and its "resistance to norms" (Kusek 38, 45) and, crucially, on its accessibility to "ordinary readers [as well as] non-literary writers" (Rak, "Are Memoirs" 323). Philosopher Helen Buss dissects how women's memoir "reveals the hidden thing, the forbidden knowledge, the shameful and guilty secret, and to make what was formerly a private matter into public knowledge" (12–13). Importantly, feminist scholars of women's life writing have established the feminine self as relational and communal. Susan Stanford Friedman posits that women's autobiographical writing shows the interdependence of their relationships, which defies Georges Gusdorf's articulation of autobiography as autonomous and individualistic, which was seen as theoretically foundational for the genre of life writing. Instead, Friedman sees life writing by women demonstrate a "sense of shared identity with other women, an aspect of identification that exists in tension with a sense of their own uniqueness" and that allows for a fluidity between themselves and other members of their communities ("Women's Autobiographical Selves" 44). Huff claims succinctly that women writers "did not follow the romantic conception of the isolated artist, but more relational and communal patterns" (5). In her groundbreaking reading of autobiographical works by Julian of Norwich, Margery Kempe, Margaret Cavendish, and Anne Bradstreet, Mary Mason identifies relationality and feminine imagery as core characteristics of women's life writing. According to Mason, "grounding of identity through relation to the chosen other, seems . . . to enable women to write openly about themselves" (22). Women's writing is marked by an insistence that their stories and identities are worth knowing (33), which is a belief upon which the writers in *Lives beyond Borders* construct their own narratives.

Paul John Eakin claims that, in fact, all life writing is relational, producing a self that stands in context with other selves. He writes that "all identity is relational, and that the definition of autobiography, and its history as well, must be stretched to reflect the kinds of self-writing in which relational identity is characteristically displayed" (Eakin, *How Our Lives* 43–44; emphasis in original).[7] In Eakin's theory, "the self's story [is] viewed through the lens of its relation with some key other person" (86). Often taking the form of children writing about their parents, this technique "affords the opportunity to speak the previously unspoken, to reveal what was hidden or suppressed" (87), such as family trauma like mental illness, alcoholism, or incest. Friedman adds that not "essences or absolutes, identities are fluid sites that can be understood differently depending on the vantage point of their formation and function" (*Mappings* 47). As I will exhibit in the following chapters, immigrant women find usefulness in this kind of relational and fluid identity in their life writing to expose systems of intersectional oppression.

In his analysis of Native American autobiography, Arnold Krupat observed a communal self that presents a "synechdochic relation of part-to-whole" (220). I connect Krupat's ethnic synechdochic self, which captures an "individual life as comprehensible foremost in relation to the collective experience of [the] tribe" with the feminist theories of relationality I mentioned above to support my discussion of immigrant women's self writing that focuses on social justice for their communities (229). For the women whose work I investigate, the self is central, but it is depicted as encompassing more than just one life to secure their communities' well-being.

Women of diverse identities have always molded life writing to fit their experiences and communication needs. Anne Goldman presents in *Take My Word* (1996) the " 'literary' qualities of 'extraliterary' texts—books marketed under the rubric of sociology, labor history, or cultural studies—in order to explore how [ethnic working-class women in the United States negotiate] the desire to speak autobiographically . . . in narratives that simultaneously write the self and represent the culture(s) within which that self takes shape" (x). Goldman analyzes, for example, cookbooks by Hispanic and African American women and women's collective narratives published by Jewish labor unions and reveals how "the speakers and writers [she] consider[s] . . . maneuver between autobiographical and politicalcultural texts, between 'I' and various forms of 'we' " (xxvii). Despite adopting a relational self, these stories "manage to be socially engaged without submerging individual voice in collective history" (Goldman xv). It is this use of innovative stylistic techniques and communal subjectivity for a political purpose that I have also observed in the books that comprise the core of *Lives beyond Borders*.[8]

Caren Kaplan, in "Resisting Autobiography" (1992), calls nonconforming autobiographical practices—like the *testimonio*, collective autoethnography, biomythography, or prison narratives—"out-law genres," which "challenge Western critical practices to expand their parameters and, consequently, shift the subject of autobiography from the individual to a more unstable collective entity" (134). Kaplan problematizes autobiography's rootedness in nationally confined identities at the expense of showing the fluidity of subjectivities and borders, which buttresses nationalistic rhetoric of intrinsic and insurmountable difference. In *Subjectivity, Identity, and the Body* (1993), Sidonie Smith includes autobiographical manifestos in this category. My study adds to these interrogations about genre boundaries and identity by looking at how the intersections of gender and immigration status influence memoir as the writers' bodies are not only marked female but also considered "alien."

Throughout, I will focus on issues of embodiment and how patriarchy, capitalism, and imperialism use gender, race, disability, and other identity markers to label, dis/respect, and besiege different bodies in distinctive ways. As Sasha Kruger and Syantani DasGupta allege, "the desire to study, categorize, understand, and ultimately demean the bodies of racialized and nonnormative others is a part of the ableist, patriarchal white-supremacist project, as is the belief that those in the center have no bodies, skin, hair, or genitalia to remark upon" (483). Because this voyeurism can make life writing a place of violence, the "key is embodiment for and by the telling self as opposed to embodiment demanded and required by the more powerful receiving other" (Kruger and DasGupta 485). The women writers in my book proudly center their identities and push back against the othering gaze to establish their memoirs not as entertainment but as political tools to "access counterhistories to dominant social narratives as well as break the silence around embodied oppressions" (Kruger and DasGupta 484).

Like other out-law genres, immigrant women's writings bring to light alternative creations of communal and individual identity and novel forms of subjectivity and agency, and they emphasize marginalized experiences, issues, and knowledge. Due to the intense connections between patriarchy, oppression, and migration that shape immigrant women's narratives, their focus is especially on techniques for survival and human rights negotiations. These women's main project with their life writing is to effect political change in their nations of birth and their current places of residence; my ultimate goal in this book, then, mirrors theirs—to further our understanding of these women's and our own social and political worlds in a way that reveals the urgency of profound political and social change.

THEORIES ON IMMIGRANT LIFE WRITING

As Whitlock asserts, "subaltern subjects are not voiceless and nor are they victims, however their visibility, legibility, and audibility are tactical, contingent, and constrained" (*Postcolonial* 8). She further confirms that life writing affords "those who lack social, cultural, and political power . . . agency and carefully defined authority" (*Soft Weapons* 18). I am interested here in how immigrant women use life writing to have their voices heard, to push back against their victimization, and to create the tactical visibility to which Whitlock refers. My study builds on earlier achievements of immigrant female life writers, who have shown that "migrant texts legitimize alternative forms of subjectivity, knowledge, literacy, and offer counter-discourses to the dominant ones" (Karpinski, *Borrowed* 226).[9] Whitlock adds that the field of postcolonial life narratives has broadened the limits of autobiography beyond the "rational, sovereign subject that is conceived as western, gendered male and . . . racially white" as well as "assumptions about autobiographical authorship and authority [that] prioritize authenticity, autonomy, self-realization, and transcendence—western Enlightenment values" (*Postcolonial* 3). The works at the heart of *Lives beyond Borders* contribute to this widening of the genre.

According to Heike Paul, immigrant literature has been "viewed predominantly in a national setting and has been analyzed as articulating . . . processes of formations of national identities along the lines of race-ethnicity, gender, and class" (1). Indeed, early critical analysis of specifically life writing by immigrants to the United States was Eurocentric in its approach. Its origins lie in William Boelhower's *Immigrant Autobiography in the United States* (1982). Boelhower's work was groundbreaking in arguing that similarities exist between ethnic groups; before him, the predominant assumption was that such literary works embody group-specific experiences. Despite its inclusive title, however, *Immigrant Autobiography* discusses only male Italian immigrants' lives and includes mostly second-generation works. Boelhower problematically treats "immigrant autobiography" as equivalent to "autobiography of Americanization."

Sau-Ling Cynthia Wong's "Immigrant Autobiography: Some Questions of Definition and Approach" (1992) challenges Boelhower's approach by showing how male and female Chinese immigrant memoirs deviate from his definitions, claims, and prescriptions. I see a similar departure from Boelhower's theory and a reconstruction of the purpose of life writing in the works I analyze. For example, Chinese immigrants, according to Wong, do not see the United States as a mythical land, but show a "pragmatic, matter-of-fact attitude" toward immigration (155). The Mexican immigrant Rosalina Rosay (whom I discuss in the next chapter), too, admires the United States as a place that offers toothbrushes, commodities so expensive in her Mexican village that her family cannot afford them. I build on Wong's astute observations in my comparative inquiry and hope to expand her findings in a more global and feminist context.

Despite critical work on life writing and migration, more studies need to address the concerns and questions that steer this book. In *Reading Autobiography*, Smith and Watson cover immigrant autobiography only sparsely and present a definition of the term under the heading "*Ethnic life narrative*" (194; emphasis in original). They offer the following brief point about immigrant life writing's importance: "Immigrant narratives and narratives of exile become sites through which formerly marginal or displaced subjects explore the terms of their cultural identities and their diasporic allegiances" (107). Autobiography as a narrative site *can* serve as a tool to negotiate cultural locations. It *can* effectively capture identity formation practices of an immigrant subject-in-process. The connection of "site" with "former" marginality seems to me a textual and cultural problem that needs to be investigated. Why can immigrants only write autobiography once they have moved from the periphery to the center? Do all immigrants necessarily desire to become part of the center? Why is their textual placement paralleled with their cultural placement?

As Paul—whose *Mapping Migration* (1999) analyzes how women migrants use creative writing to connect identity and location—proclaims, "women's immigrant writing has re-invigorated the genre of immigrant literature" (1); and much important critical work, especially in the field of American Ethnic Studies, has looked at women of diverse backgrounds and with intersectional identities in the United States. Dolores Mortimer and Roy S. Bryce-Laporte's *Female Immigrants to the United States: Caribbean, Latin American, and African Experiences* (1981) is considered one of the foundational studies of the experiences of women-of-color immigrants in the United States after the Immigration Act of 1965. Mortimer and Bryce-Laporte examine how an increase in women migrants affected the United States socially, politically, and economically as their intersectional identities increased angst about the impact of the feminization of migration particularly on issues of labor, overpopulation, and representation.

Alixa Naff's collection of Arab immigrant testimonies in the United States, *Becoming American* (1993), importantly foregrounds women's voices and the important role they played as peddlers and shopkeeper in the integration process of their communities. Huping Ling's *Voices of the Heart* (2007) collects oral histories of Asian immigrant women from a wide range of countries who settled in the Midwest. The stories speak to these women's hardships, goals, strength, and successful cultural negotiations to raise healthy families. They negate stereotypes of Asian women as silent, submissive, and passive. Martha Cutter investigates in *Lost and Found in Translation* (2005) how writing by ethnic Americans raises "questions about the feasibility of inhabiting multiple linguistic worlds and creating multiple ethnic cultures" (2), looks at how migrants develop a "new mode of voice, language, or subjectivity . . . that meshes—but also exceeds—prior subjectivities or languages" (3), and investigates a "struggle to transcode the meaning of ethnicity itself so that one can be both ethnic and 'American'" (5). In *Sucking Salt* (2006), Meredith Gadsby analyzes how Caribbean women use the cultural and historical significance of salt in the Caribbean in their fiction and poetry to fight creatively various forms of oppression and tackle hardships in their communities.

While not focused specifically on issues of gender, Rocío G. Davis, Jaume Aurell, and Ana Delago's *Ethnic Life Writing and Histories: Genres, Performance, and Culture* (2007) looks at life writers who "consciously negotiate issues of ethnic self-representation and history" (10). The chapters in their collection explore the "intersection between the discourse, practice, and social function of life writing, history, and ethnic identity" (12). Davis, Aurell, and Delago find that ethnic life narratives "challenge dominant mainstream versions which have often hidden, misrepresented, or invalidated [ethnic communities'] stories" (13) and that they bring "hidden or disenfranchised stories back to life, firstly as access to a valid identity for themselves and then as a usable past for a community" (17). Furthermore, the collection exposes how autobiographical texts can "attain a sense of group identity, which may serve as a basis for political mobilization" (18). It is this use of life writing as a means for collective identity development, community survival, and politicization around social justice efforts on which I focus my reading of immigrant women's memoirs.

Rather than centering in assimilation and ignoring the pains that come with it, the analysis of and a theory about immigrant women's life writing need to be focused on reading the narratives of immigrant women with regard to how they navigate the conflicting demands that their intersecting identity markers place on them. Especially postcolonial and poststructuralist approaches to life writing and subjectivity capture this "nonunitary, indeterminate, nomadic, and hybrid nature of a linguistically constructed identity" (Friedman, *Mappings* 47). Speaking about Asian immigrants' writings, Traise Yamamoto proposes that reading such texts as being about "'becoming an American' suggests that the writers themselves have accepted the terms and their own implied status as (former or present) outsiders" (110). Instead of consenting to outsider status, immigrant women, I suggest, courageously redefine what it means to be American. Studies about immigrants' assimilation patterns show that, in contrast to male migrants, women often do not seek to assimilate fully to the national identity of their new country of residence, but tend to create their own personal, fused identity. To them, American culture does not appear as a static concept to which one must conform, but as a flexible construct to which they can contribute (Pearce, Clifford, and Tandon 248). In doing so, gender identity seems more important to them than national identity, as for "women it is about becoming an American *woman*" (Pearce, Clifford, and Tandon 246; emphasis in original); they aim to secure for themselves and their children the erosion of traditional gender roles, more personal freedom, and education. Based on immigrant women's self-perception, it is important to question concepts such as hybridity as not merely suggesting "the assimilation of . . . immigrant practices to dominant forms but [as] instead mark[ing] the history of survival within relationships of unequal power and domination" (Lowe 67). As their life writing demonstrates, survival is at the heart of many women's migration, not the specific desire to become American.

LIFE WRITING AND NATIONALITY

Ricia Anne Chansky accentuates the power that life writing has to facilitate notions of belonging at a time when large-scale diasporic movements and waves of displacement destabilize national identities: "The potential multiplicity of national identity (identities) and the complications that arise from imagining a transnational self are vital . . . Comparatively reading auto/biographical narratives . . . holds the promise of promoting understandings of both the other and the self, as separate and intertwined agents" (5–6). She adds that "understandings of national identities are not stable; they are made, broken, and remade among the constant mutability of globalism" (14–15). *Lives beyond Borders* adds to these necessary conversations about nationality, identities, and relationality on a global scale.

Life writing as a genre is inherently tied to ideas about nationality. Analyzing trauma and self-representation in works by Dorothy Allison, Mikal Gilmore, Jamaica Kincaid, and Jeanette Winterson, Leigh Gilmore remarks that "the cultural work performed in the name of autobiography profoundly concerns representations of citizenship and nation. Autobiography's investment in the representative person allies it to the project of lending substance to the national fantasy of belonging" (*Autobiographics* 12). Autobiographical texts and their representations of the individual influence how the national community defines itself and how identity traits are used to shape policies of inclusion and exclusion and, in the U.S. context in particular, ideologies of meritocracy and individualism.

Julie Rak inserts that memoir, specifically, "is one of the genres of writing that is about the movement from private to public. For this reason, it often contains ideas about citizenship, and it is taken up within other debates about the meaning of individual experiences in the public realm" (212). Life writing has historically been used as a vessel to convey how "Western eyes see the colonized as an amorphous, generalized collectivity" (Smith and Watson, "Introduction: De/Colonization xvii). Hence, it has buttressed a master discourse "that has served to power and define centers, margins, boundaries, and grounds of action in the West" (Smith, *Subjectivity* 18). In turn, imaginations of nationalism are decidedly masculine.

Huff exposes, for example, how Benedict Anderson's highly praised *Imagined Communities* (1992) feeds sexist analytical approaches: "By focusing on mainstream national symbols and cultural practices, Anderson slights the voices and texts of women and the intricacies of their subjectivities as these influence nation-building" (7). Life writing by immigrant women, as I demonstrate, contributes meaningfully to our understanding of how women influence conversations about nationality.

After the terrorist attacks of September 11, 2001, and the invasion of Iraq, the United States has experienced a memoir boom, which, according to Rak, "participated in and reflected changes in how Americans understood themselves as citizens of a public" (35). This particularly traumatic time period necessitated a redefinition of what it means to be American, and the memoir genre promised to deliver the knowledge needed to negotiate that definition. Rak continues that "memoir makes many people feel connected, and it connects individual feelings to group ideas. Therefore, citizenship—and not narcissism—should be a key way to understand the popularity of memoirs with many American readers at the present time" (33). The memoir boom, then, constitutes an opportune moment for immigrant women to add their experiences to common, often xenophobic and exclusionary, understandings of U.S. citizenship.

Concurrently, as Leigh Gilmore establishes in *Tainted Witness: Why We Doubt What Women Say about Their Lives* (2017), the boom has been accompanied by a backlash against and discrediting of especially women's memoir and crafted a popular form of neoliberal life writing that does not acknowledge systemic oppression but puts the burden for a fulfilled life solely on the individual. Such works do not challenge systems, nor do they encourage their readers to become politically active. Texts in this subfield stand in stark contrast to autobiographies by women of color who "transformed nonfiction" "by establishing it as a newly important form for a civil rights era" (Gilmore, *Tainted Witness* 90). Maya Angelou's *I Know Why the Caged Bird Sings* (1969), Audre Lorde's *Zami: A New Spelling of My Name* (1982), and *This Bridge Called My Back: Writings by Radical Women of Color* (1981) edited by Cherríe Moraga and Gloria Anzaldúa, among others, generated a "politicized 'I' of self-representation" and offered "historical or political analysis or contextualization" to expose minoritized people's oppression (Gilmore, *Tainted Witness* 92, 93). The memoirs I investigate build on this social justice legacy with a special emphasis on issues of nationality, belonging, and citizenship.

The symbiosis between nationality and life writing, according to Whitlock, has further led to the establishment of autobiography as an "alterity industry" based in the sensationalization of suffering for a Western readership (*Soft Weapons* 15). Whitlock claims that current geopolitical situations have created an audience for memoirs that preserve a north-south divide. Purchasing global memoirs functions as "a way of indicating cosmopolitan tastes, openness, sympathy, political commitment, and benevolent interest in cultural difference" (Whitlock, *Soft Weapons* 55). Whitlock designates such life writing as "soft weapons" that can be co-opted and commercialized for their exoticization of cultural difference and used to justify Western military and other interventions in nations that are deemed threatening; at the same time, they are effective vessels "to describe experiences of unbearable oppression and violence across a cultural divide" (Whitlock, *Soft Weapons* 55). This dichotomy inherent in memoirs' affect informs my discussion of immigrant women's memoirs and their political power.

Western societies, especially, tend to see immigrants as large categories of identity, conflating their backgrounds with often toxic outcomes, such as the current political rhetoric that the United States is being overrun by "caravans" of Latin American migrants. I am interested in how immigrant women use life writing to individualize their experiences while also speaking up in support of their communities. As the women in this book describe, wide-spread conflation exists in U.S. media, popular culture, and popular opinion of all Latinx peoples, migrants from various African countries and African Americans, Asians and Asian Americans, as well as members of specific branches of Islam and different Muslim-majority countries. If life writing as "alterity industry" is written for Western eyes, the genre is complicit in reducing non-Western identities to amalgams that, I argue, can be easily abused for xenophobic purposes.

That is why it is crucial to pay attention to immigrant women's life writing, which destabilizes supposedly clearly defined concepts such as "immigrant," "home," and "nation." Jane Trenka's adoption memoir, for example, expresses traumatic struggles with being seen as neither American nor Korean and attempting to re-negotiate what family, community, and national identity mean for her. A disruption of "clear" and "established" narrative techniques—as captured, for example, in Trenka's disinterest in a chronological plot line unaffected by trauma—allows for feelings of being "at home" and "homeless" at the same time. Such redefinitions call for courage. For many members of minority groups, "home" has historically connoted shelter, for example from racism, and nurture. bell hooks, in "Homeplace (A Site of Resistance)" (1990), powerfully observes how African American women have established homeplaces as radical, political "spaces of care and nurturance in the face of the brutal harsh reality of racist oppression, of sexist domination" where the oppressed "could strive to be subjects, not objects" (384).

But just as hooks points to efforts within the African American community "to change that subversive homeplace into a site of patriarchal domination" (388), 'home' for many immigrant women conjures up experiences of oppressive hierarchy and inflexible gender roles. Instead of accepting the real possibility of "not belonging" and not being seen as a subject, they create a "relationship between home, identity, and community that calls into question the notion of a coherent, historically continuous, stable identity and works to expose the political stakes concealed in such equations" (Martin and Mohanty 296). Embracing this volatile sense of self complicates life writing's reliance on a clearly defined national background.

Autobiographical works that express doubleness on multiple identity levels can be a critical means to change national master narratives and to rupture hegemonic representations of nation, immigration, assimilation, and belonging. For example, the nine writers (including Rigoberta Menchú, Maxine Hong Kingston, and Richard Rodriguez) whom Hunsacker discusses in *Autobiography and National Identity in the Americas* (1999) "imagine new versions of the community against dominant forms of national identity in an attempt to clear space for themselves within otherwise restrictive national situations" (5). I am particularly attentive to how the ways in which immigrant women practice memoir may alleviate injustice caused by social misrecognition through which immigrant women are constituted as problematic objects, often as hypersexualized and putting at risk the existing "national identity" through their child-bearing; in giving voice to the experiences, demands, and self-interpretations of minoritized groups, immigrant women's life writing challenges narrative conventions that are non-inclusive as they are based in white, European experiences.

Because their lives are just as much informed by the people and conditions in their land of origin as by their new home, immigrant women do not position themselves as the sole heroines of their own life-writing texts but expose a plural sense of self by projecting the voices of those who are rarely heard to effect social change. Concerning this form of identity formation, Yamamoto makes a connection between (immigrant) women's life writing and other marginalized groups when she points to a "group consciousness, a sense that the individual is not an extirpated self" (108). Such a sense of self that is marked by multiple nations, cultures, and languages and perceived as communal creates notions of belonging rooted in social justice that differ from a mono-national identity, even if these women gain U.S. citizenship.

LIFE WRITING AND SOCIAL JUSTICE

While the United States signed the Convention on the Elimination of All Forms of Discrimination against Women, they never ratified it. This means that U.S. legislation is not bound to the treaty's demands "to incorporate the principle of equality of men and women in [the states'] legal system, abolish all discriminatory laws and adopt appropriate ones prohibiting discrimination against women" (CEDAW). In light of such law-making and -ignoring, immigrant women's rhetoric of human rights serves a paramount purpose of spreading knowledge about global women's rights violations. Life writing can function as a "crucial complement to legal or governmental action . . . [by] acknowledging the moral complexities of human rights abuse," and it can facilitate the "development of empathy and community" (Jolly 5, 7). Immigrant women's memoirs reveal the rhetorical ways—such as appeals to their audience's ethos and pathos—in which the authors breach the divide between the public and the private, using a personal genre as a tactic to recognize their communities' humanity and dignity.

While it is hard to gauge the influence these memoirs have on their readers—besides the information I gathered through reviews—I share Whitlock's opinion that "testimony can create a piercing and transformative 'bearing' witness that triggers advocacy, responsibility, and accountability, which move the reader and produce collective 'witnessing publics,' [even if they] are temporary and contingent collectives" (*Postcolonial* 9). We have seen such positive effects, for example, with the use of testimony in movements for truth and reconciliation in South Africa and Australia. Whitlock continues elsewhere that "life narrative is instrumental in debates about social justice" in that it may "inspire readers' imaginations to rethink communicative ethics in ways that engage with difference" without either identifying with or othering the author (*Soft Weapons* 13). Yet, Whitlock makes clear that such "empathic witnessing" demands "an appropriate cultural and political milieu" (*Soft Weapons* 77). Readers' ethical response to life writing about experiences with oppression is certainly not a given.

In this vain, each of the following chapters presents the rhetorical means by which the works discussed challenge master narratives of belonging and identity with counter-histories of oppression that can destabilize social, cultural, and political hierarchies. Immigrant women's memoirs refuse to fulfill readers' expectations for "'stock' stories [of trauma], which are familiar and therefore already known" (Cubilié xii). Such stories are often filled with clichés and do not reflect the actual voices of oppressed peoples, which furthers their dehumanization and othering. Instead, female migrant life writers demand what Anne Cubilié calls "ethical witnessing that can open up the possibility of justice" (12). Cubilié argues that ethical "witnessing . . . becomes an ongoing process rather than a narrative and demands from us, the audience to the witnessing, an equally ongoing, often failing, fraught witnessing to the witnessing" (15–16). This effect on the ethical reader renders both testifying and witnessing into political acts, which is why my case studies align with Cubilié's writers in calling for "an engaged, ethical witnessing of atrocity that opposes the disengaged, guilt-ridden viewing of atrocity-as-spectacle that many forms of spectatorship take" (11). This demand certainly will not reach all readers equally, but it promises to at least move some toward responsible and engaged allyship.

In *Narrating Contested Lives* (2015), Katja Kurz scrutinizes how human rights campaigns on female genital mutilation, child soldiers, and human trafficking use life writing to "humanize their causes" (3). While Kurz looks at texts that were bestsellers and authored by well-known public figures, her findings that life writing on human rights issues can create empathy in the reader and that it can "give value to lives and . . . define what it means to be human" are crucial for my analysis of migrant women's life narratives (35). This is especially pertinent since the implementation of women's rights as human rights is affected by the issue that "while concerns of cultural relativism arise with respect to human rights generally, it is striking that 'culture' is much more frequently invoked in the context of women's rights than in any other area" (Charlesworth and Chinkin 222). Cultural traditions are often used to explain and excuse violations against women.

Uma Narayan emphasizes how cultural relativism is intrinsically connected to essentialist, colonialist notions of Third World countries (87). It is especially in this context of culture that immigrant women's memoirs can offer valuable insight into different backgrounds that may lead to a better understanding of various forms of sexism. Linda Alcoff reminds her readers that a pervasive set-up of privileged groups "speaking for or on behalf" of the less privileged "has actually resulted (in many cases) in increasing or reinforcing the oppression of the group spoken for" (485). The women writers in this book aim to abolish this detrimental, paternalistic process. Thomas Larson proposes that memoir offers a groundbreaking medium for dissenting voices hiding behind the liberal ideology of self-development common in popular autobiographies, such as Benjamin Franklin's (188). I am interested in how immigrant women use this potential for subversive rhetoric regarding common understandings of nationality and social justice in making readers connect their own lives with the ones about which they read.

Life-writing texts have the ability to petition changes in human rights legislation. Schaffer and Smith, in *Human Rights and Narrated Lives* (2004), make persuasive connections between human rights issues, the law, and storytelling, stating that "over the last twenty years, life narratives have become one of the most potent vehicles for advancing human rights claims" (1). They claim that the "stories [survivors] tell can intervene in the public sphere, contesting social norms, exposing the fictions of official history, and prompting resistance beyond the provenance of the story within and beyond the borders of the nation" (4). After all, a memoir, *A Memory of Solferino* (1859), led to the adoption of the Geneva Convention in 1864.[10] Schaffer and Smith see life writing's power in its humanization of "categories of people whose experiences are frequently unseen and unheard" and its "legitimating process of telling and listening that demands accountability on the part of the states and international organizations" (3). These texts also provide minoritized people with a venue to "push the parameters for interpreting what constitutes a right" and to whom laws should apply, as well as with a means to offer a critique of exclusion (Schaffer and Smith 227). Schaffer and Smith discuss the human rights violations against comfort women, aboriginal tribes in Australia, Chinese protestors at Tiananmen, and prison inmates. Many of these examples have received much attention elsewhere. It is my hope to add to this existing conversation by looking intersectionally at issues of gender and migration.

Schaffer and Smith speak to the challenges in using life narratives for human rights purposes such as the need to conform a personal narrative to the "standardized, often chronological, format" of human rights abuse protocols and to offer "evidence" (37); additionally, witnesses might see themselves ontologically as "we," which goes against the standard first-person eye-witness account commonly used in human rights narratives. All works that are part of my study indeed challenge prescribed, official formats of human rights testimony and embrace a relational, communal subjectivity. Schaffer and Smith add that publication decisions have been heavily influenced by a persistent "popularity of narratives of victimization" and a demand for the "commodification of suffering" (6, 27). These requests for a portrayal of victimization and passivity are at odds with what I perceive as the main aims of immigrant women's writing rooted in a portrayal of women's strength and agency.

Immigrant women ask their readers to see them as more than objects or passive victims, but as sharing the same humanity and as worthy of the same legal treatment. Meri Danquah, in *Willow Weep for Me* (1998), for instance, appeals forcefully to Black women migrants' rights to a safe and respectful environment that grants them access to medical treatment and mental health support systems. Joseph Slaughter, in *Human Rights, Inc.* (2007), explores the connection between literature and the law, which supports my understanding that migrant women's life writing can have political implications. Slaughter states that the law and literature serve similar purposes as they are both "discursive regimes that constitute and regulate, imagine and test, kinds of subjects, subjectivities, and social formations; [and] they are 'machines for producing [and governing] subjectivity' and social relations" (8). He continues that in "contrast to the weakness of legal apparatuses, cultural forms like the novel have cooperated with human rights to naturalize their common sense" (25). Slaughter sees the bildungsroman and human rights ideals as similar since "each projects an image of the human personality that ratifies the other's idealistic visions of the proper relations between the individual and society and the normative career of free and full human personality development" (Slaughter 4).

While *Lives beyond Borders* concerns itself with memoirs and not fiction, I perceive the bildungsroman's social power "as the predominant formal literary technology in which social outsiders narrate affirmative claims for inclusion in a regime of rights and responsibilities" as also captured in the autobiographical writings by immigrant women (Slaughter 27). Like the bildungsroman, the works I analyze function "as a cultural surrogate for the missing executive authority of international human rights law, expanding its purview by projecting the social and cultural conditions out of which human rights might be recognized as commonsensical" (Slaughter 29). Especially Slaughter's concept of "human rights literacy" resonates with what immigrant women want to convey to their audience, namely, "the capacity to read [one]self and others as human rights persons, as creatures of dignity and bearers of international rights and responsibilities" (23–24). Life writing can provide a counter-discourse against aggression, indifference, or mere pity to humanize in the eyes of the audience those groups that are socially excluded because they are seen as a worthless other. Whereas the bildungsroman and international human rights law "do not begin by imagining in what the rightless . . . consist [but] by imagining the normative, rights-holding citizen-subject—an abstract 'universal' human personality" (Slaughter 42–43), I see the importance of immigrant women's memoirs particularly in their depictions of a specific, individualized, and intersectional identity experiencing oppression and rightlessness. Cubilié proposes that human rights discourse "always already presumes a body that has rights and can be protected—a body that is visible within such a juridical system" (21–22). The life writing I analyze attempts to make visible marginalized communities' experiences in a positive instead of merely pathologized realm and to establish minoritized individuals as worthy of legal protection, not just prosecution.

Their writings give immigrant women an opportunity to change their audience's perceptions of their communities, which often stand in the way of passing or executing human rights laws; such change is conceivable as "our reading practices are themselves implicated in the possibility and project of realizing a world based on human rights" (Slaughter 44), which renders analyzing these memoirs' impact on readers a socially and politically essential project. Life writing offers immigrant women the medium to add narratives about the human side of migration and rights violations to existing political and sociological representations. They themselves possess the most authority to describe their own lives and present the root causes for migration; they offer a balancing force vis-à-vis anti-immigration policies and public discourse.

As Schaffer and Smith assert, witnesses telling their stories "take risks. They hope for an audience willing to acknowledge the truthfulness of the story and to accept an ethical responsibility to both the story and teller. There is always the possibility, however, that their stories will not find audiences willing to listen or that audiences will ignore or interpret their stories unsympathetically" (6). In the end, the "powerful and relatively privileged retain the right to confer or refuse recognition" (Schaffer and Smith 232). The writers in this book aim to create forms of life writing that demand "readers . . . accept and relate to difference at the expense of a certain and secure sense of self" (Schaffer and Smith 232). As I will elaborate, in creating sympathy and solidarity in their audience, these women strive to mobilize people to political action that protects and extends social justice.

A NEW READING OF IMMIGRANT WOMEN'S LIFE WRITING

The fact that immigration is still largely discussed as a male phenomenon by politicians, many media outlets, and the broader public alike affects the production and reception of female immigrants' life writing. The persistent ignoring of their experiences results in a lack of power for these women. Miranda Fricker forcefully claims in *Epistemic Injustice* (2007) that this injustice "wrongs someone in their capacity as a subject of knowledge, and thus in a capacity essential to human value . . . [;] where it goes deep, it can cramp self-development, so that a person may be, quite literally, prevented from becoming who they are" (5). Epistemic injustice applies to immigrant women in the United States. Their experiences are oftentimes ignored, which deprives them of their agency and the right to be acknowledged as knowing more about their own lives than researchers or social workers.

Fricker identifies "hermeneutical injustice" as one of two kinds of epistemic injustice and defines it as *"the injustice of having some significant area of one's social experience obscured from collective understanding owing to a structural identity prejudice in the collective hermeneutical resource"* (155; emphasis in original). Because immigrant women often belong to less powerful social groups, based on their gender, residency status, religion, place of birth, or other identity categories, the larger community of knowers dismisses their experiences. Their life writing serves as important tools with which they try to fill those "blanks where there should be a name for an experience" (Fricker 160). They name their experiences to fight structural injustice and turn themselves from spectacles into subjects. Parin Dossa agrees that "the task at hand is to recognize [in this case displaced] women as producers of knowledge. Only at this level can we understand the extent to which socioeconomic forces are implicated in their suffering" (5). It is of paramount importance that life-writing criticism and migration studies recognize what is at stake in these women's writings. I hope that *Lives beyond Borders* will accelerate the process.

In their portrayal of immigrant women's subjectivity, the texts I analyze link politics to literature and connect power with cultural construction. As Karpinski reminds us, life writing can be impactful due to the "threat that irreducible heterogeneity and plurality of life forms, events, and idioms poses to various regimens of monolingualism, normativity, and domination" ("Migrations" 171). With their non-linear, non-singular selves, immigrant women further expand the notion of memoir as an "I" genre due to their awareness of themselves as part of collective oppression. They politicize their life writing to portray the need for changes in cultural systems that discriminate against women and necessitate their migration. Their writing is woman-centered, speaking to immigrant women's strength, determination, and ingenuity. In depicting how migration, for women, is linked to issues of resistance and survival, immigrant women's life writing challenges a pervasive "romanticization of movement, migrancy, and border-crossing" as signs of freedom and agency (Hesford and Kulbaga 307).

These memoirs make clear how migration is marked by power and privilege, how some can move freely at the expense of others, and how the regulation of women's movement is falsely seen as a measure of safe-keeping. The texts show that where women are allowed to go determines who they are allowed to be. They make readers realize the connections between patriarchy, theories of race, and xenophobic attitudes. In pushing back against fixities and binary oppositions of East/West, insider/outsider, foreigner/citizen, which pervade discourse about ethnicity and nationality, immigrant women writers procure visibility and value for their experiences and voices. They scrutinize memoir for its complicity with their oppression and manipulate the genre in order to erode the distinctions between "national" and "alien," "home" and "abroad," "local" and "global," "foreign" and "American." They promote the idea that migrant women occupy multiple identities—such as transnational migrant, woman of color, resident alien—rather than a static national self that is unchanging.

Because of their emphasis on intersectionality, female immigrants' writing strongly refutes supposed characteristics of immigrant autobiographies. In "Making Ethnic Autobiography" (1992), Boelhower claims that immigrant autobiography is characterized by a "rhetoric of consent" to American ideals and by the necessity of a dying old self and the appearance of a new American self (133, 128).[11] Examples of such autobiographies include *The Americanization of Edward Bok* (1922), a Dutch immigrant's life story, and Antin's *The Promised Land* (1912). The features of immigrant life writing change when it is produced by women without European heritage; they clearly and intentionally do not praise assimilation and conversion as the only viable paths for living in the United States.

For migrants who have faced legal and cultural exclusion in the United States, it is difficult to establish themselves as the sovereign, representative American self. Their life writing's main focus is not on describing their transition from alien status to full citizen, especially since for many immigrants becoming "American" does not necessarily mean belonging or participating in the nation-state due to sexist, racist, or xenophobic practices. Instead, they write to revise commonly accepted rules for national belonging. None of the texts I analyze in this book fits the description of "autobiography of Americanization."

Life writing portrays the self as mediated through nationality and positioned within national ideologies and values. As Rak demonstrates, memoir impacts "the way that Americans think about public events and think about themselves as citizens of a powerful imagined community" (41). In playing with the ideological connection between life writing and nationalism, immigrant women express a national doubleness to confront citizenship laws and concepts of identity formation and transnationality that are based in exclusion. Iranian writer Nahid Rachlin, for example, dedicates half of her memoir, *Persian Girls* (2006), to the life her sister leads in an abusive marriage in Iran. Her sister's letters and Rachlin's fictional stories about her sister's life co-constitute the author's subject. As autobiographies "at the limit," immigrant women's works "explore representations of personhood that are skeptical of dominant constructions of the individual and the nation" (Gilmore 13). They challenge constructions of commonly accepted definitions of identity and nationality. Their life writing proposes that difference should not prohibit belonging. Their fluid identity goes against hegemonic forms of nationality dependent on the loyalty to one nation-state, which makes immigrant women's memoirs a subversive force at the crossroads of life writing and nationality.

Instead of primarily offering retrospective writing to celebrate an autonomous individual, to illuminate one's identity formation, or to come to an understanding of oneself as a coherent self and the meaning of life, immigrant women's memoir functions as persuasive rhetoric for political action. Much like out-law genres, the writings studied here "renegotiate the relationship between personal identity and the world, between personal and social history. . . . [and they] are tied to a struggle for cultural survival rather than purely aesthetic experimentation or individual expression" (Kaplan 130). Immigrant women intentionally make the personal political even if they do not openly self-identify as feminists. For them, memoir offers a way to create a platform for the culturally silenced—such as Asian birth mothers, Black women with mental health issues, undocumented immigrants, women trapped in patriarchal marriages, and refugees.

Immigrant women's life writing strengthens women's human rights; it constitutes a timely and important tool to reach an audience that can demand change regarding the implementation of social justice efforts for oppressed groups. The United Nation's Universal Declaration of Human Rights started formalizing the discourse about human rights in 1948, and the Convention on the Elimination of All Forms of Discrimination against Women (CEDAW) of 1979 fights violence against women and the subordination of women in the private sphere. Especially women's rights provisions, however, are prone to inadequate enforcement due to weak and vague language that asks states to take "'all appropriate measures'" and, hence, provides patriarchal states immense leeway in dealing with their failure to provide for their female inhabitants' welfare (Charlesworth and Chinkin 220).

In contrast to the mostly dry, jargon-filled, and often very complicated language of human rights, life writing promises to provide insight into how the abstract nature of laws translates into actual lived experience. Memoirs by female international migrants can push, for example, for the recognition that human rights violations happen within the family, supposedly a protected sphere for women. As they are practiced right now, human rights are men's rights, based in male views of economy, work, politics, the environment, and other influences on our lives.[12] Hence, the women in *Lives beyond Borders* embrace an intersectional social justice framework disconnected from the white, male heteropatriarchy to have their voices heard.

THE SCOPE OF THIS BOOK

Rosalina Rosay's entry to the United States as an undocumented immigrant, which is at the center of her memoir *Journey of Hope* (2007), signifies the complicated relationship between Mexico and the United States. Since 1909, with the start of the first major wave of immigrants from Mexico to the United States, the two nations have been engaged in a battle about the meaning of these movements. Internally, the United States is caught between the desire for Mexican immigrants as cheap laborers and calls for their deportation to protect U.S. national identity. The legal situation is especially controversial for the more than eleven million undocumented migrants in the United States (Baker and Rytina 1). In 1977, President Carter proposed, for the first time, amnesty for undocumented immigrants, but also suggested the construction of a border fence. Twenty-five years later, President Obama's executive order "Consideration of Deferred Action for Childhood Arrivals" (DACA) implemented provisions so that undocumented immigrants enrolled in high school who entered the United States as minors were able to gain legal residence if they had lived in the United States for at least five consecutive years and were in good standing. The Trump administration ended the policy in 2017 and directed substantial sums toward extending "the wall."

While gender oppression plays a crucial role in migration processes from Central and South America, it goes ignored by politicians and the media who emphasize capitalist interests and supposed issues of national security—a deficiency that Rosay challenges vehemently in her memoir. I argue that Rosay's *Journey of Hope* manipulates the memoir genre by writing her text in the form of the relational testimonio—traditionally connected with collective social activism—but marketing it as a memoir appealing to American individualism. As a trickster text, disguising its form and ambitions to raise social awareness, *Journey of Hope* calls on readers to see undocumented immigrants as economic refugees who should not be excluded based on stereotypes but should be granted human rights.

Memoirs by female migrants from Africa, which are the focus of chapter 2, are still relatively rare in the United States. When taking into consideration the whole continent, roughly 4 percent of all annual immigrants to the United States are from Africa. Yet, many migration researchers believe the African continent to be the source of the next big wave of immigrants to the United States (Halter and Johnson 14, 7). Many African migrants report that their motivation for leaving their home country is rooted in a desire "to lift themselves individually and collectively from the strains of abject poverty, economic morass, political strangulation, and a host of epidemiological and health-related concerns" (Arthur 12). A majority of these migrants pursue the goal of improving the conditions for those whom they left behind (Arthur 7). My objective in chapter 2 is to analyze how Ghana-born Meri Nana-Ama Danquah speaks to the social invisibility of female African migrants in her memoir *Willow Weep for Me* (1998).

Willow Weep for Me focuses on Danquah's struggle with clinical depression and offers powerful observations about migration and disability. Scholars have used Danquah's work as an example of how mental illness affects African American women and how the intersectionality of gender, class, and race nourishes prejudices against them.[13] Many studies, problematically, neglect to explore Danquah's experiences as a Black, female *immigrant*. I am particularly interested in how the author adapts life-writing techniques to speak to Black migrant women's fight for survival. *Willow Weep for Me* deliberately mixes genres—memoir, self-help book, reference book—and tells the stories of multiple Black women's struggles with depression to make a powerful commentary on issues of identity, assimilation, racism, and agency.

With my discussion of Jane Jeong Trenka's memoir, *The Language of Blood* (2003), in chapter 3, I add to the field of literary criticism on transnational adoption life writing. Trenka's immigration was made possible by an elaborate transnational adoption system that brings orphans from Asia, Eastern Europe, and South America to mostly middle-class, white families in the United States and Europe. In 2004 (the peak year of global transnational adoptions so far) and 2005, the United States alone issued over 22,000 visas for transnationally adopted children from a wide range of countries. Even though the numbers have since gone down to 4,059 between October 2017 and September 2018 (United States Department of State), transnational adoptees constitute a significant immigration population whose voices are often ignored. To date, South Korea is the country that has sent the most adoptees abroad. More than 200,000 South Korean children, the majority female, have been adopted internationally. South Korea was only surpassed as the lead sending country to the United States by Romania in 1991 and by China in 1995 (Melosh 193). While children have been exchanged between countries since there have been nations, the formal and rescue-narrative-based version of transnational adoption on a large, systematic scale started with the transfer of mixed-race babies of Asian women and American GIs during World War II and, more intensely, during the Korean War.[14] Kimberly McKee calls the established system the "transnational adoption industrial complex (TAIC)," "a neo-colonial, multi-million dollar global industry that commodifies children's bodies" that ensures the supply of and demand for adoptable children via a collaboration of multiple nation states, orphanages, adoption agencies, and well-off adoptive parents (*Disrupting* 2).

McKee further discusses the system's connections with the U.S. military industrial complex that created stigmatized mixed race babies whose mothers were shunned as prostitutes (*Disrupting* 7). Since these "GI babies" "presented a possible weapon that the communists could seize upon in the ideological battle to discredit the United States and its Cold War expansionism" (Kim 48), U.S. media portrayed transnational adoptees as objects of humanitarian and religious concern. After the war ended, an underfunded welfare system in South Korea perpetuated the adoption of supposed orphans in the 1970s and '80s, a time when white babies available for adoption were becoming rare commodities in Europe and the United States due to better access to reproductive health techniques, such as birth control and abortion, and a decrease in stigmatization of single motherhood (Kim 217). While popular media and opinion tend to celebrate adoption as an act of mercy—especially for girl children who are labeled as refugees bound to suffer in their countries of birth—much scholarship has voiced criticism of the transnational adoption system, and many adult adoptees have expressed trauma through writing.

With a new generation of transnational and transracial adoptees coming of age, it is essential to look at the possibilities and limits of the life-writing genre as a critical method to process childhood experiences and to make sense of a complex identity.[15] *The Language of Blood* serves as a crucial case study due to its experimental approach to capturing Trenka's experiences. I claim that Trenka cannot encompass her doubled and fragmented self within those norms of autobiography that prefer a singular self. To confront this limitation, she expands the genre and includes, among other elements, plays, a fairy tale, and a crossword puzzle. This technique allows Trenka to experiment with her identity and to offer a platform for the voices of poor birthmothers whom the transnational adoption system pathologizes and silences.

Chapter 4 centers on acclaimed writer Nahid Rachlin's migration from Iran and her memoir *Persian Girls* (2006). Studies estimate that about one million Iranians live in the United States (Malek 357). Two major migration periods become apparent: The first period triggered by U.S. involvement in Iran encompasses immigrants between 1950 and 1977. The second wave started immediately before the Islamic Revolution of 1979, with people fearful of the new regime leaving Iran, and ended in 1986 with the Iran–Iraq War (1981–1988) (Bozorgmehr and Sabagh 6–7). Prejudice against people of Iranian descent escalated during the Iranian Hostage Crisis (1979–1981) and has persisted due to the Iranian government's fundamentalist politics. Arguably, these same stereotypes influenced President Trump's 2017 Executive Order 13769, also known as the "Muslim travel ban," which severely limited the entry of people from majority-Muslim countries to the United States. Rachlin's journey from Iran to the United States presents, much like Trenka's adoption, a particular case of female migration. Rachlin entered the United States on a student visa before the Islamic Revolution, a time when young Iranian women were only rarely allowed to travel on their own, let alone live by themselves in a foreign country. Her work speaks vividly to the sparsely examined gendered nature of the reasons for and experiences with migration.

Rachlin's memoir takes the doubleness in the previous chapters to an extreme as it portrays both Rachlin's story of seeking education in the United States to escape an oppressive government in pre-revolutionary Iran and also her sister's life in an arranged marriage in Iran. The memoir presents these women's identity as communal, with Rachlin's sister serving as a stand-in for Rachlin and seemingly living the life Rachlin would have experienced had she not left Iran. As a collective memoir that includes letters, short stories, and imagined episodes of the main subject's sister's life, *Persian Girls* advocates powerfully for women's autonomy.

Chapter 5 seeks to make connections between the published life-writing texts I analyze in the previous chapters and various forms of life narratives that have come out of the current Syrian refugee crisis. I build on conversations about historic experiences of global refugees, such as during World War II or Cubans seeking political refuge in the United States, which have been pioneered by critics such as Hannah Arendt in *The Origins of Totalitarianism* (1951). I contend that analyzing specifically refugees' live narratives can make insightful contributions to our understanding of political power, sovereignty, and bio politics, among other crucial concepts.

Books by current refugees are predictably rare at this point in time. In analyzing *Inside Out and Back Again* (2011), Thanhha Lai's lyrical novel based on her own journey to the United States as a Vietnamese refugee in the 1970s, I hope to shed light on common experiences displaced people have. I then compare Lai's writing to some of the tweets by Bana al-Abed, a young Syrian refugee girl, who has reached notoriety for her horrific updates from war-torn Aleppo. After being evacuated to Turkey, Bana was offered a book deal by Simon and Schuster, which resulted in *Dear World: A Syrian Girl's Story of War and Plea for Peace* (2017). My discussion of *Dear World* adds to our understanding of refugee life writing as an essential subcategory within the genre that deserves further attention at a time in history when we are seeing the largest movement of people globally since World War II.

The conclusion elaborates on the relevance of my study for policymakers. I suggest that connecting life writing by immigrant women with political theories of immigration could prove beneficial to decision-making processes in social, economic, and political spheres. This conclusion points to the potential for critical exchange and mutual furtherance among human rights campaigns, migration research, legislators, and studies on immigrant women's life writing.

1
A GENRE FOR JUSTICE
LIFE WRITING AND UNDOCUMENTED MIGRATION

Life writing is intrinsically connected with issues of nationality and gender and offers unique opportunities to challenge these very same, supposedly rigid concepts. It is, thus, perhaps not surprising that autobiography is one of the most important forms in Latinx literature as it "challeng[es] the sociocultural framework" of idealized versions of Americanness (Torres-Saillant 65). In this chapter, I interrogate what meaning memoir carries for undocumented female immigrants from Mexico through an analysis of Rosalina Rosay's *Journey of Hope* (2007).[1] In the context of Mexican American/immigrant life writing specifically, it is essential to "examine the various ways in which autobiographical expression emerged from social rupture and was formed within a matrix of dislocation, fear, and uncertainty that shaped contradictory but exigent responses" (Padilla 10). The examinations leading to such statements about the origin and nature of Latinx life writing have historically been based on the texts of second generation Chicanos/as and, to a large extent, male writers, which makes Rosay's memoir a fruitful case study.

    I analyze Rosay's text as an example of a mixing of life-writing genres that opens up new venues for immigrant women to voice how the intersections of gender, ethnicity, nationality, religion, and economic status affect their experiences with oppression and mark migration processes. Ultimately, I read *Journey of Hope* as a trickster text operating within the generic frameworks of *testimonio* and *métis*. With the term "trickster text," I refer to the book's ability to pose as a narrative hailing the United States, while, at the same time, it subtly pursues a very political, radical agenda to effect political and social change. Evaluating Rosay's memoir critically in such a way can contribute to our understanding of what memoir represents for undocumented migrants and provide important commentary that informs our readings of texts by immigrant women.

Journey of Hope tells the story of Rosay's poor upbringing in a village in 1960s Mexico and of her migration to and education in the United States.[2] Rosay is acutely aware that being confined to the domestic realm limits women's lives. She understands that, as Gloria Anzaldúa elaborates forcefully in her ground-breaking work *Borderlands/La Frontera*, "culture (read males) professes to protect women. Actually it keeps women in rigidly defined roles" (39), and she uses her life as an example to encourage women like herself to venture outside the realm of domesticity, which falsely carries the attribute of being the only safe space for women. Sexism and extreme economic need intersect and necessitate Rosay's migration as a young girl when her father, who moved to the United States to avoid political turmoil in his home village, refuses to send remittances back to his family. Rosay's mother, who has endured domestic violence for many years, decides not to accept this male dominance passively and instead migrates to the United States to confront her husband: "Ma realizes it will be hopeless to stay in the Pueblo. Pa will not be sending us money and there are no jobs any of us can get" (75). In order to secure survival for herself and her children, Rosay's mother uproots herself to follow her husband. While for the young women in Rosay's family moving constitutes an exciting prospect, it signifies an immense burden for Rosay's mother, who has never lived outside her village and does not speak or understand English: "Ma, who is in her early fifties, finds the crossing very difficult. The group has to run over rocky hills at night for many hours" (76). The plan is for Rosay's mother to take enough of her husband's money and make some money of her own to return to the pueblo within a few months. But without the necessary (language) skills, it is impossible for Rosay's mother to procure the needed funds, so Rosay herself joins the rest of her family in the United States.

In its detailed depiction of women's reasons for migrating, *Journey of Hope* presents its audience with a unique opportunity to hear stories of undocumented migration and the topography of displacement from a woman's perspective.[3] Rosay challenges dominant understandings within the American population about so-called "illegal" immigrants. Sonia Saldívar-Hull writes: "We have to look in nontraditional places for our theories: in the prefaces to anthologies, in the interstices of autobiographies . . . in the essays published in marginalized journals not widely distributed by the dominant institutions" (46). Rosay works as an accountant in Los Angeles and is not an established author. Her text, published by a very small press, offers such a chance for theorizing.[4] It exhibits the kind of insights to which highly praised and well-discussed authors like U.S.-born Anzaldúa have second-hand access.

Although life-writing studies and Chicano/a studies are booming sectors of literary criticism, U.S. Latinas still have comparatively few opportunities to read texts that speak to their own experiences. This is even more so the case for undocumented immigrants to the United States who are usually relegated, at times for protection of their identity, to a life of silence. With her memoir, Rosay writes against this trend, depicting undocumented migrants' everyday lives and their humanity. Place is a driving force in her narrative as she describes the artificiality of borders for families and makes clear how essential mobility and the freedom to choose a place of residence are for securing survival and personal independence.

While some critics tend to see the U.S.-Mexico border from a purely theoretical point, Rosay clarifies in her writing that it is impossible for (undocumented) immigrants to see the border merely as a metaphor. Borders silence; they arbitrarily separate communities and exacerbate movement politically, culturally, and linguistically. Undocumented writers share with the rest of the Latinx community the "experience of diasporic uprooting and the sense of living outside the dominant realm of the receiving society" (Torres-Saillant 63). But for Rosay more is at stake; publicly naming her experiences constitutes an empowering and subversive act for her as she overcomes systematic misogyny and xenophobia to promote social transformation.

Writing against undocumented immigrants' oppression and silencing, Rosay uses the oppressor's language and images to gain access to her desired audience and to influence their opinions on immigration. Through her technique, Rosay "mimes the subjectivity of universal man," a location, as Smith elaborates in *Subjectivity, Identity, and the Body* (1993), which "proffers authority, legitimacy, . . . readability . . . [and] membership in the community of the fully human" (155). As being considered human affects a community's survival, Rosay's changes to the autobiographical "I" and the purpose of the genre take on an urgent character. In reviving the testimonio with new intent for immigrant writers, Rosay's work shows how migration patterns are gendered and underscores immigrant women's fight for agency.[5] Life writing—unmarked by a stable, identifiable, preferably U.S., nationality—turns from a genre strictly recounting an individual's experience into a catalyst for social change.

UNDOCUMENTED MIGRATION AND GENDER

Journey of Hope demonstrates undocumented migration's intersectional character as it is not only racialized and shaped by class status but also fundamentally linked to gender. Rosay witnesses physical and emotional violence especially due to the misogyny of her patriarchal home culture. From the very beginning, when Rosay introduces the reader to her years as a little girl in a poor Mexican village during the late 1960s, she exhibits an astounding gender consciousness. She questions early on that her brothers do not have to do any house chores: "Pa said house chores were only for women" (Rosay 77). Realizations such as this one about the division of labor lead her to an analysis of women's status in Mexico at the time of her childhood. Rosay questions women's roles in their families and culture and demands an equal voice. She explains that her mother had ten children, not including the ones who died: "Most women my mother's age had eight, nine, ten kids, often giving birth to babies around the same time as did their oldest daughters" (Rosay 11). Her explanations speak to the lack of opportunities for women and their entrapment in family life, child-rearing, and domesticity and show that the gender oppression in her family is systematic.

These sexist limitations directly affect Rosay, as "by the time [she] was about six or seven years old [she] already knew that [she] faced a lifetime of poverty and deprivation. . . . [Her] father felt that girls did not have to be educated, since all they were going to do with their lives was to get married and have babies" (13). Gender bias manifests itself in a part of her life that is extremely important to Rosay: her education. Her enthusiasm regarding school makes her realize there can be more to womanhood than marriage. Yet, pushing her father for the right to a more extensive education is not a viable option because "you are a traitor to your race if you do not put the man first" (Moraga 95). As an education can constitute a way out of poverty and gender oppression, Rosay lives the reality that classism and sexism intersect. Because of this momentum, she does not prioritize gender over class or ethnicity. It is always clear that all three forces influence her life simultaneously.

Rosay points to the oppression of women not only in terms of missed opportunities but also in the context of domestic violence: "I was six years old when I saw Father being violent for the first time. . . . Papa comes in with a rusty old machete threatening to kill [Ma]. Ma calls him a coward. Why don't you ever do this when my older sons are here" (31). While in this instance Rosay's mother exerts power in verbally confronting her assailant and Rosay is still convinced that "he would never hurt any of us or our mother" (32), at other times Rosay makes it very clear how far the physical abuse went: "Her [Rosay's mother's] face was unrecognizable, black eyes, swollen face, and lips twice the regular size" (33). Based on her analysis of women's status in the Mexican family, Rosay understands that her mother does not have many options to exit her marriage. She clearly portrays the family as the "cornerstone of male domination" (Garcia-Bahne 44). Through cultural training within the family, devastatingly executed to a large degree also on the part of women, young girls in traditional patriarchal societies are reared and socialized to see themselves as wives and daughters instead of independent human beings.

As sexism is interconnected with other forces of oppression, the gender injustice in Rosay's family creates forms of violence besides her father's physical abuse. Rosay painfully describes how her mother "never hugs or kisses [her children] and she is worse to [Rosay] than to [her] brothers, sister, or cousins. [Rosay] know[s her mother] does not beat [her] brothers because boys are more valuable than girls" (22–23). The male-centered society in which she lives affects Rosay physically and psychologically. In essence, Rosay gets punished for not being male. Her comments reflect Anzaldúa's observations about her own mother, that "her allegiance was and is to her male children, not to the female" ("La Prieta" 201). In her memoir, *Loving in the War Years* (2000), U.S.-born Cherríe Moraga empathizes with her mother's oppression due to her class, gender, and ethnicity and analyzes that "through her son [her mother] can get a small taste of male privilege, since without race or class privilege that's all there is to be had. The daughter can never offer the mother such hope, straddled by the same forces that confine the mother" (94). Because of her low social status, a daughter cannot offer a mother any chance of social mobility, which perpetuates the oppressive cycle.

All three writers mentioned in the paragraph above describe how their mothers become accomplices to their own and their daughters' oppression, which creates a traumatic experience for Rosay as she struggles between love and hate for the woman who nurtures yet also punishes her for being a girl: "After every beating, I hate Ma and wish that she would die. I hate her for hours even though I sort of know why she is so mean" (23). Even though Rosay does not openly discuss her mother's situation as "oppression," she does not blame her mother because she understands her actions in the face of misogyny. Rosay's comments on how her mother was married very young and "had a baby every other year and nursed it for as long as possible" support my reading (23). She does not portray her mother as a villain but shows how she is a victim of multiple layers of oppression and how her actions are consequences thereof.

Journey of Hope clarifies that it is not only one's gender and socioeconomic class that decide how one is treated and which opportunities one has in life, but that these identity markers further intersect with colorism (a concept denoting prejudice based on skin tone) and bias against native looks to create unique forces of oppression for Latinx women.[6] Studies show that a preference for lighter skin and European facial structures persists among white people and systems of power based in whiteness, such as the legal and educational systems, as well as within communities of color globally due to the lasting effects of slavery and colonialism. For instance, dark-skinned women tend to get longer prison sentences in the United States (Viglione, Hannon, and DeFina), and darker girls are expelled from schools at higher rates than light-skinned girls in the United States (Hannon, DeFina, and Bruch).

Rosay explains how in her culture your skin tone and facial features significantly influence your familial and social status: "'Rosa [*sic*] is not pretty like her sister Catalina or street smart like her brother Gerardo, but at least she has light skin'" (18). Rosay's mother makes these judgments without trying to hide them from Rosay, an attitude that deeply hurts Rosay and weakens her self-confidence. With regard to concepts of beauty, Rosay's case is complicated. She has light skin, which pushes her into a higher social rank because lighter skin is associated with European heritage and might allow her to pass as white in U.S. culture. Moraga speaks to a similar influence of her skin color on her identity: "I was 'la güera'–fair-skinned. Born with the features of my Chicana mother, but the skin of my Anglo father, *I had it made*" (43; emphasis mine). In the Chicano community, just as in Rosay's village, looking white correlates with social acceptance and the possibility for economic success. Anzaldúa experienced the opposite: "What I lacked in whiteness, I had in smartness. But it *was* too bad I was dark like an Indian" ("La Prieta" 198; emphasis in original).

Rosay's native features lower her status and neutralize the benefits of her light skin tone. Rosay is keenly conscious of how her body shapes her life when she compares her appearance with those of other family members: "Ma had dark skin, but did not have the typical Indian features: small eyes, flat nose, high cheekbones, and full lips. . . . I was born with light skin, but all of the Indian features" (18). She lists in detail those features of her face that constitute the cause for her being ostracized in her family and community at large. Continuously during her childhood, people confront her with the comment that she combines "all the bad Indian features" (Rosay 71–72). Her body showing the native heritage of the Mexican people turns Rosay into the Other and lays the ground for her exclusion. Though she does not make these connections in the memoir explicitly, I argue that the criticism of her Indian appearance is a comment on her part about the remnants of racist, colonial attitudes, which denounce and attempt to eradicate native culture. The attacks she writes about exhibit the internalization of oppression that her accusers, mostly the women in her family, have undergone. They do not question the importance of Anglo looks, a sign of perpetuated colonial forces.

As she does not receive any consolation from her family, usually the main support system against racism, Rosay turns to religion for understanding and help: "I often wondered if there were any saints that looked like me. I had heard that la Virgen de Guadalupe looked more Indian. But when I saw I [sic] picture of her, I did not think she had small eyes, a chunky nose, and full lips like me" (93). Trying to find her rejected identity reflected in the most important female saint of the Mexican church, she is again disappointed. While Rosay admits that she will miss the church and priests in her village, she "will not miss people thinking that only girls who look somewhat like our virgins are pretty" (94). This comment speaks directly to the sexist collaborations of patriarchal church and society.

Although her name never appears in Rosay's writing, I read a reference to Malinche into Rosay's experiences concerning her "undesired" native features. Malinche, the native woman who was sold by her father to the *conquistador* Hernán Cortés to serve as his guide and translator, functions in traditional, male-dominated Mexican culture as the traitor figure who caused the extinction of her people. In a similar manner, Rosay becomes the ultimate outsider, physically through her appearance and also through the choices she makes in life that contradict her community's sexist culture. Anytime that Rosay does not fit the prescribed gender roles, does not follow the patriarchal rules, or speaks up for herself, a connection with Malinche can be inferred. As Saldívar-Hull explains, "individuality is devalued and selfishness decried" since "women's role in the Chicano family is primarily to serve men" (4, 30). When Mexican women like Rosay attempt to improve their lives, for example via education, they are considered narcissistic and are ostracized. The traitor woman trope originated on a national level and forced its way into the family and personal sphere where it functions as a misogynistic social control tool. Yet, its negative implications regarding national identity and gender linger as it perpetually marks Latinas as hypersexual, untrustworthy seductresses in the eyes of many in the United States.

Her desire to be educated exerts such an important influence on Rosay's identity that it generates perhaps the bravest example of her self-assertion. After her father has returned to Mexico, he demands that Rosay, her mother, and her younger brothers join him. Instead of following her father's ruling, which is expected of her, Rosay stands up for herself by refusing to leave: "He promises he will pay for me to go to high school in Mexico, but I do not believe him. I get off the phone and tell Ma I am not going back to Mexico even if he comes and drags me by my feet" (143). Contradicting the head of the household in a patriarchal family constitutes an immense act of courage for Rosay, for, if "a woman doesn't renounce herself in favor of the male, she is selfish" (Anzaldúa, *Borderlands* 39). Strong and independent, Rosay stands up for what she perceives as her rights and refuses to sacrifice her dreams and education to keep the family together. Rosay talking back to the patriarch recalls Anzaldúa's memories of challenging sexist indoctrination: "*Repele. Hable pa' 'tras. Fui muy hocicona. Era indiferente a muchos valores de mi culture. No me dejé de los hombres. No fui buena ni obediente*" (37).[7] Interestingly, both women reach this goal of standing up for themselves with the use of hybrid genres, which suggests that defying autobiographical norms constitutes an essential method of Chicana and immigrant life writing to fight for social justice and address traditions in Mexican culture that perpetuate the oppression of women.

JOURNEY OF HOPE AS TRICKSTER TEXT

I suggest that Rosay's text attempts to appeal to an American, white readership by identifying itself as a memoir while mimicking the testimonio, a protest genre that became popular in 1960s Latin America. The life-writing genre promises to be conducive toward this goal since, for "the marginalized woman, autobiographical language may serve as a coinage that purchases entry into the social and discursive economy. To enter into language is to press back against total inscription in dominating structures" (Smith and Watson, "Introduction: De/Colonization" xix). Rosay's stylistic choices mirror the risky conditions from which the author is writing as a Latina immigrant for a white audience. According to Isabel Guzmán and Angharad Valdivia, "Latina (not Latino) bodies function as a threat to racially grounded definitions of national identity" (223). Latinas, especially as undocumented immigrants, are seen as seductive, hypersexual, hard to control, and a risk to the social order and body politic because of birth rates that exceed other (especially white) communities. Xenophobic and racist fears are directly projected onto Latina bodies. These are the popular sentiments with which Rosay must work to fight the misconceptions of those U.S. citizens who criminalize Latinx bodies and want to stop immigration from Latin American countries. Rosay's narrative ruptures belief systems that have been presented as truths and inaccurate histories about immigrants from Mexico on which current U.S. politics are based.

Journey of Hope, as a tool to humanize undocumented immigration, fits Anzaldúa's concept of *Nepantla*, "which is a Nahuatl word for the space between two bodies of water, the space between two worlds. It is a limited space, a space where you are not this or that but where you are changing . . . . You are in a kind of transition" (*Borderlands* 237). *Nepantla* is a powerful concept for immigrant women's writing as it denotes a space of separation and a space of cultural and textual hybridity or métis. Rosay does not strive to become Anglo-ized, but to be accepted as a valuable member of American society despite her past as an undocumented immigrant from Mexico. This aspiration is very different from assimilation. *Nepantla* is also "a way of reading the world. You see behind the veil and you see the scraps. Also it is a way of creating awareness and writing a philosophy, a system that explains the world" (237). *Journey of Hope* constitutes such a philosophy explaining a sliver of the world about which little knowledge exists. It unveils the processes of poverty and migration and facilitates the comprehension of undocumented women immigrants' experiences.

Because such knowledge cannot be encompassed by an individualistic point of view, Rosay stretches the contours of the memoir to emphasize more forcefully her call for social change in using elements of the memoir and the testimonio. The testimonio movement began with intellectuals interviewing grassroots activists or members of the working class, supporting the idea that "no one version of history can be ultimately authoritative" (Sommer 117).[8] Offering a platform for diverse voices and experiences is the genre's goal. John Beverley defines the testimonio as located at the "margin of literature, representing in particular those subjects . . . excluded from authorized representation when it was a question of speaking and writing for themselves" (25).[9] He mentions as exemplary subjects without the right to self-representation "the child, the 'native,' the woman, the insane, the criminal, [and] the proletarian" (Beverley 25), a collection of identities that

Rosay fits on multiple counts and to which "undocumented immigrant" should be added.

Beverley proposes that "the situation of narration in testimonio has to involve an urgency to communicate, a problem of repression, poverty, subalternity, imprisonment, struggle for survival" (26). Oppressed lives lie at the heart of the testimonio movement. Rosay's text certainly concentrates on poverty, subalternity, and survival in portraying the intersections of sexism, racism, and classism as a multifaceted force affecting migration decisions. *Journey of Hope* also fits the characteristics of the testimonio as it "is the genre emerging from the Third World that permits the literate, though not necessarily literary, campesina to address the reading world in a language and on topics not sanctioned by the literary institution" (Saldívar-Hull 168). The testimonio is decidedly relational as the narrator speaks in support of the needs of their whole community. As such, it resembles postcolonial forms of life writing. As Gillian Whitlock demonstrates, for example, Olaudah Equiano's slave narrative "speaks on behalf of a collective rather than the singular authoritative 'I'" and "evokes an ethics of witnessing and sympathetic interestedness" (*Postcolonial* 5, 7). For Rosay, testimonial elements present a means to write realistically about undocumented migration, which, unless hyper-sensationalized or demonized, is rarely depicted. Even though *Journey of Hope* was not dictated to a scribe, a characteristic of most testimonials, Rosay uses this genre to translate her experiences into a text accessible to her privileged audience.

At the same time that Rosay employs testimonial elements, her book carries the subtitle *Memoirs of a Mexican Girl* to speak to its designated Anglo American audience since, as Smith and Watson explain, "participation in, through re/presentation of, privileged narratives can secure cultural recognition for the subject" ("Introduction: De/Colonization" xix). White Western readers are more likely to have a positive association with the term "memoir." Rosay perhaps also refrained from titling her book a testimonio because it might not have been "American enough." Rosay's target audience is possibly familiar with the testimonio *I, Rigoberta Menchú* (1984), which recounts the life of a Guatemalan peasant woman.[10] Likely, Rosay did not want to be connected with a story such as Menchú's, which caused controversy over whether it was factual or not, as she did not want to risk calling into question the veracity of her account. Leigh Gilmore forcefully claims that anthropology professor David Stoll challenged Menchú's narrative in a manner that turned her into a "tainted witness" by discrediting her testimony and probing the experiences of "the people in whose name she bore witness" (*Tainted Witness* 65). Rosay might have feared similar judgment. The testimonio asks readers to distrust their assumptions, take action, and change their, often very comfortable, lives. Facing the account of someone's life with these purposes in mind could set up an antagonistic attitude and deter the reader from being fully open to Rosay's message.

Journey of Hope, as the "familiar story of a child overcoming oppression and poverty through his or her own efforts[,] supports the liberal democratic ideology of much American memoir and fiction, with hints of Benjamin Franklin's ideas of self-development added to this" (Rak 135). This kind of storytelling presents Mexican immigrants as part of the rags-to-riches American myth that, to this day, shapes many Americans' understanding of nationality and citizenship. As memoir, the book attempts to attract a privileged audience interested in stories of individual success and adaptation. As testimonio, however, the text aims to create social change and overcome marginality from the bottom up, formally and through content. Like ethnic working-class women's autobiographical accounts, *Journey of Hope* "exert[s] pressure upon and must contend with the languages available" to the author, which creates "resistance if often masked" (Goldman xix). Rosay's text hides a dissenting voice behind a familiar rhetoric of Americanization and exceptionalism. It does not function as a conversion narrative because it does not depict Rosay as becoming part of white, middle-class American life. Instead, Rosay's memoir stands as a manipulation of the genre to narrate otherwise inexpressible experiences.

Much like a trickster figure in all cultures—such as the Coyote, Hermes, or Maui, "who dwell on borders, at crossroads, and between worlds" (Smith, *Writing Tricksters* 1)—Rosay's narrative disobeys conventions and relies on form variability to raise awareness and push for equality. As Jeanne Smith reminds us, tricksters "shake things up, splinter the monologic, shatter the hierarchies . . . disrupting tradition and mediating change . . . and defy[ing] homogenization" (xii); they "combine tradition and change" (xiii). *Journey of Hope* changes traditional ways of telling a life story, like a trickster "injecting multiple perspectives [in this case, on migration and gender] to challenge all that is stultifying, stratified, bland, or prescriptive" (xiii). The text poses as memoir while employing techniques of the testimonio to challenge stereotypical depictions of migrants that rarely get questioned in U.S. culture and politics. Rosay's reliance on a writing style considered less stylized and literary fits Smith's categorization of "trickster authors . . . [who] revise oral traditions in written form" (22). Importantly, tricksters are not just characters but also "rhetorical agents . . . producing a politically radical subtext in the narrative form itself" (2). I very much see *Journey of Hope* as having a "radical subtext" skillfully hidden to render its message digestible for readers with xenophobic attitudes. As such, the memoir creates a "potential for radical (re)vision" of stories told about migrants in the United States (13).

The memoir's partition into a first part called "Poverty and Deprivation," which contains Rosay's depiction of her time in Mexico, and a second part, "Hope and Opportunity," which starts with her first day in the United States, speaks to the author's trickster techniques in that it shows appreciation for her new home to tackle widespread intolerance toward her community in that very same location. These titles cater to an idealistic understanding of the United States as the land of unlimited opportunities, which does not mirror Rosay's actual life still marked by poverty upon arrival in the North. Genaro Padilla claims that such an overly positive portrayal of the oppressor, this "rhetoric of accommodation[,] . . . must be read as oppositional métis alongside other forms of narrative resistance to American hostility and hegemony" (38). Rosay's constant praising should not necessarily be taken at face value, but needs to be critically assessed as a rhetorical tool to create a favorable audience. Louise Pratt elaborates in *Imperial Eyes* (1992) that colonized subjects tend to "undertake to represent themselves in ways that engage with the colonizer's own terms" (7). As an offensive mechanism, the oppressed mix their own images and modes of discourse with the colonizers' rhetoric.

To secure survival, Rosay emulates the dominant culture's rhetoric and shows the sacrifices that immigrants make and the poor conditions they live under without complaint in order to achieve a slightly better life than in the pueblo. After multiple long bus rides and having crossed the border between Tijuana and San Diego by pretending to be American citizens' children, Rosay "wake[s] up the next day feeling like a new person" (120). But some of the issues that shaped her past are still present in the United States, the most pressing one being poverty: "I feel bad having to sleep in my brother's room. I am almost twelve and I know he likes having private time with his wife Lola, but there is no room for me anywhere else. . . . With ten people living in this small house, I am lucky I even have a bed to sleep on" (122). Compared to her idealistic preconceptions of what life in el Norte would look like, Rosay's appraisal after her arrival in the United States is more realistic and shows that undocumented immigrants' situation does not immediately improve as soon as they arrive in the North.

The common misconception that "illegal" immigrants live an easy, prosperous life by taking advantage of U.S. support systems constitutes a deeply held bias that Rosay's rhetoric tries to alleviate by emphasizing her appreciation of and gratitude for her new place of residence: "Connie [her youngest niece] is the first baby in our family to be born in El Norte. I think about how lucky she is to be born in such a wonderful country" (121). Her mentioning of her niece makes the memoir politically risky as it admires a birth that is currently vigorously debated with regard to U.S. immigration and citizenship laws. Children of undocumented immigrants like Connie are often dehumanized by being called "anchor babies," who were allegedly conceived for the sole purpose of allowing their parents to remain in the United States. Turned into inanimate tools, these children are used to propagate xenophobic claims that immigrants who are deemed undesirable will irreversibly change U.S. culture. The term also implies that undocumented migrants, and especially mothers, are fraudulent and do not value their children but objectify them as commodities (Bloch and Taylor 203). These accusations further mark foreign-born women as "sexually deviant and threatening racialized subject[s]" (Cisneros 291). Especially immigrant women of color are stigmatized as perverse and contaminating in contrast to the "sexually pure citizen" (Cisneros 292). While a public frenzy surrounds Latinas having children in the United States, an emerging trend of so-called "birth tourism," as part of which rich (mainly) Russian and Chinese women travel to the United States to give birth and receive U.S. citizenship for their children as a status symbol in their home countries, has received comparably little attention (McFadden et al.). Gabaccia claimed in the 1990s that third-world women had a higher chance of becoming U.S. citizens by giving birth in the United States than via work visas as pink-collar jobs typically held by women, such as nursing or sewing, are not in demand in the United States (39). This predicament still holds true for many immigrant women today.

Rosay opposes damaging nativist portrayals with her life writing, providing her own story and those of her loved ones as proof of the worth of undocumented immigrants for the United States. Because of this underlying agenda, she makes a point of emphasizing that wherever her family moved, all the immigrants were "like us, . . . quiet and keep[ing] to themselves" (141). Most undocumented immigrants do not make any "trouble," abuse help, or break the law; they contribute to the system to secure their survival, which constitutes an impossibility in Mexico.

During her first visit back to Pueblonuevo, Rosay realizes how much survival is a problem there: "We are shocked to see how quiet the pueblo has become. . . . Now it seems that more than half of the population is gone. . . . It feels like the life has been sucked out of the pueblo" (161). The gravity of poverty is evident. It destroys whole villages and people's lives. The miserable conditions in Mexico make Rosay revise her definition of home; she no longer seems able to consider a village that barely offers any means for survival "home." Consequently, she does not write of her return to Mexico as a journey she is excited about. Once there, she realizes that "other than my Tia Victoria's whole wheat gorditas (biscuits), [Mexican bread is] the only thing from Mexico I miss" (Rosay 161). Escaping poverty and creating a meaningful life are more important than any sentimental attachments to the place where she was born. Rosay's appreciation of the United States grows only when she becomes the first person in her family to graduate from college, which she knows "would not be possible if [she] was not in this country" (166). Rosay's writing subverts existing discursive models of life writing to sensitize the broader public toward social justice issues in the author's community. Similar to a mythical trickster, Rosay's text breaks rules and possesses the ability to transform itself. This type of genre, testimonial posing as memoir, pretends to be what it is not to translate a community's experiences for an audience likely antagonistic to many of those experiences.

The trickster text is able to get the audience on Rosay's side while at the same time demonstrating to them that they are part of the oppressive system. As such, *Journey of Hope* serves as an example of how a text can, to reference Audre Lorde, maybe not dismantle, but certainly infiltrate the master's house by using the master's tools (110–113). Smith claims that "trickster authors implicitly or explicitly invite and even demand reader involvement" (23). I propose that Rosay skillfully "tricks" readers into political and social responsiveness through offering gratitude and creating compassion. This technique fits Paula Gunn Allen's description of the "cunning crafting" implemented by women authors of color (310). *Journey of Hope* is not an apology for undocumented immigrants' existence. It teaches its readers about those individuals often taken for granted in everyday life in such roles as cleaners or gardeners.

By appealing to their own patriotic love for their country, Rosay attempts to render her readers more receptive to her explanation of what immigrant life looks like. She emphasizes her resilience in pursuing a life worth living, which has been heralded as an admirable trait in European immigrants. Through her genre adaptations, Rosay practices an "interpersonal rhetoric" common in testimonios to raise complicity in her reader (Sommer 118). She attempts to create a caring audience in letting them participate in the subject's exclusive point of view through which she invites them to draw conclusions. Especially through her childlike tone, she sets up a sympathetic relationship between the author/subject and the reader and pushes her audience to identify with parts of her life that she thinks they might find attractive, such as her longing for education. By locating her readers in her life events, she gently guides the ways in which they interpret her writing, ideally keeping them from reacting aggressively against her efforts of personalizing immigration politics.

Rosay distinctly adds to the picture that more well-known works by male writers such as Ramón Pérez's *Diary of an Undocumented Immigrant* (1991) have created about the dimensions of undocumented Mexican immigrant experiences. Writings by male undocumented immigrants reflect patterns very different from female writers: The authors describe a community mostly made up of men. The reader does not get much insight into family life, and women are often only presented as sex workers. These men's intentions are usually to return to Mexico once they have earned enough money. In their writing, they focus mainly on the process of getting jobs, not on education. Pérez, for example, does not learn English while in the United States. In contrast to these characteristics, Rosay writes to adjust the picture that male writers have created and to portray the authentic dimensions of Mexican immigrant women's experiences. Like other Latina authors she "seiz[es] the podium, tell[s her] own stories, creat[es] new images, and contest[s] the often negative and degrading images which others have used to construct the Latina" (Torres 278). While works by male writers have received academic attention, little scholarship exists on Rosay's book besides a number of reviews.[11] Critics have established a scheme for male Chicano autobiographies that includes "the journey, in the spiritual or intellectual sense[,] . . . [and] rites of passage . . . from innocence to a mature understanding of the world . . . [, which] transformed [the writers] into intellectuals with a strong writing vocation" (Flores 89). Looking at Rosay's text, I demonstrate that female immigrants' experiences cannot be confined as easily.

Readers do not learn about Rosay's achieved life goals or successful career as an adult. Her depiction of her whole community with the ambition to appeal to her audience and to call them to action are very different from male, self-centered and often self-glorifying writings that follow the original bildungsroman template capturing the narrative of a young, bourgeois man's social formation.[12] Rosay does not portray herself as a heroine, but gives a testimony of her people. Rosay works with her audience's ignorance about undocumented immigrants to procure justice for those who are perceived as "different." Readers do not get the sense that Rosay critiques Mexican culture to prove her desire to leave behind her heritage and assimilate unconditionally. Assimilation is not the ultimate goal as it often constitutes an unfeasible task for many in Rosay's community. In challenging rigid perceptions about nationality, Rosay escapes feelings of shame about her existence and claims that undocumented immigrants' lives are worth writing about and supporting.

As an "illegal" woman, Rosay has been doubly silenced for her gender and her race. Despite not mentioning a connection between her own life/writing and other texts by women fighting oppression, her choice of the testimonio with its "insistence on showing relationships" emphasizes relationality and suggests a link Rosay sees between her community's and other minorities' experiences with marginalization (Sommer 129). *Journey of Hope* as testimonio implies solidarity as it "evokes an absent polyphony of other voices, other possible lives and experiences," even if these voices are not explicitly defined (Beverley 28). Like other migrant women life writers, Rosay gives her readers an alternative view of history. She challenges fixed identities based on stereotypes, xenophobia, and the minoritization of women's perspectives on migration processes that oppose patriarchal hierarchies.

SUBVERSIVE TRICKSTER RHETORIC AND ITS AUDIENCE

Rosay uses her writing as a call for action, acceptance, and social justice. She seems well aware of the paramount position that the portrayal of her own character holds in trying to gain the audience's trust to be moved toward political consciousness; hence, her rhetorical strategies aim at portraying herself as a dependable, responsible, and honest correspondent of human rights breaches. In addition to her use of the life-writing genre, which is supposed to be rooted in "truth," Rosay establishes herself as trustworthy by presenting herself as a "good citizen" of the United States. Instead of an openly political approach, referencing, for example, the United Nations Declaration of Human Rights (1948) to present undocumented migrants as rights-bearing individuals who deserve a safe, full, and enriching life of dignity and mobility, Rosay attempts to gain her audience's trust by adopting a non-accusatory voice and emphasizing her gratitude toward the United States.

For her rhetoric of persuasion she uses concrete personal examples that show complex, layered lives to demonstrate the scope of change needed instead of lecturing about large, abstract problems. Her style is oral—with mostly simple sentence structures, a large amount of direct speech, and moments of directly addressing the audience—and less literary and evolved, which recalls the testimonio that is "primarily concerned with sincerity rather than literariness" (Beverley 26). Rosay's narrative voice is often childlike to create clarity and push for the veracity of her story. Her style is markedly female as she jumps between memories and political comments in short nonchronological vignettes, with, at times, gaps of many months in between events. Her voice is authentic, recounting a girl's experiences with a strong focus on emotions, detailed descriptions of people, naive thoughts, and an elaboration on her first falling in love. Her political agenda relies on the audience believing her account that undocumented immigrants can be trusted. After all, while "autobiographers can enjoy the privilege and the privacy of being misunderstood, . . . those who testify cannot afford or even survive it" (Sommer 130). Rosay's use of testimonial techniques speaks to the urgency of her project and the lives at stake if her story is not heard.

Through her reference to Mexican customs and food that her readers might consume themselves, Rosay caters to members of the dominant group—the people whose change in perception can most likely result in the passing or changing of laws—because of "how intimately food is related to lived cultural experience" (Padilla 224). The descriptions of the daily meals her family consumes powerfully underline their poverty: "I cannot buy a bag of potato chips. My rich cousin Leticia let me have some one time. . . . I know I probably will never be able to save up enough money to buy a Twinkie or cupcake" (16). Various food groups, such as apples, which "Ma never buys . . . because they are too expensive" (17), represent status symbols, and items associated with the United States, such as Twinkies, constitute the top of the hierarchy. By humanizing the abstract, negative image of the "illegal" immigrant through food, Rosay expands the notion of Americanness—a state most commonly associated with being a U.S.-born, English-speaking, and Christian person—with the aim of eradicating injustice against undocumented immigrants.[13]

In choosing her text's form, Rosay tries to bring about inter-ethnic understanding. Padilla writes that "in intercultural discourse between a dominant group and subject group, survival is predicated on strategically voicing one's presence" (222–223). For undocumented immigrants, survival is indeed at stake as immigration restrictions and deportations trap people in places and situations that limit their ability to thrive or even end their lives. *Journey of Hope* constitutes an attempt to appeal to a white majority with anti-immigrant sentiments because, as Anzaldúa claims, "the dominant white culture is killing us slowly with its ignorance. . . . Ignorance splits people, creates prejudices" (*Borderlands* 108). Rosay writes against this deeply rooted, destructive ignorance. She seems to agree with Anzaldúa's appeal that "we need to allow whites to be our allies" (107). It is due to this conviction, I surmise, that *Journey of Hope* does not contain much overt criticism of the United States, but concentrates on the depiction of Mexican immigrants' situations and motivations to make readers part of a movement for undocumented migrants' equitable opportunities in the United States.

As I am establishing in *Lives beyond Borders*, immigrant women's life writing renders its reader a textual subject to alter their existing biases and to effect social change. In accordance with this focus on the reader, Rosay exclaims, "I feel blessed to be here. When I was a kid in Mexico, I did not once look forward to my future. . . . And as I wait to get my diploma, I say to myself, Thank God for America" (167). Rosay's overt heralding of the United States might seem exaggerated and perhaps even disturbing to some. But exclaiming such sentiments as "I love America" is part of her trickster strategy of appealing to a white audience with a negative attitude toward undocumented immigration and of nudging them to reconsider their prejudices (166). Rosay, purposefully, puts emphasis in her memoir on education, not the pursuit of money or status symbols that might be taken back to Mexico, which male writing often exhibits. Instead, she makes clear that she seeks education to give back to the country that has offered her an exit out of poverty and made possible her sheer survival.

In her epilogue, Rosay offers the following points in defense of and as a justification for having entered the United States as an undocumented migrant: "I did accomplish my American dream of having a career. . . . I feel extreme love and gratitude towards this Great Country and I have tried to be a good citizen by contributing as much as possible. I have been a Sierra Club leader, a soccer coach, a Girl Scout leader, and a Girls Group leader" (168). The last lines of her memoir are, much like most of the anecdotes she tells in her text, designed to put the audience's supposed worries about immigrants from Mexico at ease. Instead of taking away jobs and money from American citizens, Rosay has become a "soccer mom" who gladly and gratefully serves the country. As such a widely adored cultural icon, she (implies that she) deserves her audience's trust and help. She continues:

"I have also tried to pay back this country by raising kids that do respect Mexico, but that love and have loyalty to only one country, America" (168). Using her self-portrayal as the average American mother, Rosay targets anti-immigration sentiments that question the allegiance of children born to immigrant parents. She tries to appease those attitudes with the words "love" and "loyalty," which will likely appeal to a patriotic audience.

Rosay mentions the terms "love" and "loyalty" again in the final section of her memoir, "Final Thoughts," when she explains how she became a legal resident with the 1986 Amnesty Act: "By the time the law passed I felt so much *love and loyalty* for America that in my heart I was already a citizen (I became a naturalized citizen in 1996). I also felt that this great country would not deport someone who was brought here as a child and on whom thousands of dollars had already been spent to educate" (169; emphasis mine). Rosay's comment about the magnanimity of the U.S. legal system is highly precarious. In reality, the United States has, of course, deported undocumented immigrants who were brought to the United States at a very young age by their parents, received a U.S. education, and oftentimes did not remember the country of their origin.[14] While DACA (Deferred Action for Childhood Arrivals) briefly protected this population, the Trump administration's 2017 announcement to terminate the policy renewed young undocumented immigrants' vulnerability.[15] Challenging nationalist conceptions of immigration policies in her comment, Rosay defines citizenship as not based in exclusion and difference, but in loyalty and love, of which she makes herself a credible example.

For Rosay, photos of the poor village she left behind serve as powerful pieces of evidence that speak to the necessity of her migration to secure her survival. The photos she inserts address her audience on three levels. First, far more effectively than mere verbal descriptions, they illustrate the harsh environment in and the poor conditions under which Rosay's family lived before leaving Mexico. Deserted streets, a rural farm, and the dilapidated door of Rosay's former house bring to life visually the desperation that afflicts the people in similar villages and explains the necessity for migration (116). The text details the poor living conditions in Rosay's homeland—in fact, the first half of the memoir is set in Mexico—while the physical journey to the North takes up but a small section of the book. The narrative is not centered in a mystical geographical and emotional transformation that ends in the United States as safe haven and paradise. The author's human rights rhetoric depends on her readers' understanding of the poor conditions in her homeland that necessitate migration for survival.

Second, Rosay includes a large number of images that depict religious symbols, which I argue offer another level of evidence that might make Rosay's U.S. readers trust in the righteousness of her social justice project. Pictures of the pueblo's saint, Santa Candelaria, the village's stone church (110), the church used for bigger ceremonies called La Parroquia (111), the inside of La Parroquia (112), and of a statue of Christ in the state of Guanajuato (113) conjure up an image of Mexican migrants as God-fearing, "good" people. Rosay presents undocumented migrants as sharing the same religious background and the same values of devotion and loyalty as many Americans, likely a majority of those traditionally opposed to extending rights to undocumented migrants in the United States. If they are seen as pious people, undocumented migrants might also be regarded as trustworthy.

Last, and perhaps most powerful, the photos in *Journey of Hope* offer readers friendly, smiling faces—those of Rosay's brothers and her own high school senior picture (117)—which harshly contrast the menacing images that many Americans opposed to immigration or even afraid of undocumented migrants might have been exposed to and internalized. By providing such counter-evidence, Rosay tackles one of her audience's strongest impediments against supporting her social justice cause, namely, their unfounded fears. She aims to do so without alienating her readers.

An obvious catering to her U.S. audience constitutes her address of the Mexican government and upper-class at the end of her book. In response to activists blaming U.S. trade policies for rural Mexicans' miserable lives, Rosay writes, "there was no NAFTA in the 1960's and 1970's [sic] when my brothers and sister came here because of lack of jobs and opportunities . . . . If anyone is to blame, it is the elite class and the politicians of Mexico. The rich people in Mexico would have been happy to keep us as poor ignorant peasants. . . . And the government was too corrupt and inefficient to help us" (170). She adds: "People fleeing their home country because if they stay they face a lifetime of poverty and deprivation is not a 'migration phenomenon.' It is a desperate journey of hope" (170). Rosay refrains from directly blaming the United States for creating undocumented immigration. At the same time, her explanation of the roots for undocumented immigration turns so-called "illegals" into economic refugees who deserve the same human rights protection as other asylum seekers in the United States. While war is more likely to be accepted as a justifiable reason for leaving one's home country, Rosay also pushes for empathy toward migrants who have to leave behind their homes due to poverty, gang violence, and corruption. Using such hidden strategies makes it possible for Rosay to generate political consciousness in her readers without facing them directly with that purpose, which might estrange some.

Hiding a dissenting voice in a grateful tone, Rosay presents a rhetoric of accommodation and lenience that functions as a variation of métis that subtly yet poignantly criticizes American dominion. Françoise Lionnet characterizes métis in *Autobiographical Voices. Race, Gender, Self-Portraiture* (1989) as an "aesthetic of the ruse that allows the weak to survive by escaping through duplicitous means the very system of power intent on destroying them" (18). Métis as a ruse fits Rosay's fusion of genres that appeals to those readers who have the power to change an oppressive system. As a textual technique, métis is a signifying practice especially common among slaves in the form of "survival tactics within a hostile environment that kept them subjugated, relegated them to the margins" (Lionnet 18). It denotes writing and surviving between different cultures by pushing a political strategy and combining various genres. Rosay's writing and her agenda to humanize undocumented migration match these parameters. Although Rosay is not of mixed race, like a métis woman, she has to "attempt to create a self-portrait in the interval between patriarchal cultures and colonial heritages" (Lionnet 223). She must employ a rhetoric that enables her to negotiate cultural and national locations and expectations, in the hopes of creating survival and acceptance in an adversary environment. Praising the value of the individual constitutes a difficulty for collective cultures, such as Mexican culture, and ideals associated with the life-writing genre, such as self-knowledge and self-making, are often impossibilities for undocumented immigrants. Hence, *Journey of Hope* shapes a rhetoric of the oppressed to make readers and possible change agents side with her political and social ideals.

Rosay's depictions of her education are an excellent example of the trickster text she created.[16] While Rosay genuinely praises having received the opportunity for an education, especially as a girl, she also uses her stories about school as a tool to point to examples of racism and xenophobia: "There are three Mexican-American girls in the P.E. class. They say they do not speak Spanish and they are mean like the two white girls. They call us wetbacks and I want to tell them their parents were probably wetbacks too" (129). Due to internalized racism and xenophobia, a clear separation exists among people of Mexican descent, with undocumented immigrants representing the lowest level of acceptance, exposed to the harshest discrimination. Being ignored by American students and hearing the word "wetback" are not the only racist elements with which Rosay must come to terms. The stereotype of Mexicans being lazy and unclean lingers, and so Rosay is called "dirty" by a "mean girl" when she is too embarrassed to shower in front of the other girls after P.E. class (128–129). Proving these stereotypes wrong often presents an insurmountable obstacle.

Yet, stereotypes against immigrants have much more powerful effects than merely causing discomfort. René Flores and Ariela Schachter claim that documentation status is a social construct as people judge immigrants' "legality" based on prevalent stereotypes about the former (37). For example, generalized defamation of Latin Americans as criminals, drug dealers, rapists, and violent gang members—as notoriously propagated by Donald Trump in recent years—has created an environment in which 60 percent of Mexican immigrants in Flores and Schachter's study were accused of being in the United States illegally and were met with levels of discrimination and maltreatment deemed "deserving" for that population (39). That percentage is three times higher than for Italian or Indian immigrants. Syrian immigrants, who mostly come to the United States as refugees are assumed to be "illegal" 42 percent of the time (Flores and Schachter 39), which affects and, in turn, is influenced by rhetoric around the proposed reduction of refugee resettlement efforts on the part of the current U.S. government, which I will break down in chapter 5 (U.S. Committee for Refugees and Immigrants).

Rosay reacts with defiance in the face of racism and xenophobia: "I am not afraid of getting beaten up, but I love school and learning and I would die if I ever got suspended" (135). With this expression Rosay emphasizes that immigrants, especially undocumented immigrants, are not likely to endanger the opportunities they have received through their migration, but that they are appreciative of their new privileges and do not deserve the often inhumane treatment to which they are exposed. Confirming the discriminatory bias participants in Flores and Schachter's survey had toward labeling immigrants who need government benefits as "illegal" (38), Rosay takes great care to emphasize that her family does not take advantage of the free lunch program at school since "we cannot be getting free stuff from the government after just arriving in the country" (125). In accordance with her rhetorical reliance on simultaneously praising and critiquing, Rosay stresses that her family is aware of their precarious position in American society and does not find it advisable to seek help from the government at this point. The episode commends U.S. society for offering help to the poor but also comments subtly on the shame and reproach to which those who use the services offered are exposed. In this capacity, the book offers an appropriate critique of policies promoted in 2019 by the Trump administration to limit the immigration of people who rely on or might need public assistance in the future (Trotta and Rosenberg).

Rosay's narrative is not concerned with the life of a hero—the goal of many, especially male, autobiographies—but "with a problematic collective social situation that the narrator lives with or alongside others" (Beverley 27). Like a testimonio, it presents an affirmation of the individual in the collective without the assumption that her accomplishments represent an ideal and should be imitated; instead of depicting herself above her community, she establishes herself as a firm part of it and portrays her individual identity as an example of the whole community's complexities.[17] Rather than a desire for self-aggrandizement that influences many traditional autobiographies, it is a political agenda—the push for change in the treatment of undocumented immigrants—that drives *Journey of Hope*. According to Doris Sommer, testimonios "are written neither for individual growth nor for glory but are offered . . . as a general strategy to win political ground" (109). From a position of marginality and exclusion, Rosay attempts to create change by working through an institution of power such as literature.

CONCLUSIONS

The existing reviews of *Journey of Hope* suggest that Rosay is successful in her attempt to create a caring reader.[18] The majority of readers react with sympathy and understanding in the face of Rosay's experiences and report that they see her sense of gratitude toward the United States and her determination to achieve a better life and education as the most important and moving elements of her memoir. Specifically, a number of readers comment on how the book created empathy in them through Rosay's graphic depictions of poverty, which made one reader in particular think about what they take for granted in everyday life. Based on these evaluations, Rosay appears to achieve her goal of raising sympathy in her reader.

As is to be expected, however, Rosay's experimental style fails to reach all readers. One reviewer regards *Journey of Hope* as a poorly written book that does not follow the "rules" of autobiography. They take the time to elaborate on what they perceive as the norms of autobiography and show how Rosay does not meet them. The review faults the writing for being more about Rosay's family than herself, accuses the author of having fictionalized certain parts of her account, and questions how Rosay can write so negatively about her parents, the people whom she should thank the most. Another reviewer criticizes Rosay for explaining in detail an ear infection she had instead of spending more time on her border crossing. They further declare the memoir's constant praising of America as "basic and childlike." Even though Rosay's experimentations with genre to create identification between audience and subject did not reach these readers, my findings could indicate that her narrative techniques might have the potential to serve as a tool for other female immigrants who depend on creating compassion in their readers to secure their communities' well-being.

Since undocumented immigration represents a highly confrontational political topic, Rosay's writing style could become a means for undocumented residents to have their voices heard instead of encountering an antagonistic audience. Rosay's memoir depicts a reality for undocumented immigrants that is very different from white America, a reality in which hard work and dedication do not necessarily lead to acceptance. It makes clear the constant anxiety one lives with if a discrepancy exists between one's own perception as a valuable member of a society and that very society's rejection of said perception. Rosay does not want to give anyone reason to doubt that she wants to be as "American" as American-born citizens. As an immigrant, especially an undocumented one, the burden of proof is on her. She identifies herself as a "Mexican" or an "immigrant" in contrast to American-born Mexican Americans (164), but she never leaves space for doubting that the United States is her home or that she lacks the drive to pursue her patriotic ambitions. Having her name in print validates Rosay's presence and the existence of other undocumented immigrants.

In "The Real Thing," Beverley announces that "testimonio's moment, the originality and urgency . . . or the 'state of emergency' that drove our fascination and critical engagement with it, has undoubtedly passed" (281). I argue, instead, that testimonio's significance has not decreased, but its context and use have changed. As I have shown, it provides new opportunities for writers to redefine womanhood in patriarchal societies and to fight oppression. It further offers particularly undocumented migrants the possibility to voice their concerns and reveal the complexity of their identity. Building on this chapter, *Lives beyond Borders* will continue to investigate how members of minoritized groups make modifications to life-writing subgenres to ensure that everyone's experiences receive a platform and that various forms of migration and other so-called controversial, politicized topics receive their due visibility.

2
LIVING LIKE AN ALIEN
BLACKNESS, MIGRATION, AND DEPRESSION

In her memoir *Willow Weep for Me* (1998), Ghana-born Meri Nana-Ama Danquah shares with the reader her journey to accepting her diagnosis of clinical depression. Academics have used Danquah's work as an authoritative example of how mental illness affects African American women and how the intersectionality of gender, class, and race nourishes discrimination against them. Interestingly, and problematically, these studies often neglect to fully explore Danquah's experiences as an African *immigrant* to the United States. I suggest that reading *Willow Weep for Me* with a specific focus on gender and citizenship can shed light on how female migrants of African descent negotiate oppressive forces in their lives. The image of the "alien" is fitting for this discussion. Danquah's immigration status in the United States marks her on paper as a resident alien. Likewise, her life with a disease that is foreign and inexplicable to many people heightens her position as an alien, a person who is so different that it becomes difficult to grasp their humanity.

The fact that scholars rarely investigate Danquah's identity as an immigrant is significant as it contributes to a gap in research on how African immigrants influence discourse about and representations of Blackness in the United States (Hintzen and Rahier 7). Although immigration status is an important identity marker to consider in discussions about systems of domination—especially in combination with analyses of race—studies about experiences of Black migrants in the United States lack nuance. Investigating Danquah's memoir, as well as some of her shorter essays, this chapter is interested in how the author adapts life-writing techniques to speak to

Black migrant women's fight for survival. *Willow Weep for Me* deliberately mixes genres—memoir, biography, self-help book, reference book—and tells the stories of multiple Black women's struggles with depression to make a powerful commentary on issues of identity, assimilation, racism, agency, and power.

According to G. Thomas Couser, "disability has become one of the pervasive topics of contemporary life writing" (*Signifying Bodies* 203). This is remarkable as the life stories of most people with disabilities, who are likely excluded from many social, political, economic, educational, and other spheres, often do not adhere to the themes of a conventional "success story" and often cannot be considered uplifting, which are both markers of the American myth of meritocracy (Couser, "Conflicting Paradigms" 79). In addition, internalized oppression keeps many disabled individuals from "consider[ing] their lives worthy of autobiography" (79), and "autobiography as traditionally conceived, with its inherent valorization of individualism and autonomy, presents its own barriers to people with disabilities" (88). Much life writing on disability thematizes the process of diagnosis and the success of defeating an illness. Danquah does not insist on establishing herself as a heroine who conquers the obstacles society provides her with due to her disability; instead, she writes an intersectional analysis of her life and how her access to privilege and management of oppressive forces affect whether she is believed and treated with respect and care. Much like the authors Arthur Frank discusses in *The Wounded Story Teller* (1995), Danquah uses her memoir to change the narrative about her own life from passive victim of an illness to active survivor of trauma. This process, Frank claims, can help heal both the author and the reader.

MIGRATION TO THE UNITED STATES FROM WEST AFRICA

Danquah was born in Ghana in 1967. At the age of six, she emigrated to the United States to join her mother, who had left three-year-old Danquah with her maternal grandmother to attend Howard University. Danquah received an MFA from Bennington College and works as a journalist, ghostwriter, speechwriter, and lecturer. She has edited multiple collections of essays and short stories about experiences of being Black and an immigrant.[1] Danquah openly writes about her struggles with clinical depression and how cultural forces of collectivism combined with racism and sexism make it hard for her to get to the bottom of some of the root causes of her illness, such as her father's abandonment of her family, the sexual abuse she experienced from her mother's partner, and being raped in high school. She now lives primarily in Accra, Ghana.

Danquah's native Ghana gained independence from the United Kingdom in 1957 and elected its first president in 1960. The author and her parents' migration falls into the time period between 1966 and 1981, during which the country was politically troubled and economically challenged after the overthrow of Kwame Nkrumah's government led to a series of alternating military and civilian governments. As a native Ghanaian, Danquah joined a wave of West African immigrants from Guinea, Senegal, Sierra Leone, and Nigeria whose ancestors were forcibly transported to the United States as part of the slave trade and who are now migrating to North America in significant numbers. While most Africans, initially, tended to move to old colonial centers, like London, harsher immigration restrictions in European countries and new, laxer laws in the United States in the latter half of the twentieth century (like the initiation of the Diversity Lottery and the Amnesty Act of 1986) brought about a shift in African migration patterns (Halter and Johnson 16). Even though researchers predict that the numbers of African migrants to the United States will soon exceed numbers from Asia, migration from the African continent is not exhaustively researched because African American Studies tend to focus on the forced migration of enslaved people and Migration Studies primarily concentrate on Europe, Latin America, and Asia as sending countries.[2]

Foreign-born Black people in the United States are often overlooked even though they offer the opportunity to illuminate systems of racial hierarchy and oppression. In a country that used to mark Italians and Greeks as Black, voluntary African migration might encourage new consideration of how race is socially constructed. Due to a racial hierarchy that persistently locates Blackness at its bottom, relations between Black African immigrants and African Americans can be tense since, as Marilyn Halter and Violet Johnson explain, "some West Africans resist the label of 'Black' because . . . they see it as eclipsing their unique cultural identities and . . . they arrive with preconceived pejorative ideas about [African Americans] that can manifest itself as disdain or arrogance toward them" (183). In an effort to preserve their survival in a racist and xenophobic society, African migrants attempt to distinguish themselves from those whom they consistently see being oppressed. Danquah attempts to break with this defensive silo mentality by establishing a community in her memoir with other Black women and women of color who live with a mental disability.

MENTAL ILLNESS, GENDER, RACE, AND NATIONALITY

"Even though I have lived in America for most of my life, it has always been difficult for me to think of myself as an American," Danquah writes in her introduction to *Becoming American* (xiii).[3] She recounts continuously having to negotiate her identity. While this process is certainly not uncommon for many immigrants worldwide, these negotiations gain a more complicated character when combined with depression and other forms of mental illness, especially since "immigrant women's voices on mental health (read: societal issues) have often been silenced. Policy makers, service providers and medical practitioners alike render these women socially invisible" (Dossa 4–5). *Willow Weep for Me* actively fights this invisibility.

Danquah remembers that as a child she "did not believe it was possible for people to 'become' American; . . . . the only way to be an American was to be born in America. There just wasn't any room for in-betweens. . . . So I learned to view America as a place, not an identity" (*Becoming American* xiii). Danquah's learned notion of Americanness is based in exclusion, which mirrors conservative, xenophobic propaganda on migration and citizenship. Her statement connotes a persistent feeling as an outsider, an alien after her move to the United States, which likely had huge implications on her mental well-being. The creation of a secure national identity is made even more difficult for her by people in the West African immigrant community who tell her that she is becoming too American, which she cannot decipher as either a positive or negative comment. Thus, the "process of becoming felt like a betrayal of what I was and, ultimately, of who I was. . . . I didn't want to exist in the in-between" (*Becoming American* xvi). The limbo state created by losing grip of your birth nationality while never reaching "full" Americanness is daunting. Danquah does not perpetually refer to her country of birth in her memoir and emphasizes her Africanness more than her Ghanaian roots (perhaps expecting readers' probable ignorance with regard to African nations), which helps her negotiate so powerfully a sense of existing in-between nationalities, cultures, and different states of (mental) well-being.

In an online essay, Danquah exemplifies how her African descent was used against her:

> the one word that . . . was quite curiously often used as an insult was "African." Many a classmate, in anger or spite, had called me an African. The harshness of the tone in which the word was said, coupled with the context, left no room for

doubt; it was to be interpreted as something negative, intended to shame. . . . It was always a perplexing situation in which to find myself because, well, I am an African; but for me, it was and continues to be a source of pride. ("I Am What I Am")

When analyzing Danquah's justice efforts with regard to mental disability in her memoir not in isolation from her other writings, it becomes evident that ignoring her geographical origin is rather negligent. It is clear that exposure to xenophobic stereotypes has always been a part of her life in the United States and that negotiations between pride and shame about her background have influenced her identity construction.

In *Willow Weep for Me*, the author expounds on her immigrant status: "Like many other immigrant children, I grew up trying to find my own personal balance between two distinct cultures. I have always felt torn between the rigid mores of Ghanaian culture and the overly permissive attitudes of Americans" (33–34). Exacerbating these forces that pull her in different directions, Danquah remembers that for her parents she "was melodramatic, thin-skinned, and whiny, just like their image of the average American" (34). The parents' fears of her daughter becoming too Americanized clearly focus on Danquah's ability to handle her emotions in a private manner. This culturally challenging attitude toward open expression of feelings affects how many immigrant groups deal with depression. Depression, therapy, and psychopharmaceuticals are often seen as white and American, which makes it harder for immigrants, and especially immigrant women, to seek help. In Ghana specifically, mental illness is routinely blamed on witchcraft, and women who suffer from mental diseases are designated as witches and blamed for their own sickness (Ofori-Atta et al. 592). While Ghana led the way among African nations by passing a Mental Health Act in 2012, the country had only three psychiatric hospitals and twenty psychiatrists for its 25.9 million inhabitants in 2017 (Gberie). Consequently, the most common treatments for mental illness remain sending patients to "cleansing" camps and to isolate and reject them from regular life (Ofori-Atta et al. 592).

Despite these historical and cultural influences, most articles about *Willow Weep for Me* ignore Danquah's references to her nationality. Anna Mollow, for example, writes about how gender, race, and mental illness come together in Danquah's memoir. She offers helpful background information when she points out that "people of color, especially African Americans, are less likely to be diagnosed with depression or prescribed medication when they report their symptoms to a doctor" (73). Racism impinges on mental health treatment in that people of color are seen as more aggressive and more frequently in need of institutionalization than white patients. African Americans especially often lack the option to determine and control their care themselves. Mollow points out how Danquah's "autopathography" exposes depression as a complex amalgam of personal and social influences: "By showing how the convergence of racism, sexual violence, and poverty literally made her ill," Mollow writes, "Danquah insists upon the validity of depression as a diagnostic category while at the same time contesting hegemonic accounts of its etiology" (83). Mollow offers an important intersectional analysis of Danquah's literary attempt at depathologizing mental disabilities. In a footnote, she mentions that Danquah does not linger on her migrant status, which keeps the author from analyzing that part of Danquah's identity.

In contrast to this neglect of her citizenship status, Danquah herself mentions in a conversation printed after the main text of her memoir that she "felt that nationality and ethnicity have the same impact on one's perception and acceptance of depression as race and gender do. . . . It was another layer of silence and stigma that I had to break through in order to respond to my condition" ("A Conversation" 277–278). Truly intersectional discussions of depression need to include nationality in order to capture all forms of privilege and oppression at play. In her memoir, Danquah echoes this sentiment: "I am black; I am female; I am an immigrant. Every one of these labels plays an equally significant part in my perception of myself and the world around me" (225). Immigrant women are prone to mental health challenges because of how racism, classism, sexism, and xenophobia shape their lives and put pressure on them to "make it" and not let their community or home country down. As Parin Dossa asks poignantly, "How can one maintain a sense of well-being when powerful institutions—health/biomedicine, welfare, legal and others—erase and appropriate one's lived reality?" (12).

Danquah's personal assessment of the influence location of birth has on migrants' mental health is especially important in the context of African migration since common images of Africans stigmatize them as "helpless victims, poverty stricken, a marginalized group with less social or human capital, . . . dependents of the welfare state . . . . [which] inhibits their full integration and incorporation into the affairs of their host societies" (Arthur 5). Accepting the diagnosis of mental disabilities can intensify negative stereotypes against migrants of African descent, and xenophobia affects the diagnosis, support, treatment, and judgment that African migrants, and especially women, can expect.

Studies show clear connections between depression and immigration status. Stephanie Potochnick and Krista Perreira "found that migration stressors [such as traumatic events, reason for migration, discrimination, and documentation status] increased the risk of both depressive symptoms and anxiety" (470). With the help of support networks, these stressors' influence decreases over time. Especially undocumented migrants and members of mixed-status families are prone to depression and anxiety. Not only do people with a migrant background deal with depression inducers, they also struggle with stigma and barriers when seeking information about and treatment for mental health issues. Tahany Gadalla at the University of Toronto "found immigrants are less than half as likely to get professional help for depression compared to self-identified Canadians" (Chua). Notions of depression as a purely Western concept, the fear that acknowledging mental disabilities will bring shame on the family, and a lack of cultural sensitivity training for mental health personnel contribute to this lack of help. Potochnick and Perreira's as well as Gadalla's observations have been found to affect—even if in differing ways—most migrant groups in many countries. According to Amelia Derr's survey, migrants from Africa (which Derr does not separate into different countries) cite "stigma" against mental illness and the preference for "alternative care" as the most common reasons for not seeking medical help (269). Based on the above findings, I claim that considerations of nationality and citizenship status need to be part of any reading of Danquah's memoir.

In *Willow Weep for Me*, Danquah goes into great detail about the myriad factors that affected her mental health state from a young age. After her friend Jade talks about the racism she experienced in school and admits to having wanted to be white, Danquah explains: "Top that with being a foreigner. . . . It wasn't just the white kids with me. It was everybody. I hated being different. I used to come home from school and stand in front of the mirror and practice talking like the kids in school, walking like them. Hell, I wanted to be them. All I knew was that I had to be someone other than who I was" (91). Her skin color intersects with her migrant status and creates feelings of self-hatred in the author. Danquah elaborates on the racism she experienced: "They mocked my accent that refused to roll *r*s or clip vowels. They pinched their noses and slid away from me as I opened my lunch box," and they called her the "African Monkey" (104). Danquah's schoolmates clearly bullied her not solely based on her race but because of her remnants of a foreign accent, her nation's culinary traditions, and her facial features. While these children likely did not consciously act in this manner due to outright racist convictions, their behavior is shaped by their socialization in a racist *and* xenophobic society.

Understandably, "these experiences . . . shattered any personal pride . . . and replaced it with uncertainty and self-hatred" (Danquah 105). Early ostracization negatively affects Danquah's mental well-being as she experiences intense self-loathing caused by her foreigner status. As Dossa's study of female Iranian refugees in Canada shows, for women, "wellness is an integral part of the process of reconstructing lives and recapturing meaning in a new land" (12). Without a balanced level of mental and bodily wellness, Danquah's episodes of self-doubt and depression increase and make it hard for her to believe that anyone would take her struggles seriously, which, as the medical studies above underline, complicates Danquah's acceptance of her mental illness and her search for adequate treatment.

Gender plays a significant role in immigrants' experiences with mental illness. While data show that immigrant men across races and ethnicities are less likely than immigrant women to use mental health services (Derr 270)—probably due to toxic conceptions of masculinity that mark mental illness as a weakness that makes one "less of a man"—it is her Black womanhood that acutely affects Danquah's life with depression. Stereotypes about immigrant women of color—which, as I have discussed in the previous chapter, mark them as hyperfertile, hypersexual, and inassimilable, among other labels—converge with those about African American women—pigeonholing them as strong and angry—and affect Danquah's ability to take adequate care of herself:

> Clinical depression simply did not exist . . . within the realm of possibilities for any of the black women in my world. . . . The one myth that I have had to endure my entire life is that of my supposed birthright to strength. Black women are *supposed* to be strong—caretakers, nurturers, healers of other people—any of the twelve dozen variations of Mammy. Emotional hardship is *supposed* to be built into the structure of our lives. It went along with the territory of being both black and female in a society that completely undervalues the lives of black people and regards all women as second-class citizens. (Danquah 18–19; emphases in original)

Persistent and internalized racist images of African American women as sacrificing themselves for others to save their community make it almost impossible for Black women to acknowledge their own weaknesses and health struggles, much less to seek support when living with a mental disability. Danquah explains further how this postulate of strength diminishes empathy toward Black women and "how hard it sometimes is for black women to be seen as vulnerable and emotionally complex" (20–21). Racist and sexist assumptions about them dehumanize African American women and, by extension, non-American-born African women, which thwarts a compassionate discussion of depression within that demographic.

Chimamanda Ngozi Adichie's bestselling novel *Americanah* (2013) has brought this neglect to a wide readership.[4] The novel recounts the migration and return stories of two young Nigerians and offers powerful observations about race and immigration status in the United States and United Kingdom. Adichie depicts how West Africans experience racialization upon arriving in the United States and Europe, which causes periods of depression for many migrants. But, "depression was what happened to Americans, with their self-absorbing need to turn everything into an illness. [Ifemelu] was not suffering from depression; she was merely a little tired and a little slow. . . . because panic attacks happened only to Americans. Nobody in Kinshasa had panic attacks. It was not even that it was called by another name, it was simply not called at all" (Adichie 194–195). Ifemelu, the main character, struggles with depression as she experiences extreme poverty while studying in the United States to the point where she has to prostitute herself; and yet, the concept of depression evades her. As a result, "her self-loathing had hardened inside her. She would never be able to form the sentences to tell her story" (Adichie 195). Due to the inability to understand her condition and seek help, Ifemelu's condition worsens.

She eventually finds an outlet for her story and her opinions on racism and sexism in her blog, *Raceteenth or Various Observations about American Blacks (Those Formerly Known as Negroes) by a Non-American Black*, which turns into her main source of income. After her nephew attempts suicide, Ifemelu is convinced that "his depression is because of his experience" as a young Black immigrant male in United States society (470). One of his first comments when he visits Nigeria constitutes an admiring exclamation that he has never seen so many Black people in the same place (518). Ifemelu herself, upon her return to Lagos, remarks that "I feel like I got off the plane . . . and stopped being black" (586). Adichie makes the convincing claim that racism is complicit in the creation and perpetuation of mental health issues. In her introduction to *The Black Body*, Danquah echoes the social construction of race when she states that she does not "remember ever being aware of [her] blackness before" her migration (13). In contrast, once in the United States, she was "always keenly aware of [her] blackness nearly every second of every day, of how the adjective *black* suddenly seemed to precede every nominative description of [her]—*black* student; *black* girl; *black* friend" (13; emphasis in original). This racist qualifier, Adichie and Danquah agree, negatively influences the self-esteem and mental health of immigrants of color.

Adichie makes clear that it is not only racism but also its intersection with sexism that creates a specific form of domination for Black women—whether native born or with a migrant background. In a blog entry, Ifemelu writes sarcastically: "In describing black women you admire, always use the word 'STRONG' because that is what black women are supposed to be in America. If you are a woman, please do not speak your mind as you are used to doing in your country. Because in America, strong-minded black women are SCARY" (Adichie 274). Strength as a racist and sexist descriptor prevents Black women from expressing who they truly are, which has severe negative consequences for their mental health.

Tamara Beauboeuf-Lafontant, in "Strong and Large Black Women" (2003), expands on the connections between the Mammy trope, associated with African American women's strength and extreme selflessness, and Black women's mental well-being. She argues that even though an insistence on female strength could be interpreted as positive—considering that, commonly, femininity is associated with passivity and fragility—in the case of African American women, it is read as a sign of their abnormality and their exemption from oppression. They are expected to have the ability to withstand any adversity, which, supposedly, makes it unnecessary to exert empathy toward them, to support them, or to change the oppressive status quo. Such assumptions are devoid of a deeper understanding of the intersectionality of Black women's lives as "the strength demonstrated by and seen in Black women is too often a sign of their resignation to the oppressiveness of their social context" rather than a sign of social power (Beauboeuf-Lafontant 114–115). This dehumanization further causes Black women to neglect their own desires, hardships, and abilities.

Studies consistently show that many Black women consider themselves too busy taking care of others to worry about their own health. With this prioritization in mind, it might not seem surprising that Danquah expresses guilt for feeling overwhelmed with her life, which presumably differentiates her from most other Black women who have always worked multiple jobs and raised children: "No one ever made mention of these women griping about depression. It was a luxury that they couldn't afford. What made me think that I was so special?" (195). Silence within Black communities and society at large about mental health issues rooted in social stressors enhances in Danquah the notion that her depression is only a sign of neediness. Add the already existing "difficulties poor women face when they try to get health care" due to the intersections of their gender, race, class, and level of ability, and the prospects for Black women to receive adequate mental health treatment are bleak (Silliman 66). Once Danquah finds the strength to accept her disability and seeks treatment, it is difficult for her to locate a therapist she can afford because the providers who work pro bono have long waiting lists. She eventually sees a doctor who uses a sliding scale to calculate fees, but her class status—which is, of course, deeply connected with her race and gender—makes it hard for her to afford transportation, child care, and medication (189).

Disability is, certainly, a stigma used against all people who are differently bodied. In her groundbreaking *Unruly Bodies* (2007), Susannah Mintz analyzes how works by eight women with various physical disabilities "display corporeal difference to demonstrate the damaging effects of not disease or impairment but, rather, of the cultural mythologies that interpret those conditions in reductive or disparaging ways" (1). Unlike the biomedical model of disability which labels disability as physical or mental characteristics that are abnormal and need to be permanently fixed, thus creating "deviant bodies and legitimiz[ing] inequitable distributions of resources" (Gomes et al. 1), many feminist scholars see disability, like race and gender, as socially constructed.[5] Likewise, many people with a biological impairment describe not feeling disabled until they have to negotiate a society (like buildings without wheelchair ramps or videos without subtitles) that does not consider their needs.[6] Most societies worldwide are designed for people who are young, robust, and without infirmities, in fact, for strong men (Wendell 110). People with impairments are othered; like with race and other identity markers, many project what they are afraid of onto those with a disability instead of thinking of disability as a constant possibility for everyone (e.g., because of age or an accident). A cultural obsession with so-called normalcy, youth, strength, and beauty makes it especially difficult for women—whose bodies are judged more harshly than men's—to be accepted as full human beings. As Mintz elaborates, many women with disabilities powerfully challenge the pathologizing medical discourse in their life writing, and I see Danquah doing the same in *Willow Weep for Me*.

Both Wendell and Mintz are basing their theories primarily on physical disability, which makes Danquah's writing about her experiences with a mental disability a crucial addition to feminist disability studies. Danquah's memoir builds on the works analyzed by Mintz, which present a "keener, more critical understanding of how gender and disability interact in the formation of a woman's identity" (2). Its intersectional analysis of disability reveals that gender, immigration status, race, and class play an essential part in the nuances of how patients with a mental illness are portrayed:

> I have noticed that the mental illness that affects white men is often characterized, if not glamorized, as a sign of genius, a burden of cerebral superiority, artistic eccentricity—as if their depression is somehow heroic. White women who suffer from mental illness are depicted as idle, spoiled, or just plain hysterical. Black men are demonized and pathologized. . . . When a black woman suffers from a mental disorder, the overwhelming opinion is that she is weak. And weakness in Black women is intolerable. (20)

Media and popular culture are complicit in the use of disability to uphold the patriarchal status quo by taking away agency from women, portraying men of color as animalistic, and shaming and denigrating Black women. The "strong Black woman" expectation constitutes a debilitating conundrum for Danquah: she is expected to be strong, but strong Black women are reviled, as exemplified in mainstream commentary about such women as tennis player Serena Williams or former first lady Michelle Obama, who are put down for their physical strength and their emotional and intellectual stamina. So Danquah is supposed to be strong, but, because of her disability, does not see herself as capable of living up to that standard; at the same time, she cannot afford to not be strong in order to protect her daughter while knowing that she would also be critiqued for her strength. For Danquah, the double bind created by xenophobic, racist, and sexist social structures is truly disabling. Due to this conditioned reluctance of Black women to recognize any forms of weakness in themselves, it should come as no surprise that Danquah's initial attitude toward depression is ridicule: "Leukemia, cancer, heart disease, AIDS, even schizophrenia—*those* were illnesses. But depression? I wasn't buying it" (87; emphasis in original). Depression is not sanctioned as a legitimate disease for many marginalized groups.

The precarity and lack of community support Danquah experiences due to her status as an immigrant woman of color add to her self-doubt and inability to discuss and work through her fears. Since the strong Black woman rhetoric perseveres outside of as well as inside African American and African immigrant communities, it is difficult for Black women with mental health issues to share their experiences, which makes Danquah's memoir, in which she speaks not only to her own life but to other Black women's struggles, an interesting case study. Danquah received skepticism from the Black community about her willingness to discuss depression. Comments like "'take your troubles to Jesus, not no damn psychiatrist'" demonstrate a deep-seated skepticism against depression as a white illness but also against a medical system that is designed to benefit white patients (Danquah 21). Unsurprisingly, once she does begin treatment, Danquah finds it difficult to talk about her family during therapy sessions "because in African as well as African American cultures, talking about one's parents is frowned upon; only an ingrate would do such a thing" (35). Such an extreme distinction between private and public spheres heightens prevalent notions of victim-blaming.

Danquah writes that, as a child experiencing sexual abuse by her mother's boyfriend, she initially asked herself: "What kind of a man uses his erect penis, like the pointed, glistening tip of a blade, to butcher the trust of a child?" But, inadvertently, this question would morph into self-centered criticism: "What kind of child allows this to happen? It was never his fault, always mine" (124). Danquah shares that she was unable to talk about the abuse because she was socialized to think she had brought it on herself. Victim-blaming is an outrageous problem for all women who have suffered sexual violence, and statistics for Black women experiencing child sexual abuse are similar to other races and ethnicities, hovering around 40 percent (Ramos, Carlson, and McNutt 154); but the way in which U.S. culture hypersexualizes and exoticizes women of color necessarily impacts these women's self-esteem and how they think about their own bodies and ownership of their sexuality.

In trying to come to terms with having been raped in high school, Danquah tells herself that she "felt violated, but [she] told [her]self [she] had no right to. [She] had given Wayne [her] virginity without the least bit of resistance. [She] was so ashamed. . . . [She] grew detached from [her] body" (121). Because she is not offered an outlet to work through her trauma, Danquah internalizes her experiences with sexual violence as self-hatred, adding to the self-criticism she already practices because of her skin color and nationality. Studies on the short- and long-term effects of specifically child sexual abuse suggest that survivors deal with depression, anxiety, PTSD, and addiction for the rest of their lives (Ramos, Carlson, and McNutt 161). Yet, as Blanca Ramos, Bonnie Carlson, and Louise-Anne McNutt's results indicate, "social expectations about being strong, cautious about not calling attention to the violence of their partners, and valuing group over individual preservation may pose additional sources of stress" for abused Black women (162), which makes them less likely to seek and use the help of formal services (156). Ramos, Carlson, and McNutt add that "Black women are often socialized to be 'superwomen,' who can handle all stresses and problems, including those stemming from" interpersonal violence (162). Research on child sexual abuse and its consequences for immigrant children is rare, but it is likely that this particular intersection of identities and feelings of alienation could heighten levels of trauma.

Because of the severity of these long-lasting effects, Danquah's adaptations of the memoir genre to accommodate her negotiations of nationality and disability are geared toward helping others in similar situations as herself. Her literary efforts stem from the observation that "when there aren't dismissive questions, patronizing statements, or ludicrous suggestions, there is silence. As if there are no acceptable ways, no appropriate words to begin a dialogue about this illness. And, given the oppressive nature of the existing language surrounding depression, perhaps for black people there really aren't any" (Danquah 21). Danquah recognizes the potential for language or a complete lack of language to perpetuate the oppression of people, and acutely people of color, with an invisible disability. To counter this force, *Willow Weep for Me* provides the vocabulary and stories needed to have informed conversations and make positive decisions.

Danquah offers, for example, a list of the causes for postpartum depression (taken from an advice book which she cites at the bottom of the page) from which she likely suffered (38). The mothers' race and class status play an enormous role in whether or not they are diagnosed correctly and receive treatment. Between 13 to 19 percent of new mothers experience postpartum depression, but the rate among new mothers of color is closer to 38 percent (Keefe, Brownstein-Evans, and Rouland Polmanteer). Yet, women of color are less likely to be screened for the disease and to receive appropriate services upon diagnosis. Because of the intersectionality of oppression, women of color are more likely to be uninsured and, thus, less likely to be able to afford treatment (Abrams, Dornig, and Curran). They are also more prone to ignoring symptoms of mental illness due to the justifiable fear that their children might be taken away from them by the state as, for example, 53 percent of African American children will be investigated by child protective services before the age of eighteen compared to roughly 37 percent of all children (Kim et al.).

Danquah assumes that if, during her pregnancy, doctors had asked pertinent questions, the symptoms of her depression would have become clear; at the time, however, she did not have the knowledge to bring up the topic herself. The stigma that new mothers who suffer from depression are necessarily bad mothers negatively influences whether society views postpartum depression as a valid mental stressor in all women. Widespread assumptions that women with disabilities are incapable of providing adequate care for children, that they "lack the dexterity and maturity to mother" causes these women's wish to become mothers to be "frequently met with skepticism and even contempt" (Mintz 144). Influenced by such oppressive stereotypes, Danquah did not feel comfortable discussing her mental state with her doctors.

Danquah's intersectional writing about motherhood connects her disability and gender with her race. The risks of being labeled a bad mother are even higher for women of color, especially Black women, who are confronted with much harsher judgment regarding their parenting than white women. Indeed, Danquah felt extremely "ashamed and selfish" for not functioning as a "good" mother to her young daughter as she "didn't want to take care of anybody else" (71, 72). The lasting impacts of the racist stereotype of the "mammy" has idealized (older, large, dark) Black women as loyal, maternal, submissive caregivers toward white children, while portraying them as neglectful toward their own children (Wallace-Sanders). Nonwhite mothers tend to be labeled as fraudulent and lazy, as having children for the sole purpose of collecting government assistance, and they are blamed for the structural challenges they might experience by claiming that they hold "inferior cultural beliefs and values" (Bloch and Taylor 202). As a damaging consequence, children of color—especially African American and Native American children—are taken from their families and placed into the foster care system at a disproportionate rate. For example, in 2000, African American children made up 16 percent of the United States child population but constituted 38 percent of children in foster care (Summers). Many of these children experience abuse under a broken system or are offered up for adoption, which often severs all ties with their biological families.

I explore how this connection of racism, classism, and sexism shapes perceptions of "good" motherhood further in the next chapter on transnational adoption. For Danquah, it directly affects her resistance to applying the term "depression" to her life: "Considering the circumstances—a high-risk pregnancy, poverty, domestic violence, single motherhood—I thought I was doing pretty well. After all, I wasn't on welfare, I wasn't smoking crack or abusing my child" (58). Danquah has internalized sexist ideas about Black women as "welfare queens" and "crack mothers" that demonize women of color as necessarily failing mothers. Such low expectations cloud Danquah's ability to measure how well she is doing and keep her from taking care of herself.

Danquah's descriptions of depression do not remain solely personal. In powerful ways, she offers a social investigation that compares the root causes and effects of racism, xenophobia, and depression. In response to the acquittal of the police officers in the Rodney King trial, Danquah remembers thinking, "all black people had just been told that our lives were of no value, especially in the hands of white justice" (42). She reads the trial as a clear sign of the degradation of Black humanity in the United States. During the riots that followed the trial, she "listened as the television reporters referred to the predominantly black crowds as 'packs,' 'herds,' words generally used to describe animals, not human beings" (43). *Willow Weep for Me* offers a strong critique of Black people's dehumanization and asks, "when would any black people—ever be able to find peace and happiness in this world?" (44). The effects of racism push those touched by them into a deep-seated hopelessness. It is in this disparity that Danquah sees a parallel between racism and depression: "Everything was out of order, out of control. . . . This is how the world feels to me when I am depressed. . . . living feels like a waste of time and effort" (44). In a pervasive way, both racism and depression make you lose ownership of your choices and desires. Likening the severity of depression, an involuntary illness, to racist prejudices allows the author to speak out against intolerance that shatters people's lives.

For Danquah, the process of naming functions as a tool to show the world who you really are and as a complicated mechanism to cope with xenophobia, racism, and mental disability. The fluidity that she assigns to self-naming and identity challenges life writing's prevalent reliance on a stable nationality—much like Rosay does with her memoir, as discussed in the previous chapter. Danquah describes negotiating her national identity as similar to struggling with different personalities due to depression: "Many names and skins have been shed in order for me to evolve into the person I now am" (103). Danquah's birth certificate states her first name as Mildred; her middle-name, Nana-Ama, however, was always her family's preference; but in an attempt to find acceptance with her American schoolmates, she went by her second middle-name, Mary, as she hoped that a "plain, simple, 'American' name would provide [her] with what [she] wanted most desperately: . . . Invisibility" (108). Danquah believed that an American-sounding name could afford her assimilation, the precarious ability to escape xenophobic and racist comments. Re-naming herself is not idiosyncratic to Danquah's life but rather a practice that immigrants have been using globally in an attempt to avoid discrimination, ridicule, and people's unwillingness to learn how to pronounce names correctly. Studies support immigrants in the choice of adopting Anglicized names, as data show it makes them more likely to receive positive treatment in schools and on the labor market (Bertrand and Mullainathan; Zhao and Biernat), which has led to a persistent trend of immigrant parents giving their children names common in their country of residence instead of their country of origin (Gerhards and Hans). Eventually, Danquah decided to change the spelling of her name to Meri because "it wasn't a persona" (130). She created a new self that encompassed her identity more naturally.

While it was, at first, important to her to depart from Mildred, "the self [she] so despised" (108), later on, acknowledging "the core reasons for the feelings [she] had learned to call 'depression' meant saving Mildred, claiming [her] past, however traumatic" (109). Shedding her past in the form of her name did not facilitate for Danquah the ability to work through her trauma caused by abandonment, violence, and discrimination. For fellow Ghanaian Akuyoe Graham, as she describes in her essay "The Remembering," renaming (even if not implemented legally) initially offers opportunities of assimilation: "In [an] attempt to become as colorless as possible in England," she straightens her hair, speaks with a British accent, and renames herself Katherine. Her metamorphosis appears to work, as on "the phone [she] could pass for a member of Parliament" (Graham 70). But the benefits of that change are short-lived since she acknowledges that it "seemed as if [she] was an embarrassment for black[s] and a painful reminder of the ancestors who had sold them away into slavery" and that, for Caucasians, she was an "'exotic'" other because she did not fit their stereotypes of "'savage'" Africans (70–71). Giving herself a British name does nothing to change the racist social system of Graham's country of residence.

In her essay "Break Skin, Break Spirit" (2009), Danquah takes up again the issue of naming with an intense connection to racism:

> Granted, there's nobody standing over us with a freshly oiled whip waiting for us to say the new name that we have been given—but we still don't have total freedom. Freedom to name who we are. . . . Being black in America can still so easily be about the surrender of identity, the relinquishment of your sense of self. It can still so easily be about using whiteness, definitions of the dominant culture, as your Rosetta Stone, as a way to translate yourself to others and, sometimes, even to yourself. (233–234)

Danquah makes a crucial reference to slavery and its remnants in contemporary United States society for African Americans and non-U.S.-born Blacks alike. The right to name yourself and your experiences is intricately connected with agency, humanity, and reaching your full potential. Naming herself and being able to name her illness create for Danquah a sense of authenticity. Pursuing this goal, *Willow Weep for Me* shares her and others' insights into mental and bodily healing in ways that innovate the memoir genre.

MEMOIR AS A TOOL OF HEALING

Willow Weep for Me broadens the genre of memoir because it functions as an interesting amalgam between personal story and self-help/advice book that seeks to empower others, especially immigrant women of color with a disability, more than it aims at celebrating the author's life. As such, I see the memoir building on a rich heritage of African women's autobiographical texts, which Carole Boyce Davies interprets as "not a statement on a 'self' after success but an insertion of a 'self' within a historical and social framework which accepts [African women's] invisibility or silence. Within such a context, [African women's] autobiography also becomes political statement [that] submerges [the] self within a larger frame of family or cultural history" (187). Danquah particularly expresses this relationality with other disabled people and in the cultural and political framework of disability as socially constructed identity. Perhaps because of her mistrust of the medical establishment, Danquah, early on, recognizes the healing powers of literature, which might have been an influential reason for choosing the memoir genre to spread her social justice message. When she discovers Audre Lorde, Anne Sexton, Adrienne Rich, and other confessional writers in a class taught by a supportive instructor, Danquah starts writing poems herself to give "birth to [her]self. . . . In art, [her] words, [her] feelings, were suddenly credible" (129). It is telling that Lorde and Rich, who saw writing as feminist practice to support political activism and created feminist theory through their personal reflections, serve as inspiration for Danquah. Writing restores a sense of self-worth in her of which her environment has deprived her.

Crucially, research in the health sciences supports the positive correlation between writing exercises and treating depression. The study "Writing for Depression in Health Care," published in 2013 in the *British Journal of Occupational Therapy*, finds that writing (under supervision of a therapist) benefits patients with depression as it helps them gain self-knowledge and distance from their experiences and offers the opportunity to organize thoughts and feelings (Cooper). In 2015, Di Blasio and colleagues wrote in *Psychological Reports* about the benefits they see for clients with postpartum depression and post-traumatic stress disorder who engage in expressive writing practices. For Danquah, as for many of the patients in these studies, putting her experiences on paper validated them, calmed her, and gave her a new perspective on dealing with oppressive elements in her life—a technique she wants to share with her readers. Suzette Henke designates such writing that offers therapeutic benefits for those working through trauma "scriptotherapy." The healing aspect of facing suppressed traumatic memories constitutes a large component of Danquah's life writing. Importantly, I also see *Willow Weep for Me* as an example of Linda Martin Alcoff and Laura Gray-Rosedale's concept of "survivor discourse," which, as the authors argue, is intrinsically political (220). Danquah's memoir is not merely confessional but serves as a witness account that draws attention to the mental state of those being shamed for living with a disability as well as survivors of racism, xenophobia, and many other forms of abuse. It aims at restoring agency and helping to transform healing victims into resistant survivors.

Indeed, writing and reading "literature became the most immediate and effective way for [Danquah] to ease [her] feelings of confusion and isolation" (Introduction, *Becoming American* xv). But despite the fact that some literature was empowering for Danquah to read, it became obvious to her that most texts are not meant to speak to people like herself and do not encompass experiences to which she can relate. She reads, for example, many works about immigration but "none of them contained any information that even remotely seemed to relate to [her]. There wasn't anybody on the *Mayflower* who looked like [her]. Or on Ellis Island. . . . Where were the accounts of immigrants' experiences through the eyes of a black African-born woman"? (xv; emphasis in original).[7] In Danquah's perception, mainstream literary, critical, and historical expressions normalize whiteness and Europeanness and leave out the lives and contributions of those who are deemed "other"—a condition that my analysis of immigrant women's life writing attempts to remedy. This lack of diverse representation has enormous effects on such concepts as citizenship and mental health and influences whom communities are willing to accept as part of their own. *Willow Weep for Me* addresses this exclusive homogeneity and offers representation to readers who, like Danquah, often find themselves at the margins.

Danquah hopes that her memoir can fill a gap in the literature about mental health since books on depression are mostly written by Caucasian authors (183). This imbalance might suggest that depression mostly affects white communities; countering this impression, Danquah emphasizes that "depressive disorders do not discriminate along color lines, people do" (184). While white patients are afforded empathy, media coverage accuses Black people of causing their own mental instability, for example through the use of illegal drugs. This racist assumption isolates people of color and forces them "to suffer alone because we don't know that there are others like us" (Danquah 184). In sharing her story candidly, Danquah helps lift the stigma against mental illness within the African/American communities.

In his study of West African Immigrant Women's Memoirs, Odun Balogun (2009) remarks how Danquah uses literary techniques, especially repetition, to stress "the extreme nature and severity of her disease in order for the reader to better recognize the heroic level of the endurance, perseverance, and psychological power it took for her to be able to overcome it" (447). In my reading of Danquah's memoir, the self-centeredness that Balogun detects is much less prevalent. While it is important for Danquah to emphasize the strength it took her to admit to her illness, I do not see her writing about it to celebrate herself but as a way to encourage others not to shy away from going through that same necessary process. After all, "Illness. It seemed like such a weighty word" (Danquah 87). Instead of portraying herself as a heroine, Danquah focuses on her readers' anxieties and preconceptions about mental illness to assuage their fears and offer practical reassurance. Balogun continues that the memoir's structure supports the claim that "it is erroneous to think that depression is a symptom of laziness, sloth, and weak-mindedness on the part of irresponsible individuals who cannot face up to the often difficult task of living. On the contrary, [Danquah] insists, depression is a serious disease provoked by a combination of complex social, psychological, and biochemical causations" (447). Because of this educational focus, *Willow Weep for Me* at times reads more like an investigative essay or an advice book than what many readers might expect of a personal memoir.

Misperceptions about the disease, stereotypes against those afflicted by it, and a general lack of conversation about mental health that might create more empathy make it difficult to overcome fears of being marked as an outcast, a concern even more crucial for those who are already marginalized due to their race, ethnicity, citizenship status, or other identity categories. Through the title of her memoir, Danquah extends feelings of comfort and shelter to those who experience marginalization. She explains that the title is taken from Billie Holiday's song "Willow Weep for Me," which in turn alludes to Desdemona's song (based on a sixteenth-century popular composition) in act 4, scene 3 of William Shakespeare's *Othello*, a tragedy about race, immigration, assimilation, and violence against women. Danquah reprints the following stanza of the song: "willow weep for me / willow weep for me / bend your branches down / along the ground and cover me / listen to my plea / hear me willow and weep for me" (46). These particular lines, which reappear in the song, encourage the creation of a protective and empathetic environment. The author explains that, as a young child, "it struck [her] as odd and unfair that a tree so beautifully delicate and regal like the willow should be forever associated with tears" (47). The willow represents a metaphor for Danquah herself and everyone struggling with depression: Despite the fact that they are wonderful and complex human beings, they are marked to the outside solely by the symptoms of their mental illness. To refute this reductive attitude, Danquah "wanted a title [for her book] that would reflect the courage, devotion, and resilience that it takes to contend with depression" (262), a title that counters stereotypes of the depressed as lazy, self-involved, and demanding.

Debating the title choice, Danquah was concerned that it could imply that "black women [are] victims" (262), which would contradict her emphasis on their resilience and "the necessity of the long-overdue inclusion of black women in discussions about depression" (262). Instead of offering a platform for women's voices, the title might be associated with negative images of victimization. As women of color, particularly, tend to be pushed by the media into the dichotomy of either being strong and assertive or pitiful victims, the concern to take even more power away from them is a valid one. But when Danquah conducted more research on the history and attributes of the tree, she found that the willow functions as a symbol of pleasure, glory, and kindness. Its bark contains the chemical salicin, a component of aspirin (263). As "the willow is a healing herb" and not at all merely a suffering, useless piece of flora (262), Danquah decides on it as a fitting image for the perseverance and strength it takes to live with and fight depression—a vital message she communicates to her audience.

In order to achieve the goal of describing adequately what life with a mental illness is like, Danquah adapts the genre to include other women's stories about their experiences with depression and builds a community of support and knowledge to be shared with her readers. Through a detailed examination of Anita Hill's 1991 congressional hearing in which she testified that Supreme Court Justice nominee Clarence Thomas had sexually harassed her, Leigh Gilmore establishes that Black women are at heightened risk of being turned into tainted witnesses, of not being seen as credible knowers (*Tainted Witness*). It seems likely, then, that Danquah felt the need to capture multiple Black women's lives with mental illness to establish credibility. Hence, a whole chapter in *Willow Weep for Me* recounts details about a friend's mother and her struggles with Seasonal Affective Disorder (SAD). When she first meets Patricia Bledsoe, Danquah is "expecting her to be old, feeble, and withdrawn, what [she] imagined someone who had been depressed for over three decades would look like" (60). Even though she deals with depression herself, Danquah admits to being influenced by public stereotypes about people with mental health issues in her initial assessment. Instead, Patricia is "beautiful, and full of energy" (60), proving how problematic and insufficient stereotypes and classification attempts are as they do not include individual stories. Just like with postpartum depression, Danquah defines SAD, using Dr. Norman E. Rosenthal's *Winter Blues* (1993), an established reference on the disorder, to emphasize the realness of her friend's mother's experiences.

As Danquah herself does earlier in the memoir, Patricia explains in detail the shapes depression takes in her own life: she first noticed the illness, which was "like nothing [she] had ever experienced before" (61), at the age of twenty-eight with the main symptom of overwhelming guilt. She notes that she became obsessed with cleanliness and death, had suicidal thoughts, and was offended when neurologists suggested she should attend therapy sessions because in the early sixties "even white folks weren't doing that" (62). Seeking treatment seemed like such a foreign concept to her, not only because of her race, that it prevented her from finding meaningful help. Once she does find the courage to meet with a therapist, she is initially diagnosed with "housewives' syndrome" and told that she should find a job (63). The sexism in this "diagnosis," which merely tells women that they need to fight their boredom and which recalls Betty Friedan's collection of white, middle-class women's stories in *The Feminine Mystique* (1963), is apparent. Not until she finds a doctor in the African American community who prescribes electroshock therapy and antidepressants does Patricia feel taken seriously.

After this initial introductory meeting with Patricia, Danquah reunites the reader with her in a later section in the memoir where they learn about the possible reasons for Patricia's illness: Patricia recounts that she was abandoned by her mother at age three (eerily paralleling Danquah's own life), which caused her immense "emotional deprivation" (241). While her mother does return to get Patricia when she is in third grade, she is emotionally abusive. Patricia becomes pregnant at seventeen and leaves her abusive husband at nineteen. Her life experiences underline Danquah's point throughout the memoir that mental illness is intricately connected to life circumstances and opportunities and not an issue of willpower and merit. Because the United States is still at its core a sexist, racist, and xenophobic country, the stressors in Patricia's life are of relevance to all women of color, especially those with an immigrant background.

For Danquah, sharing personal stories constitutes a consciousness-raising tool that helps her understand that her experiences are not unique or abnormal. When Danquah and her friend Jade discuss a personal journal entry, the former initially shows herself reluctant to think of herself as depressed: "I hardly think that's cause for medication or a trip to the loony bin. Everybody gets that way sometimes. . . . We get down, we deal with it, we pick ourselves back up and we move on" (Danquah 84). Her denial seems rooted in both the strong Black woman stereotype and American Dream rhetoric, which labels everyone (and, above all, an immigrant) weak who is unable to "pull themselves up by their own bootstraps." This attitude proves, of course, deeply problematic, chiefly for women of color with a mental disability, as it neither acknowledges unearned racial, gendered, and citizenship privilege as a deciding factor nor takes into account biology. When Jade counters this rejection by explaining that she takes Prozac, Danquah becomes "frightened. People on Prozac were said to be unpredictable, even violent" (84). She cannot evade negative prejudices that mark people with a mental illness as necessarily dangerous and out of control. In connection with racist claims that brand all people of color as aggressive, these misperceptions create an unsafe environment for Black women with chronic depression. Therefore, denying the illness becomes a survival mechanism. Jade tries to assuage Danquah and explains that chronic depression is a legitimate condition that is belittled by an overuse of the term: "People who are just having a bad day should use another word" (86). During this conversation, the first of its kind for Danquah, she experiences a "sudden surge of strength and determination. [She] wanted to know more" (85)—a desire that she hopes to incite in her readers, too, as knowledge might lead to activism.

In a relevant manner, *Willow Weep for Me*'s lack of self-centeredness provokes the calls for social and political action in Guinea-native Kadiatou Diallo's memoir, *My Heart Will Cross This Ocean. My Story, My Son, Amadou* (2003). Diallo's son, Amadou, was shot nineteen times by a street crime unit in New York City in 1999. Her son's death is what triggers his mother to begin writing her own autobiography, in which she speaks out for African women's rights and against police violence targeting Black men in the United States: "The one last thing she can do is to try and give her child back his story, the greatest and least obligation she can fulfill" (5). Like Danquah, Diallo uses her memoir not solely to depict her own life, but to educate her readers on a social justice issue and to call them to political action. *My Heart* starts with an intricate portrayal of the violence and poverty that plagued West African Guinea after French occupation. Diallo describes how she underwent female genital mutilation and was given away as a child bride at thirteen to a man sixteen years older. While her husband eventually gets a second wife and abandons her and their children, Diallo still manages to become an affluent business woman.

Interspersed with Diallo's story that demands equality for women, the reader learns about Amadou and other young people who look for better living conditions abroad: "At the embassy in Conakry, the young men and women stand in lines for hours, sometimes days, hoping the clerk behind the window will announce their number" (214). Poorly equipped hospitals, lack of electricity and clean water, old school supplies and books are just some examples that Diallo lists to emphasize the lack of opportunity for young people in West Africa and to incite understanding for their desire to migrate. But while Amadou did not see a future for himself in his home country, he was well educated and not destitute, which is the opposite of what the media reported after his death. For them, he was an "unarmed West African street vendor" who was poorly educated and lacked English skills (244). Diallo is certain that "this label stole [her son's] story" (246). In the United States, African migrants, like other minoritized communities, have their stories written *for* them. For Diallo, to dedicate her own life story to the survival of young Black men in United States society denotes how much is at stake for African migrants and how memoir can be conducive to educate and demand social change.

Rooted in a similar social justice focus that connects migration, race, gender, and class, Danquah's objective for her memoir is twofold and based in an activist point of view: she aims to disseminate her own experiences to provide support for immigrant women of color with depression and to educate those readers who are unfamiliar with mental illness. Additionally, she advocates for a reform of therapy practices. Danquah describes how she starts taking Zoloft, which makes her emotionally numb (202). Her doctor also prescribes an anxiety-controlling medication, but when she cannot afford to buy it, she begins self-medicating with alcohol (203). Only when she stops taking Zoloft does her desire to drink go away (221). Like with Patricia, her friend's mother who suffers from SAD, Danquah comes to realize that medication does not improve the racist, sexist, xenophobic reality that disables her every day as a Black woman.

Dossa observes that "as marginalized communities are often considered to work within the confines of their own traditions and cultures[, t]heir critique of the larger system is barely acknowledged" (161). Mostly ignorant of anything but Caucasian "norms," many health care professionals tend to blame a person's culture and community for their mental health concerns more readily if the patient is a member of a minoritized group. According to Dossa, this "focus on culture detracts attention from social, economic and political factors that exclude and trivialize the concerns of racialized minorities" (163). Danquah asserts that if a therapist "could not 'fathom' [her] reality as a black person, how would he be able to assess or address the rage, the fear, and the host of other complex emotions that go hand in hand with being black in a racist society? For whatever reason, seeing a black therapist had never crossed [her] mind, until then" (224). Consequently, she uses her memoir to demand "cultural sensitivity" from medical personnel "as . . . culture plays an important role in both the patient's illness and treatment" (224–225). If a therapist cannot imagine the harshness of their patient's quotidian experiences, how can they fully understand that patient's struggles, empathize with their hardship, and decide on an adequate course of action. Danquah suggests that it would be immensely beneficial if she could work with a therapist who has "knowledge [about her experiences as a black woman], preferably, that [she does] not have to give him/her [her] self" (225). Emphasis on sensitivity and diversity training in medical schools could go a long way toward improving medical care for all.

CONCLUSIONS

"There is beauty on the other side" (266); those are the last words of the core part of Danquah's narrative. While the majority of *Willow Weep for Me* concentrates on the struggles associated with being a Black immigrant woman with chronic depression in the United States, it seems important to the author to leave her readers on an optimistic note and with practical advice. Danquah admits that "reluctantly, [she is] on medication" (258). She acknowledges that she needs this medication, but, at the same time, she is concerned that "there is something that seems really wrong with the fact that Prozac is one of the most prescribed drugs in this country. Maybe I just don't want to accept the reality that so many of us are in pain" (258). Weary of doctors' eagerness to prescribe pills and hoping to give her readers a sense of control over their own bodies, Danquah offers advice on how to treat depression with music, meditation, exercise, diet, and vigilant monitoring. In an acknowledgment that racism, sexism, and xenophobia disable people, she also hosts monthly meetings for Black women to offer them a healing space to share their experiences in a consciousness-raising setting. Before she lists the criteria for depression, which I have discussed above, she cites the poem "Alive in the World" by Jackson Browne. One line stands out: "I want to live in the world, not inside my head" (Danquah 267). Through her memoir, Danquah attempts to facilitate for her readers the ability to live more fulfilled and less isolated lives.

In a 2011 interview, Danquah identifies herself as an activist:

> I'm . . . interested in grassroots politics, in everyday people becoming active and realising that they are empowered to navigate their own future and the future of their land. To that end, I'm interested in issues of social justice, especially ones that concern themselves with ending violence against women, exploitation of children for labour, trafficking of human body parts, eradicating poverty and bridging the gap between the haves and the have-nots. I try to do my part to raise awareness about these issues. ("Interview")

I see Danquah practice her activism, much like Rosalina Rosay whom I discussed in chapter 1, via her adaptations of the memoir genre that accommodate the experiences, identities, and needs of underserved communities such as Black and immigrant women with mental health problems. Jane Jeong Trenka, whose life writing is the focus of the following chapter, pushes such generic revisions even further in her call for attention to the rights of transnationally adopted individuals.

3
TRANSNATIONAL ADOPTEE LIFE WRITING
OPPRESSED VOICES AND GENRE CHOICES

In contrast to the other migratory movements (from Central and South American, Africa, or predominantly Muslim countries) discussed in *Lives beyond Borders*, transnational adoption is usually not perceived as gendered male because most adoption of this kind, especially from Asian and African countries, is presented as the rescuing of girl children and labeled as a necessary end product of Western support for refugees rejected by their country of birth (see Volkman; Park Nelson). I argue that investigating transnational adoption through the lenses of migration and gender can assist in assessing systems of power and privilege that affect adoptees' experiences. In her memoir, *The Language of Blood* (2003), Jane Jeong Trenka explores the identity of children adopted from Korea.[1] In the process, she adapts life writing's generic boundaries and its relationship with national identity by inserting, among other elements, letters, third-person stories, a play, and a crossword puzzle. By means of these stylistic choices, she contrasts her own self-perception with the way she is consumed—that is, perceived and stereotyped—by U.S. society. She critiques white privilege for condoning structural racism and discriminatory assimilation practices, which force a toxic, fake identity onto many adoptees.[2]

While not all adoptees perceive their relinquishment as a traumatic experience, much literature finds that the adoption process—especially closed adoption, which grew out of a desire for secrecy on the part of upper-class unwed women and became standard in the 1960s (Carp 112)—can harm children.[3] In the opinion of adoption scholars such as Nancy Newton

Verrier, this denial of a child's birth-past exacerbates a "primal wound" of separation that—similar to Cathy Caruth's understanding of trauma as "unclaimed experience"—can cause PTSD-like symptoms (such as anxiety, distrust, and depression) in adopted children. In *Lost and Found* (1988), Betty Jean Lifton offers an overview of medical and psychological studies that diagnose adoptees with higher rates of varying mental illnesses. Margaret Homans, too, sees trauma reflected in adoptees' writing: "Like (or as) trauma narratives, adoption narratives are often obsessively oriented towards an irretrievable past, and like (or as) trauma, adoption compels the creation of plausible if not verifiable narratives" ("Adoption Narratives" 7). With its historical focus on self-creation and self-determination, life writing offers valuable opportunities for adoptees to make sense of their identities. Additionally, as I will demonstrate in this chapter, Trenka uses the genre as a tool for social activism in examining transnational adoption as a consequence of globalized oppression and in offering an intersectional analysis of transnational adoptees' and poor birthmothers' lives.

In the United States, international adoption has been more popular than domestic transracial adoption. Barbara Melosh's *Strangers and Kin* (2002), an extensive history of stranger adoption, illustrates how, in 1949, Pearl S. Buck's Welcome House laid the groundwork for a transnational adoption market as it brought roughly five thousand Amerasian children to the United States. Likewise, the founding of Henry Holt International in 1956 systematized the adoption of Korean children by U.S. couples. Many prospective adoptive parents who feared contested domestic adoption were attracted to international adoption and its promise of geographically removed birth parents (Melosh 192). While during the 1950s and 1960s most adoptees were orphans or abandoned biracial children fathered by American soldiers, most adoption cases by the 1970s involved full-Korean children born out of wedlock due to increasing divorce rates and teen pregnancies in a society that experienced rapid industrialization and urbanization. After a baby boom and a rise in children conceived out of wedlock had initiated a market for adoption in the United States in the 1940s and '50s, the 1960s and '70s—marked by the legalization of abortion, easier access to birth control, a decline in teenage pregnancy, and a larger social acceptance of single parenthood accompanied by more access to social assistance mechanisms—saw a decrease in desired white, able-bodied children available for adoption (Carp 196).[4] Indeed, a " 'healthy white baby' was a request deemed 'unrealistic' by social workers in the 1970s" (Melosh 162). In 1985, transnational adoptions peaked in Korea with 8,837 children sent abroad. Melosh explains that the "pluralistic ideology and ethnic diversity of a 'nation of immigrants' rendered American society more open to adoption than any other country" (166). And, in fact, the United States has historically been one of the main recipients of Korean children; for example, between 2004 and 2015 roughly 80 percent of Korean adoptees were settled in the United States (Condit-Shrestha 366–367).

The multifaceted mechanisms of adoption are estimated to have generated approximately fifteen to forty million dollars for the Korean economy by the 1980s (Condit-Shrestha 372). Kimberly McKee's concept of the "transnational adoption industrial complex" (TAIC) is especially powerful because it captures the willfulness of the creation of adoptable children in light of increased demand in the West. Striking support for this claim provide the facts that 90 percent of Korean adoptees have been children of unwed mothers and that until July 2015, when the Single Parent Family Support Act passed in 2011 took effect, adoption agencies ran about 50 percent of all unwed mothers' homes in the country (Bae 306).

Looking at the transfer of children as a TAIC implies that the cultural, political, and socioeconomic circumstances that make especially developing nations, like Korea, send children abroad in large numbers are the purposeful effects of lasting colonial and imperial exploitation by European countries as well as the United States. While perhaps sustaining the adoption market is not the primary goal of said practices, it has certainly been a welcome and accepted side effect.[5] Indeed, as John McLeod points out, colonialism has always been invested globally in the breaking and making of certain families. He writes: the "social production of vulnerable children, rendered on their own and available for state-endorsed ownership at the service of a colonial mission, was a core business of empire, discovered far and wide across colonized space and a ready result of the inequities it wrought" (McLeod 207). As Trenka makes clear in her memoir, adoption is not merely a private but a very political issue with far-reaching implications.

The Language of Blood exposes the challenges many transnational adoptees face when trying to fit into narrow, socially constructed concepts of hybridity and critically analyzes the use of transracial adoptees as symbols of a supposed post-racial, colorblind society. Together with the voices of other adoptees, the memoir creates "a counterpublic that challenges the [TAIC] and the fetishization of [adoptees'] bodies within mainstream adoption discourse" (McKee, *Disrupting* 5). Trenka struggles with trying to define herself. Is she American, Korean, Asian American, an adoptee, an immigrant, an exile, or an ex-pat? Despite her insecurity about her identity, she writes powerfully against images that portray her as a "fraud" or a "grotesque hybrid" (Trenka 215).[6] Through her writing, Trenka reclaims expertise about transnational adoption from researchers, social workers, and white adoptive parents. My reading of *The Language of Blood* points to vital connections between adoption studies, Women's and Gender Studies, and Race and Ethnicity Studies and demonstrates how transnational adoptees might use life writing not solely as a genre of self-representation, but as a tactical strategy to have their communities' humanity and dignity recognized. Adoption life writing challenges idealizing master narratives of belonging, home, and national identity with counter-histories of oppression and discrimination that can destabilize social, cultural, and political hierarchies and our understanding of life writing's link with nationalism.

In *Adopting America* (2011), Carol J. Singley offers insights into how literature from Puritan settlement to the early twentieth century used adoption as a trope to create various forms of "American-ness." She argues that "literary representations of adoption reflect national mythologies" (Singley 5). Adoption functions as a symbol of individual and national progress, long used to prop up ideologies of meritocracy and the American Dream. The movement to seal adoption files in the early twentieth century, which became standard in the 1970s, intended to erase children's national birth identity in support of the American nationalist project. In more recent literature, according to Singley, "adoption rises again in importance as a hallmark of a multicultural American society, but ambivalence continues, reflecting both pride in American hybridity and attachment to naturalized, traditionally patriarchal family structures" (15). While much literature employs adoption as supposed proof of the end of racism in the United States, other literary works, including much of the life writing by transnational adoptees, questions adoption's complicity with nationalism and white supremacy.

Within this literary context, life writing offers an effective site for the examination of transnational adoptees' identity formation and their political agendas. In *Subjectivity, Identity, and the Body* (1993), Sidonie Smith elaborates that "autobiographical practices become occasions for restaging subjectivity, and autobiographical strategies become occasions for the staging of resistance" (156). In addition to offering retrospective writing to come to an understanding of oneself as a "coherent" self, Trenka's memoir functions as a tool of persuasion to push for political action in the form of the complete overhaul of the TAIC. On her (now taken down) blog, *Jane's Blog. Bitter Angry Ajumma*, she published her adoption file, explains the fraudulent system of creating "paper orphans," and expresses the hope that she "will live to see the day when adoption as it is practiced today is viewed as the archaic, primitive, and exploitative practice that it really is."[7] In defining what it means for her to live as a Korean transnational adoptee as well as calling for changes to the adoption system, Trenka practices what Scott Lyons calls "rhetorical sovereignty," the "inherent right and ability of peoples to determine their own communicative needs and desires . . . , to decide for themselves the goals, modes, styles, and languages of public discourse" (449–450). This freedom to shape autobiographical communication according to one's rhetorical situation and needs allows Trenka to recover self-determination and respect.

Adoptee life writing gives insight into intersectional systems of oppression—such as the possible ostracization of transracial adoptees, the exploitation of poor women in favor of childless, Western, middle-class families, as well as the perpetuation of global, economic injustice—and reaches a wide population in ways that the social sciences at the forefront of this discussion usually do not have at their disposal.

TRANSNATIONAL ADOPTION AND OPPRESSION

The space for adoption to be an altruistic act certainly exists, and Trenka indeed received pushback for her memoir's open criticism of adoption. Kristi Brian explains that those who analyze the adoption industry critically risk being accused of "overpoliticizing a problem that should only be about giving a poor child a nice home" (151). She further claims that "thinking of adoption as quite possibly the beginning of a disaster rather than an automatic happy ending may be a more realistic way to think about the child transfers that land thousands of children of color from around the world into white nuclear families in the United States every year" (170). Because Trenka's work challenges the dominant cultural imaginary, *The Language of Blood* offers an alternative perspective that is marginalized by public opinion.

In its critique of transnational adoption practices, Trenka portrays herself as doubled: she is legally American and trained to think of herself as white, but, at the same time, society treats her as a perpetual foreigner who does not fit in. Describing herself, Trenka says on her blog, "I live with two distinct legal identities that never meet." Her racialized body parallels the memoir's textual body: Trenka wants her book to be read as a memoir, according to her subtitle, but she also vehemently resists traditional autobiographical norms. Through her adaptations in form, she attempts to challenge socially constructed versions of "truth" and resists a definition of the self that depends on a distinct nationality.

Like Rosay in her portrayal of undocumented immigrants' humanity and Danquah's emphasis on the experiences of Black immigrant women with mental illness, Trenka uses her personal writing as a political tool to give voice to those who are not heard—adoptees as well as culturally silenced birthmothers—to promote a person's rights to preserve one's birth identity and to determine freely who you are. In discussing Trenka's modifications of the genre, I demonstrate what forms life writing assumes for people who find themselves excluded from the larger systems in which they live. It is not my intention to diagnose and objectify adoptees' experiences as is often standard practice. Instead, I aim to understand how some adult adoptees critically question their upbringing through writing their lives and publicizing the voices of oppressed communities, such as poor birthmothers.

According to Rocío Davis, "Asian North American memoirs of childhood are challenging the construction and performative potential of the national experience, particularly in the experiential categories of epistemology and phenomenology" (1). Adoptee memoirs like *The Language of Blood* add substantially to the important discourse of the construction of nationality, citizenship, and U.S. identity. In their introduction to *Outsiders within: Writing on Transracial Adoption* (2006), Jane Trenka, Julia Oparah, and Sun Yung Shin stipulate that "over the past fifty years, white adoptive parents, academics, psychiatrists, and social workers have dominated the literature on transracial adoption . . . . The voices of adult transracial adoptees remain largely unheard" (1). Thanks to texts such as *The Language of Blood* and the work of many adult transnational adoptees, the politics and perceptions of transnational adoption have started to change.[8] Yet, the number of transracial adoption memoirs, which hold the power to question the "dominant narrative of transnational and transracial adoption as a remedy for racism" (Park Nelson, *Invisible* 9), is small, and we need more critical, literary analysis of these works.

Trenka's identity negotiations shape her memoir from the beginning. Transmitting the supposed voice of a newborn, Trenka describes her birth identity on the second page:

> My name is Jeong Kyong-Ah. My family register states . . . my birth, the lunar date January 24, 1972. . . . My ancestry includes landowners, scholars, and government officials. I have six siblings. I am a citizen of the Republic of Korea. I am from a land of

pear fields and streams, where Buddhist temples are hidden in the mountains, where people laugh loudly and honor their dead. (14)

Shortly after this explanation, however, we learn how migration has changed Trenka's identity:

> Halfway around the world, I am someone else. I am Jane Marie Brauer, created September 26, 1972, when I was carried off an airplane . . . . My . . . birth certificate declares my date of birth to be March 8, 1972. . . . My ancestors were farmers, factory workers, a sometime Bible salesman. I have one sister . . . I became an American citizen at age 5, when I stood before a judge and pledged allegiance to the flag of the United States of America. I come from a land of plains . . . where Lutheran churches foot the corn fields, where stoicism is stamped into the bones of each generation. (15)

Working against a common attitude that sees adoption as a tool to "save" children from horrible living conditions, Trenka subtly introduces her negative stance toward interracial adoption early in her memoir:[9] Trenka's identity and personal history change to the point that her date of birth cannot stay the same; already the citizen of a country, she becomes a citizen of the United States only at the age of five;[10] born into a fruitful, wild nature and to a welcoming, joyful people, she is moved to a monotonous landscape populated by a passive people. The dichotomy between the environments that shaped her sets the tone for Trenka's isolating experiences of displacement and fragmentation. The term "created" stands out forcefully. It connotes the idea that one's birth country, culture, and parents can be permanently erased from one's identity to create an "unproblematic," unified self.

Tonya Bishoff echoes this insistence on a second birth upon arrival in the United States in her poem "Unnamed Blood" when she writes "i was squeezed through the opening / of a powerful steel bird" (37). Like in Trenka's narrative, a plane functions as leitmotif in Bishoff's narration: Instead of a mother's body, Bishoff's American alter ego is birthed by a plane, representing the tendency among many adoptive parents to create the notion that adoptees' lives began only after adoption (see, for example, Lifton's *Lost and Found*). This approach to adoptees' identity formation, also called the "clean break" ideology, was "most popular in the first half of the twentieth century, . . . [when b]irth parents were figuratively erased out of existence. . . . [as] birth certificates were legally doctored, with the birth parents' names removed and replaced by those of the adoptive parents" (Jacobson 91). The intention was to cut out the children's past to make it seem as if they had never lived any time and anywhere else but at "home." A necessary by-product of this practice is the complete obliteration of birthmothers.

Homans asserts that the "problem is not simply that birthmothers have been discouraged from sharing their stories. In culturally prevalent views of stranger adoption, the birthmother is not meant to survive, much less to speak" ("The Mother" 35). Much like women of color in the United States who are vilified as bad mothers, as I have discussed with regard to Danquah's memoir and disability in chapter 2, Korean birthmothers are unable to live up to ideological notions of "good" motherhood and are punished for it. Capturing the epitome of patriarchal views on women's bodies, poor birthmothers (especially non-Caucasian ones) are widely seen as birthing vessels that can be discarded after the child is born.

Elaborating on adoptive parents' desire to change their children's lives completely, Emily Hipchen and Jill Deans point out that "the act of adoption . . . assumes that one's identity can be re-written, re-scripted, through language, laws, and customs" (167). Often, this attitude is supported by the parents' wish "to impose a new identity upon the child, through naming" (Grice 58). As Trenka's narrative suggests, many adoptees refuse to be silenced in such a way, reject such imposed passivity, and "resist being defined as victims condemned to half-lives between cultures" (Trenka, Oparah, and Shin 4). While some adoptive parents leave a trace of their children's birth identity in their (middle) names, Trenka decides for herself to use her Korean name as a tool of empowerment: "Jeong. Kyong-Ah. . . . Jane Marie Brauer. Jane Marie Trenka. Jane Brauer Trenka. Jane Kyong-Ah Jeong Brauer-Trenka. I finally choose Jane Jeong Trenka: one name from each family. I wear it like a scar and a badge . . . I deliberately choose my name, my clan, my place in the world as it has borne me and created me" (238). Very similar to the naming process Danquah undergoes, which I discuss in chapter 2, Trenka achieves self-definition by incorporating elements from all her life stages into her identity. She embraces her national doubleness as a strength instead of a circumstance that necessarily weakens her. Her names remind her of her traumatic past and point to the pride she carries within herself.

As the field of Adoption Studies has made clear, issues of power, race, and white privilege pervade adoption processes. The adoption system is shaped by white parents' desire for healthy, able-bodied, non-Black/

non-Latinx children who can be taken far away from their birth parents to avoid familial interactions (Jacobson 37). Brian explains that, because of "race-evasive and power-evasive thinking" that presents race and culture as interchangeable (37), "forces of violence . . . continue to weave their way through adoption stories" (x).[11] A lack of cultural and racial literacy on the part of her adoptive parents complicates Trenka's fight for a self that integrates both her nationalities: "The a-word, adoption, was not mentioned in our house. Neither was the K-word, Korea. There were no books about adopted children, no celebrations of adoption day or naturalization day, no culture camps to attend" (39). While contemporary health professionals recommended that adoptive parents conceal the fact of adoption from children because it was seen as psychologically more beneficial for the latter (Carp 135), the lack of practices Trenka lists above hinder her identity formation and leave her helpless against racism and xenophobia, which has devastating implications for her.

Ignoring a child's skin color and heritage can yield traumatic consequences, which is why adoption agencies that follow ethical practices now require prospective adoptive parents to undergo complex training; many newer adoption manuals, too, offer adoptive parents advice on being proactive about a transnationally or transracially adopted child's possible experiences in a racist and xenophobic environment.[12] Gail Steinberg and Beth Hall's *Inside Transracial Adoption* (2000), for example, admonishes adoptive parents to avoid "mak[ing] kids choose between family and race! Children can't make such a choice without negating parts of themselves. In order to feel whole, they must feel connected to all of the worlds they inhabit" (17). Yet, they also address their readers by asking: "Are you the kind of person who tends to read more than one book at a time . . . ? If you enjoy complexity, then the demands of transracial parenting will be less challenging for you than if you are the sort of person who strives for a life of simplicity" (Steinberg and Hall 13). These questions, in my opinion, fit the oversimplifying rhetoric of many adoption self-help books—the cultural narratives, which Trenka reacts to and writes against—on such topics as stress-reduction or social networking skills. While the generalizing and distorting tone of such statements strikes me as highly inappropriate for the sensitive topic of adoption, Steinberg and Hall do point to the necessity of acknowledging a child's identity since it "is important that your child feel accepted into your family for who she is; *not for whom she might think you want her to be*" (212; emphasis in original). Adoptees' identity should not be forced to conform to adoptive parents' fantasies of children never born, for the idea that adoptees' birth identities can be completely erased is a myth.

As her parents' child-rearing strongly contrasts the above recommendations, Trenka comes to believe that her parents, devout Christians, adopted her and her sister to please God and to fulfill God's command to multiply. Addressing the Lutheran Social Service that helped her parents with the adoption process, she writes, "show me that in 1972 there was absolutely no information about what to do with a transracially adopted child, and that there is still no information available to them in their area, that you never gave them any support or follow up. If their ignorance was beyond their control, maybe I could forgive their callous actions" (193).[13] Trenka's parents refuse to talk about their daughters' Korean origins in an effort to erase all early memories. At that time, the well-established practice of forced assimilation was only slowly beginning to be replaced by efforts to preserve birth culture. Through the 1960s, "children were to be mainstreamed—'Americanized'—as quickly as possible," and any differences were supposed to be ignored (Jacobson 3–4). Such assimilation forces pressure adoptees much more than other immigrants since they do not have ethnic enclaves to fall back on (Brian 65).

In the 1970s, a rise in transnational adoption, more openness in adoption processes, and criticism regarding the adoption of African American and Native American children slowly led to a shift toward efforts of "culture keeping" "intended to allow for the acknowledgement of the child's specific and unique origins . . . in a way that does not necessarily jeopardize the feeling of exclusive kinship adoptive parents crave" (Jacobson 93). So-called "culture camps," which resemble weeks-long summer camps focused on adoptees' birth cultures are now particularly popular. Such programs might, to a certain extent, serve as a balancing force to assimilation pressures. Amanda Baden carefully suggests that "as a form of racial-ethnic socialization, culture camps may be effective for reducing depression and anxiety levels" as her pre- and post-tests correlate lower levels of depression with higher levels of ethnic identity in adoptee campers (27). The camp experience further helped participants "gain a sense of themselves as adopted persons and develop a degree of comfort with their adoptive histories" (Baden 28). Lori Delale-O'Connor, nevertheless, notes tendencies to push a nationalist agenda in the culture camps she observed, which concentrated only on "the 'acceptable' aspects of children's birth cultures: that is, those aspects that do not contradict or create dissonance with mainstream American culture" (214). The camps in Delale-O'Connor's study mostly provided generic information constructed by white American adoptive parents and avoided controversial topics that show a clash of American and birth culture values (214, 216); hence, in some cases, culture camps might be turned, intentionally or not, into a tool to promote nationalism and assimilation instead of offering practical approaches for children to feel more secure in their identity and deal with life in a racist and xenophobic society.

In addition to culture camps, some families might opt for a return visit to their child's country of birth. Studies suggest that these visits can have positive effects on the adoptees' sense of identity and might help them answer questions about their origins; they also likely support the adoptive parents' understanding of their child's birth culture and might strengthen their efforts to keep a connection to it (Ponte, Wang, and Fan 117). Often, such trips include visits to orphanages and abandonment sites, which can be an emotional experience for adoptees and adoptive parents alike (118).

While nowadays adoption agencies offer "engagement with a foreign culture" as an attractive feature of international adoption (Jacobson 53), at the time of Trenka's adoption, as described by Lifton in *Lost and Found* (1988), "inherent in the adoption process [was] the expectation that the child [was] to regard the birth parents *as if* dead—if not literally, then certainly symbolically. They [were], in other words, taboo" (14; emphasis in original). In fact, professional diagnosing practices were complicit in upholding white adoptive parents' power as they labeled adoptees as "neurotic" (Lifton, *Twice* 98), "disturbed," and stuck in a "family romance fantasy" for wanting to find their birth parents (Carp 117), a desire pathologized as "unnatural or a sign of mental instability" (Carp 163). Additionally, Trenka's adoption predates any critical discussions of whiteness so that "critiques of racialized entitlement were eclipsed by assumptions of generosity and goodwill" (Brian 51). Likewise, adult adoptee voices were not present at the time and are still not heard enough today.

While Trenka's sister, Carol, who was adopted with Trenka at the age of four and a half, seeks complete assimilation, Trenka resists this approach. The estrangement from her parents makes the author think of herself and her sister as "replacement children . . . . last resorts; consolation prizes in the fertility lottery; the children who came into the family to replace the biological child, the child who was really wanted. . . . To our parents, we are reminders of their infertility. . . . We are reminders of inadequacy, of incompleteness" (207). Her adoptive parents' frantic insistence on the absence of a Korean part of their daughters' identity keeps reminding Trenka that she is not the white, male, American child that her parents had hoped for, but that she is an imperfect version of who they wanted her to be. These feelings add to her perception of herself as a "mail-order child" (Trenka 97), not a full family member but property, a consoling object to make her parents feel better about themselves no matter the cost to the child.

The Language of Blood portrays the roots for Trenka's trauma in a system built on the exploitation of poor women that made her adoption by unfit people possible.[14] The connection between women's oppression and adoptees' global movements demands further theoretical attention. As the title suggests, Eun Kyung Min's "The Daughter's Exchange in Jane Jeong Trenka's *The Language of Blood*" (2008) makes reference to Gayle Rubin's seminal essay "Traffic in Women: Notes on the Political Economy of Women" (1975). While in transnational adoption—similar to patriarchs marrying off their daughters—"children are exchanged in a systematic exchange of money and bodies in which *children* do not have full rights to themselves" (Min 25–26; emphasis in original), adoption, unlike marriage, does specifically *not* create reciprocal kinship among families (Min 126). Because the exchange does not happen solely between men, the context changes.

I would like to explore these parallels between the exchange of women and children further. Rubin argues that the origins of the exchange of women lie in business transactions between people in power. Transnational adoption, too, was designed by higher authorities to benefit the privileged. While the media portrayed adoptees as objects of humanitarian concern, the system of exchange was in fact inaugurated to strengthen the United States' fight against Communism. Tellingly, many transnational adoptees were heralded as "gifts," but because this denomination made Korea sound like a benefactor instead of the parents like saviors, now the term "chosen child" is used more frequently (Kim 48).[15] Min adds that the terminology of "choice makes the adoptee yet more dependent on and indebted to the adoptive parents, by fixating on that moment in which the adoptee was supposedly rescued from danger and brought to safety" (127). The rescue narrative is a well-documented element of adoption, beginning with portrayals of official national "rescue missions," such as "Operation Babylift," which facilitated the migration of children fathered by U.S. servicemen in Vietnam. Narratives by white adoptive parents as well as media coverage about transnational adoption tend to emphasize opportunities for upward mobility and assimilation in the United States compared to countries of birth (Melosh 194).

In the case of transnational adoption from Asia, the rescue narrative is intrinsically connected with Orientalist perceptions that justify the relocation of children from a supposedly uncivilized and "backwards" East to a civilized and "progressive" West (McKee, *Disrupting* 19). Oriental, in this context, does not simply mark a geographic location, but implies racist theories about power hierarchies. In *Orientalism* (1978), Edward Said explains Orientalism as those romanticizing forces that describe the West as superior and justify the domination and invasion of a backward East. Still today, these convictions enable global imperialist policies and the perception of people of Asian descent as a threat.

To many people, it is "clear" that Trenka was "saved," "rescued by adoption; had [she] stayed in Korea, [she] would have been institutionalized, after which [she] would have turned into . . . a prostitute. The standards by which [Americans] judge . . . good living—a college education, American citizenship, a white, middle-class upbringing in a pre-approved home—would not have been available to [her]" (Trenka 226). This "rescue mission" rhetoric surrounding adoption is steeped in imagery that sexualizes Asian women and is detrimental because it feeds into the "Orientalist fantasy of an uncivilized and cruel East that is unable and unwilling to care for its own people" (Wills, "Claiming America"), which legitimizes the global export of children at the expense of investing into social systems in the sending countries. In her follow-up memoir, *Fugitive Visions* (2009), Trenka further highlights the dire consequences of this willful, systematic ignorance: "My body survived. . . . But so much of me . . . didn't survive. . . . The destruction of the identities and histories of the adoptees wasn't at all personal. It was just methodical. . . . Our adoptions would take our language, our culture, our families, our names, our birth dates, our citizenship, and our identities in a perfectly legal process. And the world would view it as charitable and ethical" (89).[16] The common idea that adoptees are necessarily saved from prostitution and death is not factual, as Trenka attests that her sisters who stayed in Korea do not lead a destitute life.[17] Conversely, as Brian elaborates, depression, addiction, suicides, and incidences of stalking, caused by "racial hatred and isolation, gendered violence, and structural inequality," are so common among transnational adoptees that adoption does certainly not offer a guarantee of a less violent life than in the birth country (x–xi).

The rhetoric of rescue not only creates a sense of infallibility surrounding the adoptive parents, but also vilifies birthmothers and cultures with no regard to the oppressive root causes for transnational adoption, such as extreme poverty and misogyny. As Homans clarifies, birthmothers are dehumanized as a "result of an insufficiency in language that reflects and perpetuates the social non-being of the birthmother" ("The Mother"

45). In my adapted theory of Rubin's patriarchal exchange, adoption works as an exchange medium not of grown women but children in an environment in which female children are excess and waste and are abandoned instead of used for kinship bonding. To force them into participating in the exchange, sexist constraints are put on poor birthmothers. Brian argues that "a woman's strategy for survival . . . demands a constrained choice that ultimately benefits the state in the form of hard currency that adopters from the global North willingly pay to satisfy a desire" (179). Capitalist requests for ownership perpetuate transnational adoption. As with Rosay's mother in *Journey of Hope*, discussed in chapter 1, the attempt to secure her children's sheer survival pushes Trenka's mother to initiate the immigration process for her children. Although the cultural backgrounds of these life stories are far different, the mothers, due to the oppression they experience, must go to extraordinary measures to do what they think is best for their daughters.

Poverty and an abusive husband create an environment in which Trenka's mother is forced to give birth to her youngest daughter outside in the snow instead of in a hospital. Once Trenka is born, her father almost suffocates her because she turned out to be "only" another daughter. To avoid any responsibility for her, he accuses his wife of having had an affair and even goes as far as throwing Trenka out of a window in an attempt to get rid of her (6–7, 116). He finally succeeds in pressuring his wife into bringing Trenka and her sister to an orphanage. At the orphanage, however, conditions are so poor that Trenka nearly loses her life again. When her mother realizes the risk, she rescues her daughters. But seeking shelter from an abusive husband, working multiple jobs to feed her children, and knowing that growing up in Korea without a father causes great shame, Trenka's mother, or *Umma*, comes to the point where she believes that "if she had kept [Trenka], [she] would have been either dead or a beggar" (Trenka 229). As physical proof of this dire prediction, Trenka's older sister arrives in the United States extremely malnourished and legally blind. Fitting my adaptation of Rubin's analysis, patriarchal forces cause the exchange, as the man in power enforces the adoption, not to create kinship but to profit from it nevertheless. The patriarchal nation-state then benefits financially from the abandonment and resulting migration.

Through her memoir, Trenka shows her readers how this predicament of unbalanced exchange can put a traumatic strain on the relationship between a transnational adoptee and her Western, adoptive parents. In addition to a silencing intrafamily atmosphere, Trenka experiences growing up as a child of color in an all-white neighborhood in small-town Minnesota as oppressive.[18]

Her adoptive parents' vehement insistence on ignoring her skin color and ethnicity hinder Trenka in her identity formation process. Addressing this issue, Trenka, Oparah, and Shin propose denoting international adoptees as "*transracial*" adoptees to emphasize "how relentless our racialization has been through our lives" (2–3; emphasis in original). With regard to the community beyond their families, Korean adoptees' racial features can turn them into a consumable commodity—an Oriental Other whose "exotic" features serve as entertainment for the community—and perpetuate their silencing.

Trenka critically analyzes the influence of common perceptions about Asians as unassimilable foreigners in the United States on her own behavior: "I never bitch about my rights or blame my problems on the whites . . . If I ever were discontent you'd never even have a clue" (97). She realizes that she has fully internalized her role as the obedient Other, both in her family and in American society at large. Rather than letting her voice be heard, Trenka is trained to comply with the muzzling forces of the white cultural majority. In light of her social stifling, writing a memoir about her experiences with racism strikes me as a powerful message against a system that marks adopted children of Asian descent as docile and passive.

Trenka is not the only Korean adoptee who works through her status as the Other in her autobiographical writing. In her essay "Homeward Bound: The Journey of a Transgendered Korean Adoptee" (2006), Pauline Park explains that "it's true that I had known no homeland other than the United States, but to strangers I was Asian, and therefore a foreigner. My Asian features automatically defined my status as the other, the outsider. Because others challenged my Americanness, I came to doubt my own sense of belonging. I belonged neither here nor there" (126). Trenka's work prefigures these feelings of exclusion, of being culturally constructed as an Other, and shows that the ostracization of Korean adoptees works systemically. She writes: "The liberal Minneapolis brand of truth is colorblind, and it can usually be summed up on a bumper sticker. It says all it takes is love to make a family. Race doesn't matter" (129). Unfortunately, this prevalent attitude does not reflect many transracial adoptees' experiences, as colorblindness turns into a racist tool that silences existential aspects of adoptees' identity. Because, as Sally Haslanger notes, a "group is racialized [if] its members are socially positioned as subordinate or privileged along some dimension (economic, political, legal, social, etc.), and the group is 'marked' as a target for this treatment by observed or imagined bodily features presumed to be evidence of ancestral links to a certain geographical region" (44). As much as race is a social construct with no basis in biology but created to establish social hierarchies, and as much as adoptive parents insist that genetics do not determine their adopted children's fate, people's perceptions of one's race have very real, everyday influence on how we are able to navigate our environments. Thus, as Kim Park Nelson asserts, colorblindness works as "a system of race denial in which everyone is imagined to pass as White" (122). Such repudiation keeps adoptive parents from acknowledging the racism that necessarily marks their children's lives.

Colorblindness, Gina Samuels explains, leaves adoptees "feel[ing] disconnected from racial 'knowledge of themselves' and 'set up' to expect a colorblind experience of race that their stigmatized racial appearances prevent them from accessing" (88–89). Parental colorblindness, practiced by ignoring children's racialized bodies, "crumbles in practice" as it discounts structural injustices based on domination and subordination (Fogg-Davis 34). It is merely an abstract ideal of an imagined society that does not place value on a person's skin color, which is at odds with contemporary American society, in which "race-based socioeconomic inequalities and race-based stigma" very much exist (Fogg-Davis 35). Based on these realities, Samuels recommends that "raising children with a sense of racial normalcy may require color-conscious, not colorblind, parenting, expanding beyond one's own experience of race to include the insights of others who do share the child's racialized status and experience" (92). Some transnational adoptees never achieve this "sense of racial normalcy" as parents fail to include people of different races into their lives and colorblindness violently disturbs their self-perception.

In "Home, Adopted" (2006), Jill Kim SooHoo comments on the negative effects of colorblindness: "I grew up thinking I was white. I was so sure I was so white, in fact, that when someone called me a 'Jap,' I thought it meant Jewish American Princess" (248). While SooHoo's confession likely makes the reader smile, her words speak to the powerful impact of ignoring racial and ethnic roots on children's self-understanding. Trenka expresses these feelings of existential confusion in her memoir as well:

> Like a true Twinkie, I had checked "white" in the box on all my college forms. Real reason: I didn't want to be Korean. Korea was a place that couldn't be talked about at home; . . . Korea was the reason my face was mutated . . . Self-deluding reason: what is on the inside is what matters. I checked "white" because I was *culturally* white. Every semester my little forms came back from the registrar's office corrected to "Asian-Pacific Islander." My liberal, diverse, private, Lutheran school . . . stuffed my mailbox

with offers for tutoring in the English language, oblivious that I
was one of the few people who tested out of freshman writing.
(129–130; emphasis in original)[19]

The gap between Trenka's self-perception and how others see, judge, and categorize her, made visible in print on official forms, is immense and causes Trenka again and again to question her self. These acts of cultural policing in addition to her parents' ignorance about her birth culture implant in Trenka a negative stance toward Korea as a place that marks her as the "mutated" Other. Trenka's college experiences demonstrate that her environment did not accept her as American but rather as a foreigner needing help with day-to-day life in the United States.

Trenka reflects in her writing the painful contradictions inherent in transnational adoption: "How do I explain . . . that my seemingly flawless assimilation into America has yielded anything but joy and gratitude? How do I explain my ambivalence? . . . I feel ashamed and unworthy of the gifts that have been given me; . . . What an unworthy, spoiled, ungrateful, whining, American brat" (227). Trenka struggles with the forces that conditioned her to be solely thankful for her adoption. The fact that her environment is able to accept only an Americanized Jane, a being without Korean roots, makes it difficult for Trenka to come to terms with her intense longing for completeness: "How can I weigh the loss of my language and culture against the freedom that America has to offer . . . ? How can a person, exiled as a child, without choice, possibly fathom how he would have 'turned out' had he stayed in Korea? How many educational opportunities must I mark on my tally sheet before I can say it was worth losing my mother?" (229). In an environment in which two-worldliness and hybridity seemingly constitute impossibilities and which confronts her with a "burden of gratitude" (Trenka 229), Trenka struggles between the comfort she experiences in the United States and the mourning of her birth culture; at the same time, she forcefully rejects the need to feel guilt whenever she allows herself to question the decisions others have made for her about her life and identity.

TRENKA'S STYLISTIC CHOICES AS RESISTANCE

In "The Birth of Contemporary Adoption Autobiography" (2003), Jill Deans reminds her readers of the long history of adoption life writing, including narratives about nonformalized adoption during captivity and slavery. When looking at formal, legal adoption in the United States, Florence Fisher's *The Search for Anna Fisher* (1973) emerges as one of the first life-writing texts to "politicize and polarize adoptive identity in specific ways" (Deans 240), which initiated a movement of adoptee activists who used the genre to call for the opening of adoption files. According to Deans, adoptee life writing "illustrates the foundationalist problematics of all autobiography in the subject's inability to recapture an 'original' self. It works to reconcile the 'post'-identity with its own indeterminacy and betweenness, to exist as a site for struggle and possibility" (239). Trenka adds to this rich history of domestic adoption autobiographies and memoirs an intersectional and transnational focus, as the complexity inherent in transnational adoptees' identity challenges life writing's complicity with nationalism, which Trenka explores through her unorthodox stylistic choices.

Emily Hipchen postulates that adoption life writing "can be used as one of the limit cases for individuality, a particularly weighty ideology in the United States where our important myths require both that our ethnicity, our places, and our kin are apparent and that people imagine themselves absolutely in control of their destinies, their successes and failures" ("Adoption Geometries" 236). I would add to Hipchen's list that U.S. myths also demand a stable national identity.[20] She further suggests that "life-writing scholars can think with adoption about how we understand contested ideas of relationality, embodiment, and family" ("Adoption Geometries" 240), all concepts explored in this book. According to Hipchen, adoption creates a necessary relationality among "adoptee, biological parent/s, . . . adoptive parents, . . . adoption agency, extended family members, nations and their treaties" ("Adoption Geometries" 232); adoption experiences are "polytemporal" and exist in a three- or four-dimensional cloud (Hipchen, "Adoption Geometries" 239, 240). It is my intention to expose here how *The Language of Blood* beautifully captures the characteristics of adoptee life writing that Hipchen catalogs.

By adapting the autobiographic genre to fit her experiences, Trenka powerfully reflects on the struggles against narrow ideas of what is "authentic" and "the norm." As the fragmented Other, Trenka had to rework notions of a national subject. And, as Deans argues, life writing gives her the space and power to do so since in "speaking for itself, the adoptive identity invents a vocabulary for loss, recovery, and discovery" (256). Trenka has to redefine a central concept of autobiography, "home," and re-imagine her homeland(s) for her audience. Mark Jerng writes that Trenka's breaking of the rules of life writing speaks to her "anxiety over maintaining the boundaries and frames in which the adoptee is placed" (155). Adapting memoir, for Trenka, parallels her multidimensional efforts to accommodate her identity as a transnational adoptee. She "frames her life in terms of 'facts' and reality just as much as she frames it in terms of fairy tales or dreams and no framework is 'truer' than the other" (Jerng 153). "Truth" as defined by official, patriarchal, nationalist discourse does not constitute her work's main focus.

With her stylistic decisions, Trenka builds on rich traditions within life writing, and particularly the subgenre of adoptee life writing. A fragmented narrative style has been widely used in Western fiction, especially by women, to convey a fragmented female self. Virginia Woolf and Gertrude Stein come to mind as authors who have prominently used fragmentation techniques in their works. For adoptee life writers, fragmentation takes additional layers. Homans explains that "life stories of adopted people often have complex narrative lines, since to the already insurmountable difficulty of any human effort to know and fix one's origin is often added the extra difficulty of lack of information" ("Adoption Narratives" 4). While the chronological linear plot centered in the search for one's birth family is common, using a fragmented narrative has shown widely effective for adoptees to express their selves. In *The Wounded Storyteller* (1995), Arthur Frank confirms that, in the face of traumatic experiences, suffering, and oppression, it can become impossible to create a coherent storyline. To him, such "chaos narratives" necessarily consist of a patchwork of fractured memories, emotions, and visual as well as aural elements (97ff). Emily Hipchen, for example, structured her *Coming Apart Together: Fragments from an Adoption* (2005) through vignettes that contain invented and then revised life stories for her family members. Jeanette Winterson's *Why Be Happy When You Could Be Normal?* (2011)—whose title is based on a quotation from her adoptive mother in reaction to Winterson's sexual coming-out—is organized as a palimpsest often with multiple layers of meaning. Winterson explains that with her fragmented writing style she "want[s] to show how it is when the mind works with its own brokenness" (169). In her study of adoption narratives, Hipchen found a prevalence of descriptions of fragmented body parts, which, to her, "emblematize the way these narratives complicate identity as it is formed in relation to the family body" ("Images" 169).

Moreover, Trenka's use of fairy tales and myths can be found in early adoptee memoirs such as Florence Fisher's *The Search for Anna Fisher* (1973) and Lifton's *Twice Born: Memoirs of an Adopted Daughter* (1975), in which Lifton intermittently identifies with Oedipus, the Minotaur, and a fabled Japanese shape shifter. Some of Trenka's approaches to telling her life—such as a collective identity and story lines fabricated through literary bricolage—also resemble (diasporic) Korean life texts, which Heui-Yung Park examines in *Korean and Korean American Life Writing in Hawai'i* (2015). Further, Trenka's use of a doubled self as well as mythical depictions recalls the ways in which Maxine Hong Kingston's *The Woman Warrior* (1976) establishes a montage of a collective and ambiguous national identity. Trenka makes all these approaches to telling a life her own and adds an intersectional lens as well as a multimodality that goes beyond photographs to push her readers toward an activist mindset.

One of the first frameworks Trenka presents is the narrative segment *Highway 10, A Play for Imagining*, which interrupts her more conventional autobiographical writing. In accordance with the stage directions of Trenka's play "*all exits . . . must be locked, preventing anyone from leaving before the end of the play*" (16; emphasis in original). The directions further explain that the play takes place for "*approximately four hours, or long enough to make the audience feel uncomfortable and trapped*" (16; emphasis in original). In creating this oppressive atmosphere, Trenka accentuates the feelings of culture shock and alienation that she and her sister underwent upon arrival in the United States. The play describes the conversation a husband and wife are having after picking up their newly adopted girls from the airport. When the mother asks Carol, one of the adopted girls, if she is okay and Carol does not understand her because she does not speak or understand English, Fred, the father, loudly yells at the young girl, "Your mother asked you a question" (Trenka 17).[21] Fred clearly lacks any insight into his adoptive daughters' situation as well as basic transcultural skills. Trenka uses this play in defiance of autobiographical standards that demand a self-centered I-narration to introduce the foundation for the relationship between her and her parents that would cause her traumatic self-loathing and depression. While she could clearly not have remembered these events because she was still an infant when they occurred, the play sequence uses imagined memories to relate how transnational adoptees might come to terms with the adoption experience and how they navigate a sense of belonging or a lack thereof.

The play emphasizes the trauma that Carol as a four-and-a-half year-old experienced: "*At the end of the movie sequence, the Korean memories are completely erased . . . CAROL has willed herself to become a girl with no history and is now ready to start her new life*" (18; emphasis in original). Because her adoptive parents wish for her to be someone else, Carol is (in Trenka's rendering) brainwashed into forgetting her origins and into living the life her adoptive parents have designed for her. The term "erased" connotes a forceful, almost violent act, which matches the scene's hostile atmosphere. Through her inclusion of the play, Trenka is able to portray her adoptive parents' selfish desire to create a child who is completely their own and whom they do not have to share with another family and nation.

Taking liberties with autobiographical models allows Trenka to conceptualize racism in a manner that reaches her audience more forcefully than a first-person narrative might. In the section entitled *The Ice House Restaurant, A Musical*, she depicts a regular dining-out experience with her parents. The musical begins by setting a prejudice-filled atmosphere in which the restaurant patrons stare at and talk about Trenka's family. Some diners ask: " 'Do they speak Chinese? How big will they get? . . . Feel their hair! It's so thick! . . . Rice-Picker! . . . Would you like to adopt this stray dog? . . . How much did they cost?' " (34). These comments vividly speak to the exoticization and objectification in American society that many Asian adoptees, especially girls, have to confront. The oral aggressors compare adoptees to animals roaming the streets in need of a "forever home" and intrude into the children's private sphere by physically touching them to be able to appraise their value better. Trenka and Carol experience these obviously racist remarks as cruel and hurtful, but their parents remain oblivious to this scene. The parents' conduct portrays a shocking example of their culturally instituted ignorance about raising children of color. Set in a public space, the musical scene emphasizes the social context of small-town, homogenous America that contributes to the sisters' ostracization. Trenka's parents do not live or act in isolation. Their attitudes are conditioned and supported by the environment in which they raise their children. While for other adoptees a close-knit community that holds its members responsible for their actions might be comforting, Trenka experiences the rural atmosphere as cooperating with her adoptive family in excluding herself and her sister.

In its positioning of the readers as members of the audience, *The Language of Blood* attempts to make them aware of their Western, white, and privileged gaze that often fetishizes transnational adoptees and interracial families by drawing attention to the supposed "unnaturalness" of their constellation. Like the works of trauma survivors in Anne Cubilié's study, Trenka presents to "readers an alternative to a distanced and 'safer' spectatorship of atrocity through the invitation to engage in performative relationships of witnessing" (17), which might propel some into action. *The Language of Blood* places the readers as an element of the racist, capitalist system that creates the necessity for adoption and turns Trenka into an exoticized object. The audience's attention is intrusive and resembles efforts of public surveillance that observes difference, objectifies adoptees as curiosities, and isolates them. As part of its political agenda to move readers to action against transnational adoption, the memoir calls for awareness in people's complicity in the othering of transracial adoptees.

Like many transnational adoptees who, according to Brian, say that they learned the meaning of racism through their own parents' prejudices (73), Trenka recounts memories that make it clear that her parents held discriminatory beliefs. Both times that Trenka introduces boyfriends, who happened to be of Asian descent, her father "mocked their faces, as if they were not human, but dark stupid monkeys. He mutilated their long names, which he could not and did not want to pronounce correctly" (66). Her father ridicules these men based on their physical appearance and declares them inferior to himself, a Caucasian American. He treats them as exotic foreigners and turns them into an Other that can be denigrated. In his role as father and head of the household, he functions as a stand-in for the United States as a patriarchal nation that superficially claims to embrace "good" migrants but exposes deeply troubling ideas about gendered and racialized hierarchies. In reaction to her father's xenophobia and racism, Trenka asks: "Who do you think I am?" (66). Knowing that she looks similar to her boyfriends, she comes to suspect that her adoptive father, on some deeper level, must see her, too, as a being worth less than himself. This realization creates a strong sense of self-loathing in Trenka, "the kind you get when you discover that you must be one of two things to your dad, either invisible or ridiculous; the kind you get when you hate your own face . . . the kind you get when you want to love your father but hate him instead" (66–67). Caught in this dichotomy of being labeled as either nonexistent or a freak, Trenka begins to hate not only her body but also her father.

In an act of defiance, she scratches her Korean name into the wall in her bedroom. But despite this powerful act of renaming and doubling herself, of going back to a past self that seems more authentic, her self-hatred persists and leads her to perm her hair—which her adoptive mother adores as it seemingly removes Trenka from her racial community—and to dye it lighter, which tellingly remains an unsuccessful endeavor (67). She also frantically peruses teen magazines' tips "to make myself beautiful, but my face wasn't getting any less round, my eyebrows wouldn't stop growing downward, and the curling-the-eyelashes trick usually ended up in a smashed-spider legs look" (67). Much like we have seen in previous chapters with Rosay and

Danquah, Trenka unsuccessfully strives to fit socially sanctioned patriarchal and sexist beauty standards to leave behind her outsider status.

Trenka's exposure to racism does not end with her childhood. Orientalist stereotypes also affect her as an adult. On a flight back to the United States from Korea with her white husband, an American stewardess assumes, without attempting to verify her conjecture, that Trenka is the wife of a Chinese passenger sitting next to her and would want some milk just like her "husband." When Trenka reacts confused about the stewardess' gestures, the flight attendant proceeds to explain the concept of milk to Trenka in simplistic English (248). Persistent social prejudice against women of Asian descent makes it impossible for this woman to think of Trenka as independent, American, and fluent in English. After this incident, Trenka decides to "let *him* [her husband] do the talking, since it's clear that he speaks English, [and] [she] make[s] sure that he talks to immigration officers first when [they] go to the counter together upon arrival in America, since it's clear that he's born and bred American" (249; emphasis in original). Since her language skills, identity, and citizenship are constantly questioned, Trenka develops a profound unease about belonging in the country that she considers home.

Fueled by the model minority myth, American society tends not only to conflate people of different Asian backgrounds (e.g., see Holland and Palaniappan), but, more importantly, Asian Americans with Asians (see Kawai). This ignorance marks people of Asian descent with a permanent home in the United States as eternal foreigners: "Asian Americans are permanent houseguests in the house of America. When on their best behavior (as defined by the hosts), they are allowed to add the spice of variety to American life and are even held up as a 'model minority' to prove the viability of American egalitarian ideals" (Wong, "Denationalization" 6). The racism inherent in the model minority trope—which homogenizes people of Asian descent and heralds them as the "good" kind of minoritized person that all other minorities should look up to—is even more complex for adoptees who were not born in the United States and whose "Americanness" is thus challenged even more. Because Trenka's body is declared deficient, it cannot be the site of a centered U.S. nationalistic vision. Pushing back against this predicament, her hybrid life writing expresses and normalizes an essential, life-affirming duality.

For female Asian adoptees, racism is often paired with strong forces of sexism. As an Asian woman, Trenka is rendered invisible on multiple levels: she is considered part of an Asian community that is judged as a model minority that quietly assimilates into the mainstream without causing too much "trouble," and she is culturally constructed as a demure, servile Asian female. Paradoxically, invisibility is paired with a level of hypervisibility caused by the hypersexualization of women of Asian descent. Objectified and infantilized, women of Asian descent remain sites of an Orientalist patriarchal imagination. Trenka brings this to her audience's attention by including the following personal advertisement in her memoir: "**SWM, 29, SEEKS ASIAN**—You: Submissive, petite, long hair. Your master is 6'3", brown/brown, 185 lbs. Looking for fun. Will respond to all that send pictures" (79; emphasis in original). This blurb resembles countless ads that can be found in newspapers and on the internet, constituting a billion-dollar pornography and mail-order bride system.

Portraying Asian females as pretty, weak, and easily adaptable (read: submissive), these ads connect with the cultural ideologies at play in the adoption complex. Adoptees' commodification starts before the actual selection process, steered by "market-driven approaches" that "prioritize meeting parents' . . . desires" (Brian 166). Asian children are highly marketable in adoption circles since stereotypes about people of Asian descent are regarded as more positive than assumptions about African American or Latinx communities, which creates a system in which "nonwhite orphans abroad are deemed more rescuable and desirable than domestic nonwhite children" (Dorow, "Producing Kinship" 71). Due to their skin color, adoptees from Asia are supposed to be racially more flexible, to be able to "pass" (Dorow, *Transnational Adoption* 21). As a "buffer race," "honorary whites," and a "model minority" (Brian 57), Asian adoptees are seen as assimilable, devoted, and intellectually and professionally successful so that they should necessarily adjust well to life in the United States. This presumed flexibility makes it seemingly easier for adoptive parents—most of them white, middle-class couples—to practice a "reproduction of whiteness" (Dorow, *Transnational Adoption* 21), to insist that their adopted Asian children are white. While domestic adoption is classified according to race, transnational adoptees are categorized by birth country, which positions them "somewhat outside of the American racial hierarchy" (Brian 26). Oftentimes, it is this pretense of racial flexibility that leads to the ignoring of racism.

Trenka does not comment on the afore-mentioned personal ad or integrate it into her text; but, as the introduction to the chapter in which she describes her traumatic experiences of being stalked in college, this section speaks to a strong connection between stereotypes about Asian women and the physical and emotional violence to which she was exposed. Earlier in the memoir, Trenka explains that debilitating stereotypes about women of Asian descent as "exotic, petite, lotus blossom, pale, fragile, docile, geishas" are intricately linked to perceptions of Asian children as "China dolls, whiz kids, happy, cooperative, obedient" (65). She establishes her adoption and her experience of being stalked as both caused by the objectification of women and girls of Asian descent.[22] In *Fugitive Visions*, Trenka spells out this correlation even more directly: "The property of what you can become obsessed by when you see an 'available child' in a catalogue—That which makes this one your adoptive mother . . . . The property of whom you can become obsessed by, when you see her in an open window—That which makes this one your stalker" (130–131). Whether as prostitutes, picture brides, war brides, mail-order brides, or mail-order children, Asian females' entry into the United States has been historically rooted in their sex/uality, which lays the ground for their dehumanization.

Capturing her critique of adoptees' objectification, Trenka expresses discomfort with the language that surrounds her entrance into her adoptive family: "'We chose you,' my mommy always says. To me that means from a store, because when you go to the store you look at the rows of dolls and you choose. . . . I could also be returned to the store" (24–25). Their commodification through the adoption market leaves some transnational adoptees uneasy about their acceptance into their adoptive families and culture and makes them vulnerable to physical and emotional violence. Because of their race and sex, Asian female adoptees may be Orientalized, othered, and considered inferior, especially by white men, who tend to stereotype them as sexually serving. This attitude might likely have been the source of motivation for Trenka's stalker, who plots to kill her. Trenka underlines the connection between her adoption and her stalker in emphasizing the racial motivations for his crime when she cites him as saying upon their first encounter, "You're nothing but a Korean in a white man's society. You're a gook, you're a chink" (83). She shows her audience the very real effects of being considered a sexualized racial Other, a commodity, a non-human.

In a factual manner, Trenka explains minutely the events surrounding her period of life with a stalker. She recounts meeting her stalker for the first time and bringing recordings of messages he left on her answering machine to campus police, who lose them. She describes how she was not taken seriously by officials because she was a young woman and that she specifically remembers the "humiliation" she felt (85). When she tells police that she knows who broke into her car, they do not believe her, actively silencing her by means of epistemic injustice, which, as Miranda Fricker explains, implies "prejudicial exclusion from participation in the spread of knowledge" (162). After he is finally arrested, it is revealed that her stalker had a weapon and had planned to rape and kill Trenka (87). The invalidation and dismissal with which she is met have damaging consequences. Trenka feels "impotent, frozen, blind," "silent," and "useless" (88). The sounds of her stalker shooting at her father haunt her so that she "emerged from college four years later beaten up emotionally, intermittently suicidal, with no further plans because [she] didn't think [she] would live that long. [She] hated [her]self—for what [she] had brought on [her] family, for being worthless, for being someone whom no one would take seriously" (89). Her experiences throw Trenka into years of depression, partly spent in hospitals, where she felt devoid of "dignity" (93).

Trenka's silencing continues as the lawsuit against her stalker begins. At the time, no laws existed in Minnesota against stalking, and Trenka never got to testify in court: "I never told my story" (92). It is only when she comes across Judith Lewis Herman's *Trauma and Recovery* that "for the first time [she] knew [she] wasn't crazy," but that she had undergone the "psychic equivalent of terrorism" (Trenka 93), which manifests itself in post-traumatic stress disorder. In presenting the facts about her stalker and her ensuing mental illness, Trenka underscores the trauma that transnational adoption can cause. Even if her story is an extreme example, sharing these occurrences might serve as convincing evidence for her readers to begin questioning the prescribed good nature of the transnational adoption system.

Similar to her work with the audience in the *Ice House* scene, Trenka, in the section about stalking, addresses the reader with "here's the story, and I won't even charge you admission" (82), implying that her life provides entertainment that the audience seeks. Her critique of a gaze that enjoys adoptees' life stories as "trauma-porn" is powerful. But instead of outright calling the audience racist and sexist, which might make them feel attacked and could cause their resistance to the memoir's political message, Trenka subtly reaches out to the audience's emotions and especially their likely wish of being seen as anti-racist and pro-equality in hopes that they might support policy changes with regard to transnational adoption.

Trenka returns to the traumatic objectification she experienced in a stand-up comedy routine entitled "Don't Worry, I Will Make You Feel Comfortable. A Monologue for Imagining." As part of this routine, Jane, "generically Asian" (97), manifests that "no matter mail-order bride or mail-order kid—Oriental Woman love you long time" (97). Through the use of parody in both the personal ad and the comedy routine, Trenka harshly critiques cultural productions that belittle and abuse women of Asian descent. In its spoofing exaggeration, the monologue again turns Trenka into a spectacle and her readers into a willing audience. The highly provocative exclamation reiterates how stereotypes mark Asian women as passive and docile beings, which enables their consumption as exotic objects whether on the sex work, marriage, or adoption market. The idea that adoptees are "mail-ordered," picked from a catalog and paid for like objects, further contrasts public opinion that adoption is a process of pure altruism, affording poor children the opportunity of a fulfilled life.

As my analysis of the above segments shows, Trenka's modifications of the autobiographical voice challenge the pact of truth that is supposed to exist between the author—who vouches for the story's authenticity with her name—and her readers. According to Philippe Lejeune's "autobiographical pact," the "I" has to guarantee that the name on the book matches the life that is narrated, which needs to be the main focus of the narrative: "What defines autobiography for the one who is reading is above all a contract of identity that is sealed by the proper name. And this is true also for the one who is writing the text" (Lejeune 19). "Lejeune's emphasis on the synonymy of the author, narrator, and protagonist as the pivotal definitional criterion, and the exclusion of 'You' as a significant and agentic presence" is supposed to ensure that the claims made in the text are accurate and that the narrator is faithful to her personal memory (Stanley, Salter, and Dampier 278). But, in the context of adoption life writing, authorial authority is often more complicated and necessitates, as Trenka shows, a "you." The sense of bodily self-determination and, thus, the patriarchal privilege that the original pact assumes—and which, as I have mentioned, women have always pushed back against in their life writing—do not accommodate the distinctive form of relationality that adoption creates.

The Language of Blood expresses this relationality via letters from Trenka's Korean self, Kyong-Ah, to American Jane: "Dear Jane, you are a brave young woman, keeping me alive. I am like a parasite; I exist only because you do. . . . People do not see me even though we share a heart, a face, a mind, and a body. . . . Take care of me. Take care of this body because . . . it is really mine. That face you see—mine. The hand you use to eat and work—those too are mine. You are living a borrowed life. Don't forget" (139). This letter elucidates how Trenka feels as if her upbringing in the United States has split her into two separate, yet dependent personalities. Kyong-Ah had to sacrifice herself, had to "lend her life" to Jane, in order for Jane to exist. But Kyong-Ah has not vanished; she is part of

Jane despite her adoptive family not acknowledging that. Kyong-Ah is alive in the "language of blood," in Jane's body. This letter, which distinguishes the subject and object as different people designated by different names, stands as an explicit example of Trenka's nationally doubled self and the pain Trenka experiences.

With this creative doubling, Trenka echoes the experiences of other transracial adoptees. Catherine McKinley, for instance, uncovers seemingly multiple versions of herself in *The Book of Sarahs* (2002) as her mentally unstable biological mother birthed three daughters whom she all named Sarah. As a Jewish–African American biracial woman, McKinley comes to terms in her writing with the fact that a clear-cut racial, biological, and family identity does not exist for her. To this triad of identities, Trenka adds a conversation about a national self that is also reflected in Deann Borshay Liem's film *First Person Plural* (2000), in which Liem investigates her inseparable link with the young girl whose identity she was made to assume when she was sent to the United States for adoption.

Molding autobiographical conventions to fit the extraordinary parameters of her life allows Trenka to analyze how many adoptees' identities do not fit into any neatly definable category. A crossword puzzle of terms such as "fraud," "metamorphosis," "neither," "both," "seem," "ambivalent," "paradox," "freaks," "loss" constitutes a powerful example of the complex intersections that mark Trenka's identity (225). The inherent enigmatic and challenging nature of a puzzle underlines many adoptees' efforts to make sense of their identities: the struggle of being considered "neither" American nor Korean, the seeming impossibility to be "both," the gap between what you "seem" to be and who you actually are. The puzzle also demonstrates visually how language entwines cultures for adoptees. To make the words that designate Trenka's identity fit the frame, they depend on other words, some speaking to a very different part of her self. Just as the letters of words standing in for different cultures intersect, her identities intersect as well.

The alignment of the words in Trenka's puzzle invokes Ferdinand de Saussure's (1916) structuralist approach to meaning and offers insight into how Trenka sees herself. According to Saussure's analysis of semiotic systems, the horizontal (or syntagmatic) axis of meaning denotes possibilities of combination whereas the vertical (or paradigmatic) axis involves differentiation. While syntagmatic relations between words connect vocabulary present in a text at the same time, paradigmatic relations relate to words not present in the text. When applying this approach of reading signs to Trenka's puzzle, patterns emerge that emphasize her conflicting views of her identity. Most words in the puzzle that are aligned horizontally and thus might denote options for combination have a negative connotation. Those words include "Janus," "fraud," and "paradox." Vertically, signifying difference, the puzzle offers words like "Korea," "memory," and "ambivalent." This alignment can produce, among others, the following interpretations of the puzzle: Because Korea and America are both oriented vertically, they constitute contrasts. Temporally, they cannot be present at the same time, which speaks to Trenka's difficulties of combining her Korean and American heritage. On the other hand, the horizontal axis of combination might generate a sentence like "Trenka is Janus *and* a fraud *and* a paradox," which reinforces some adoptees' identity conflicts. In using this stylistic element, Trenka emphasizes the trauma imposed on her and visually presents the feelings of confusion and incompatibility that shape her life in a more forceful manner than would have been possible through narrative alone.

Complementing this visual representation, Trenka captures her struggles with the constant burden of being judged by and having to explain herself to others, of "defying either-or solutions of being Korean or American, birth child or adopted child, abandoned or rescued, universal citizen or unique individual" (Dorow, *Transnational Adoption* 264), in the labels "fraud" and "grotesque hybrid," which she uses frequently to describe herself as a daughter and an American (215). Forces of assimilation clash with Trenka's innate feelings that there is more to her than white, American culture. As Trenka, Oparah, and Shin elaborate, transracial adoptees "cannot be contained by national borders or simple dichotomies. [They] refuse to assimilate into white culture or to submit to narrow ideas about cultural authenticity" (14). Adoptees' identities transcend artificial geographic and cultural norms, which nation-states rely on to uphold their power, and they refuse to be used as pawns in geostrategic, political battles.

Aware of the complex processes that influence her identity, Trenka chooses the term "exile" as a fitting term to capture her self: "I hadn't thought of myself as an exile or immigrant before—just a lucky adoptee. But now, I see that 'exile' is the word that fits me best. The language of exile is filled with gains and losses, culture and family, memory and imagination" (227). While the identity category "adoptee" seemingly connotes passivity, the term "exile" captures Trenka's identity more holistically, including the suffering Trenka experienced being torn from her birthmother and culture. *The Language of Blood* promotes a tolerance for a transnational identity not bound to merely one nation and culture and not defined through difference or exclusion. Notably, despite her opposition to socially constructed dichotomies, Trenka herself frequently essentializes identity and nationality in her memoir and, thus, mirrors the adoptive parents in Heather Jacobson's study who did not see their children as Chinese American or Russian American but either Chinese/Russian or American (90).

Trenka forcefully separates Korea and the United States and fights for her readers to see that hybridity is not a culturally accepted option. This becomes especially apparent in her numerous mentioning of the word "true." She is, for example, looking for a "*true* self" and behaves like "a *true* Twinkie" (74, 129; emphases mine). While she criticizes terms such as "freak" and "Other," she uses them herself. It is almost as if she sees herself like this through society's eyes and posits the sight. With the help of this attitude she might, paradoxically, feel more secure. Instead of living in a limbo of identity, essentializing and using society's denominations for her might give her a firmer sense of existence. Trenka's struggles with self-knowledge demand that she experiment with the generic forms of life writing to be able to include emotions and experiences outside of patriarchal and nationalistic postulates.

LIFE WRITING AS A TOOL FOR HEARING SILENCED VOICES

I agree with Kim Park Nelson that the desire for and commodification of children's bodies plays a major role in adoptees' immigration processes and that an urgency exists "around the erasure (legally, and often culturally) of any vestige of immigrant identity for adoptees to acculturate them into American family and society" (*Invisible* 153–154). I am aware that adoptees exert far less agency and choice than other immigrants in their movement between spaces—in fact, to a degree that is comparable with the lack of choice refugees experience in their relocation, which I will explore in a later chapter. McKee calls Korean adoptees "hybridized citizens due to their ability to enter the United States outside of immigration quotas regulating the entry of Asian bodies" due to the privilege of their white parents ("The Transnational Adoption" 9). She investigates how they "exist simultaneously as privileged immigrants, yet probationary Americans" (9). Their lives are a clear reminder of the interlocking nature of privilege and oppression, a major focus of Trenka's narrative explorations.

Besides adoptive parents' demand, I also see Trenka express economic and political pressures at the heart of adoption migration, especially in the form of sexism. Whether it is a strong bias *against* female children that leads parents to abandon their daughters, the desire of white, middle-class families *for* young, healthy, and affordable Asian girls, or extreme poverty against which single, often abused mothers are helpless in their attempt to keep their children alive, the oppression of women is a major cause of transnational adoption. To create the adoptability of children, biological mothers' vulnerability is exploited, and social and economic inequalities and marginalizations are taken advantage of, many times by establishing arbitrary levels of "good" motherhood that especially poor mothers struggle to attain (Briggs 283).

As we have seen with Rosay and Danquah, immigrant women, in writing about their lives, do not prioritize themselves but turn the genre into a tool to advocate for social justice. With her focus on the experiences and suffering of her birthmother and others like her, Trenka braces McKee's request to look at adoption as an issue of reproductive justice, which "makes explicit the ways adoption is a reproductive technology rooted in the disruption of women of color's ability to parent" ("Adoption" 75). McKee explains that reproductive justice takes into consideration a person's race, class, gender, nationality, ability, and other characteristics when looking at issues related to parenting; it thus offers "new opportunities to understand adoption outside of reductive celebrations of adoption as a gift of love" (McKee, "Adoption" 75). Reproductive justice elucidates how many white, Western women's bodily autonomy is complicit in poor (often non-Western) women's oppression, which pathologizes the latter, paints them as sexually promiscuous and not deserving of and/or wanting a child, and negates their "right to parent with dignity" (79). Some scholars and activists hold that to honor birthmothers' lives "riddled with institutional abuse of power and interpersonal violence," they should be paid reparations that would move conversations about adoption away from adoptees and adoptive parents and lessen the romanticized appeal of search and reconciliation narratives in favor of strengthening birthmothers' rights, which are the basis for healing (Hsu 317f).

Mindful of the multifaceted forces of economic, racist, ableist, and sexist oppression against poor women, which influence most forms of female migration, Trenka begins her memoir with a letter from her culturally silenced, biological mother, which pushes back against "the dominant adoptive-parent focused discourses of transracial adoption" (Park Nelson 294). The letter reads: "I'm ashamed that I couldn't take care of you earlier. . . . How reproachable [a] mother I am! . . . To image [*sic*] your lovely face, this is my only hope" (Trenka 9–10). To hear a birthmother's voice longing for "a child she never wanted to give away in the first place" is a rare occasion in conversations about interracial adoption (Trenka 113).[23] "If you could recognize a child's mother as a human being, would you still think of taking her child from her as a charitable act? . . . If you knew the true nature of desperation, would you still use the word 'choice' as a synonym for the relinquishment or abandonment of a child?" (85). Through her life writing, Trenka strives to depathologize poor Asian birthmothers, whom the rhetoric of saving inherent to transnational adoption demonizes as inadequate mothers and often as prostitutes, resembling the overwhelmingly negative portrayal of African American birthmothers as well as mothers addicted to drugs (Brian 155); the image of the incompetent non-white female caregiver also recalls the fears that Meri Nana-Ama Danquah experienced about losing her child as a Black mother with a mental disability, discussed in chapter 2.

Through exchanging letters with her mother and visiting her twice, Trenka comes to understand that her "mother's hard life" was shaped by poverty and sexism (115), and she sympathizes with "how her mind was split from grief after [two of her daughters] were taken away and she carried a dog on her back, as she used to carry her daughter" (116). As just one example of how her mother's psychic wounds manifest themselves, this anecdote shows that while some adoptees have begun to work through their trauma via writing, most biological mothers report feeling trapped in their loss of a child. For example, memoirs by U.S. birthmothers—such as Margaret Moorman, Janet Mason Ellerby, and Karen Salyer McElmurray—exhibit the guilt, loneliness, emotional pain, and often devastating depression caused by having been pressured into giving their children up for adoption.

Adult Korean adoptee activists, like Trenka, have begun fighting for support and the rights of their birthmothers as they "recognize that their own acceptance in Korean society is intimately related to the acceptance of unwed mothers in Korea" (Brian 144). Understanding that "narratives of rescue hide how power and privilege have influenced which mothers have been able to raise the children they bear and which have been able to adopt" (Jacobson 31), social justice groups, such as TRACK (Truth and Reconciliation for the Adoption Community of Korea)—of which Trenka is a founder and which consists of adoptees, unwed Korean mothers, and other supporters—work on providing birthmothers with alternatives to adoption.

Representative of many biological mothers, Trenka's mother's story is a desperate one from the beginning, marked by economic disparity and sexist oppression: "Three months after marrying into a poor family, she was pregnant, widowed by the war, and starving" (Trenka 48). Like

Rosalina Rosay in *Journey of Hope*, Trenka realizes that not her mother's own decisions or life choices are responsible for her and her children's life trajectory, but large-scale social conditions: "The characters [in many Korean families] are always the same: starvation, lost family members, bitter cold, poverty, men unable to support their families, drunkenness, disappointment, despair. . . . What does the world care about one woman with three lost children?" (49). Trenka identifies poverty and a sexist society with "Confucian morals, whose patriarchal traditions instructed them to abandon our mother when she was hungry and pregnant" as the root causes for her adoption—not her biological mother's inability to be a "good" person and mother (49). Trenka comes "to understand the beautiful, terrible culture of my mother, [and] learn[s] that her experiences were not so unique in a land where boys are more valuable than girls, where women carry the weight of duty on their backs, as they do their babies, so that by the time they are old they are permanently bent over, eyes to the ground" (117). Similar to Mexican culture, which made life much harder for Rosay than for her brothers, Korean patriarchal traditions oppress poor women to the point where they are forced to give up their children.

Despite her emotional and physical scars from a life shaped by poverty and domestic violence—Trenka's father had bitten off parts of her nose—Trenka's biological mother's strength in the face of adversity comes through: "Her stories worked their way through my skin and into my blood. I felt her bravery seeping in . . . transforming me into her daughter" (117). Umma works hard all her life to raise her children and decides to give up two of her daughters to secure their survival, and, even though all odds are against her, she fights to get in contact with Trenka and her sister in the United States: "It is not supposed to happen this way, and I have never heard another story in which a Korean birth mother finds her child . . . Who but Umma could have done it—with no money to bribe, no helpful husband, no English skills, and hardly an education? She had only her determination" (71). Trenka is amazed by her mother's strength in a society whose goal it is to keep women dependent and helpless. Trenka's respect for the women in her family who successfully navigate patriarchal gender roles extends to her older sister: "She cared for her own children and husband, her mother-in-law, her mother, our little sister, and me. . . . Nothing—not our father's abuse, not poverty, not the indifference of those who allowed her to grow up without innocence—could ever extinguish the kind of beauty and courage that is the essence of Eun-Mi" (181, 182). Despite having to fight patriarchal and capitalist forces that attempt to push them into passivity, Trenka's mother and older sister refuse to give up their agency to ensure a good life for their families.

While Trenka is deeply hurt by her adoptive parents' ignorance of her birth culture, she realizes that they, too, suffered under an oppressive society that prescribes gender roles and what a family has to look like. She makes a connection between her biological mother, who has to fight poverty and abuse, and her adoptive mother, whose oppression stems from persistent social and religious blame and stigmatization vis-à-vis childless women. The traditional, rural environment that her adoptive parents inhabit makes it very clear that "women are wives and mothers. They must be mothers, not just wives, and if the children are not born soon, people talk. . . . What is a woman without a family? . . . What was wrong with her body?" (Trenka 19). Society automatically faults her adoptive mother's body for not having given birth to a child; never do voices mention the possibility that her husband might be the biological source for their childlessness. Either way, remaining without children is not an option in Trenka's adoptive parents' religious community, and so adoption is a forced solution.

Yet, despite similarities between Trenka's mothers, McKee reminds us that "birth and adoptive mothers are located on opposite ends of the motherhood spectrum, where, although both mothers are stigmatized for their reproductive failures—motherhood or pregnancy—adoptive mothers are considered brave and humanitarian" while poor birthmothers are labeled deviant (McKee, "Adoption" 83). Hence, adoptive mothers tend to receive much support in their desire to become a parent, while birthmothers have limited options to raise their own children. Oppression for Trenka's mothers works at different economic, social, and emotional levels, and yet annihilates exit options for both of them out of their respective environments, works transnationally, and, ultimately, perpetuates a system of adoption that, in Trenka's opinion, causes trauma and violates the human right to a nonfractured identity.

Similar to Trenka's journey, Katy Robinson, in *A Single Square Picture* (2002), returns to Korea to hear her birthmother's story. While she is able to reunite with her birthfather and her brothers and sisters, her family and Korean bureaucracy make it very clear that they do not support her search for her mother and even tell her lies about her mother. What Robinson does learn is the harsh reality that "Korean society did not easily forgive women" (193), especially women like her mother who had an affair with an older, married man. Robinson, like Trenka, realizes that her mother had no other option but to give up her daughter and directs her anger at her father who had children with various women whom he then abandoned. I compare Robinson's account to Trenka's memoir as both women understand that their birthmothers' state of oppression causes their adoption instead of these women's behavior as "bad mothers." Both women use their life writing not to celebrate their own accomplishments but to defend their mothers. Their stories offer a platform for the voices of a specific group of oppressed women. In doing so, they support a solidarity movement between adult adoptees and birthmothers that emerged in South Korea in the early 2000s "as both groups experienced growing social consciousness regarding the ties between unwed mothers' rights and adoption" at a time when more adult adoptees returned to Korea and more unwed mothers decided to raise their children on their own (Bae 304). And yet, especially poor unwed mothers continue to face "extreme social prejudice" and often live in isolation (Bae 308).

The Language of Blood and *A Single Square Picture* are also worth comparing for the women's reactions toward their identity and their birth country. Robinson feels "disposable and rootless. A drifter, passed randomly from one set of hands to another" (17)—sentiments that Trenka certainly also describes. When Trenka arrives for the first time at the Seoul airport, the two passport lines for "Korean" and "Foreigner" confuse her because she does not know which one she should join. Of course, Trenka is aware that she holds only an American passport, but, at the same time, she was born Korean. Categorizing people by nation in a way that discourages flexibility can pose an insurmountable hurdle for people with a more complex identity, such as transnational adoptees. In fact, most adoptees Park Nelson met "articulate national, cultural, and racial duality or multiplicity" (183). Trenka eventually experiences her Korean identity taking over, her "heart beating loud in [her] ears with the anticipation of metamorphosis: the thrill of becoming Korean again . . . alive inside the belly of [her] motherland" (120). Her emotional reaction collapses ideologies of mothering with ideologies of nation.

Seeing her nation as a nurturing mother, while widely common in nationalistic rhetoric, is rather ironic in Trenka's case since Korea, as a nation, does not offer poor female children many options, and at one time sent them off in masses as adoptees. The image of metamorphosis, the physical changing of the body, as well as the image of Korea as a welcoming caregiver and protector, are indicative of Trenka's longing for what she was forced to leave behind. Her positive re-encounter with Korea makes it even more disappointing for Trenka to accept that Korea initially rejects her, that in

Korea, too, people see her as a foreigner, mainly due to her lack of language skills. Adoption creates an identity limbo for many adoptees that can be prevented only by overhauling the transnational adoption complex.

CONCLUSIONS

In her epilogue addressing the reader directly, Trenka reveals that she deliberately created "mythologies" in her memoir. She also speaks to the version of "truth" that stories portray that is far different from the "truth" that official (adoption) documents convey. *The Language of Blood* specifically sets out to show how truth is constructed and can deceive, even in a memoir. It is, hence, "pointless to try to evaluate Trenka . . . on the basis of [her] reliability or the truthfulness of [her] descriptions of [herself] and [her] li[fe]" because the book's formal adaptations of the life-writing genre comment on the constructed truth of cultures and ideologies of race as well as their material enacting in society (Wills, "Aporetic Origins" 88). Trenka honors her mother's life in recreating it in detail in *The Language of Blood*, using storytelling in a similarly empowering manner as her mother. Umma told her life story to anyone who would listen because "she hoped that this act of storytelling would redeem her, that through the telling, people could see what she wanted to be and not what she had become" (Trenka 115). This resolve stands as a strong reminder that life stories, written and oral, can be empowering tools to portray experiences that dissent from officially accepted versions of history.

Throughout her book, Trenka makes a point of mentioning how other adoptees' must have felt similarly dehumanized in researching their adoption process: "I count myself lucky because I have more stories and more documents than most. . . . Who decided that the truth present on official documents is more truthful than stories? Documents are only partial truths" (232). If Trenka is successful, readers will accept her claim that adoptees are the true knowers of their own lives and should have full access to all the information about the circumstances of their adoption. To render her negative assessment of the adoption process more trustworthy, Trenka points out the perversity of the legal situation: "Don't scream because she, a perfect stranger, with probably minimal qualifications, can sit there and read my file with all my information in it and all my family's information and all the crap that determined my life and *I am not allowed*" (197; emphasis in original).[24] Although some states began changing laws around opening adoption files in response to the Adoption Rights Movement that started in the mid-1970s when a critical mass of adoptees had grown up (Carp 185,137), many never defined exactly what constitutes "good causes" for opening adoption files (Carp 43), leaving many adoptees at the mercy of individual clerks and judges. The situation's absurdity underscores Trenka's establishment of adoptees as experts of their own lives who, unethically, are kept from owning their histories.

Many see sending children across the globe as an example of a successful system of transnationalism. Transnationalism as a contemporary buzzword denotes a sense of privilege, a possible escape from restricting gender roles and poor education toward geographical places that allow for choices and freedom. In contrast, Trenka explains in *Fugitive Visions*, "transnationalism is not supposed to look like sisters trying to rebuild their relationship after being unwillingly separated, families struggling to talk to each other" (109). She argues that transnational adoption is rarely a choice or voluntary and not necessarily a form of rescue. She argues that transnational adoption should cease because poverty, war, imperialism, and patriarchy should not force families to split up or cause mothers to give up their children. These destructive strategies employed in the name of nationalism operate at the cost of children and poor women's humanity. According to Trenka, transnational adoption does nothing to improve conditions in the sending countries, and it certainly does not help birthmothers. Brian puts it this way: "U.S. demand or willingness to absorb another state's children hinders social welfare reforms," decreases reproductive rights, and fails to change norms of family patterns and child-rearing in the sending states (104, 150). An adoption system that privileges people based on their nationality, race, gender, and socioeconomic class does nothing to alleviate the hard choices women must make under structural constraints to preserve their humanity. In the next chapter, Nahid Rachlin takes the previous authors' relational and doubled writing style further to explore said patriarchal constrictions in the context of religion.

4

(RE)NEGOTIATING THE SELF

COLLECTIVE MEMOIR AND BORDER CROSSINGS

Matt Rees, contributing editor for *Time* magazine, writes in his review of Nahid Rachlin's *Persian Girls* (2006) that the book "paints the exotic scents and traditions of Tehran with the delicacy of a great novel." Novelist Patty Dann, too, applies the term "great novel" as a benchmark for Rachlin's work. Both reviewers appear struck by the fictional powers of Rachlin's work, and yet, the text they comment on is entitled *Persian Girls: A Memoir*. These statements suggest that the genre boundaries of Rachlin's autobiographical writing are not clear-cut for her readers. In this chapter, I discuss how Rachlin molds the life-writing genre to create a collective memoir with a communally constructed subject to depict Iranian/immigrant women's lives and how they are shaped by intersectional forces of gender, religion, class, and nationality.[1] The Trump administration's 2017 issuing of a travel ban targeting Muslim-majority countries stands as a stark reminder that experiences by Muslim women must receive more recognition.

Persian Girls' collectivity works on two levels. Through the use of letters, fictional stories, poems, and song lyrics, among other elements, Rachlin portrays herself as part of a global community of women fighting oppression. On a more specific level, the memoir establishes Rachlin's self as doubled: parts of the memoir are entirely devoted to Pari's, Rachlin's older sister's, traumatic experiences in an arranged marriage and her possible suicide, indicating that Pari lives the life Rachlin would have faced had she stayed in Iran. In accordance with Eakin's proclamation that all life writing is relational, *Persian Girls* presents a "proximate other to signify the intimate tie to the relational autobiographer" (*How Our Lives* 86; emphasis in original). In the case of Rachlin, I argue, there are multiple "proximate others," as she refuses to see herself within limited identity boundaries and gives voice to the female members of her family, who are culturally silenced because of their gender. Through her presentation of the "I" within a collective, Rachlin challenges identity constructions and writing norms that insist on a clear national consciousness and sense of belonging.

IRANIAN IMMIGRANT WOMEN'S MEMOIR BOOM

Rachlin's book constitutes part of a plethora of memoirs by Iranian American women that have appeared since 2003.[2] Most of these works were written by women who were either born in the United States, emigrated to the United States at a young age with their whole family, or left Iran after the Islamic Revolution of 1979. *Persian Girls* stands out because Rachlin, as one of only a few female Iranian immigrants before the Islamic Revolution, has a rare story to tell.[3] Her writing offers insights into the influence gender exerts on migration, a young Iranian woman's experiences at college in the United States, and the lives of married and divorced Muslim women in Iran.

The recent burst of autobiographical writing among women of Iranian descent might come as a surprise. Life writing does not have a strong tradition in Iran, especially among women. Traditional Iranian culture does not foster a climate conducive to self-reflective works, as it "is such a strong part of Iranian culture to never reveal private matters. . . . Private lives are trivial and not worth writing about" (Nafisi, *Things* xv). More specifically, in "a society concerned obsessively with keeping the worlds of men and women apart, with an ideal of feminine as silent, immobile, and invisible, women writers have not found it easy to flourish" (Milani 2). Autobiography, a genre that expresses autonomy and draws attention to the individual, cannot be taken for granted by women living amidst patriarchal traditions and a religiously fundamental political regime. Writing that fosters self-authorization can constitute a political tool to fight the oppression of women. Rachlin uses this power not only for herself but for other women in her family, creating a communal voice about women's strengths. Her social justice rhetoric might be received differently in the United States from that of the other women I discuss in this book since, after 9/11 and the wars in Iraq and Afghanistan, American readers have started to look to life writing with a Middle Eastern background as a source for cultural information on a "country and a people that have been deemed 'evil' and an imminent threat to Western society" (Malek 362), as well as for political assertion, either justifying or condemning military engagement in the region (Whitlock, *Soft Weapons* 128). Many Western readers exert empathy especially toward the problematic, stereotypical figure of the "oppressed Muslima" (Rak 172). Based on this special opportunity to reach a larger audience, I am interested in how experimental and communal life-writing techniques can create a space for immigrant women's voices.

The emergence of memoirs by Iranian American women has not received only positive attention. Some critics have suspected women of Iranian descent of using their texts to justify Western military intervention in their homeland by insinuating that Islam is "incurably backward and that Arab and Islamic societies indeed deserve to be dominated, undermined, or worse" (Ahmed 247). Nima Naghibi, for example, argues that "by marketing the East . . . as a place both inviting and threatening, these texts lend their implicit support to colonial intervention" (82). Many of these memoirs have been accused of exoticizing Iran and of perpetuating the biased division between East and West, which depicts the East as inferior to the advanced West. Azar Nafisi's *Reading Lolita in Tehran* (2003) was particularly criticized for portraying "the native informant confirming mainstream stereotypes about Iran and celebrating western civilization" (Elahi 39). Critics took offense with the book for depicting Iran as a backward nation without explaining the injustices that led to the Islamic Revolution. While Rees's review of *Persian Girls* makes reference to Iran's "exotic scents and traditions," Rachlin, who must have been familiar with the criticism against these memoirs by Iranian (American) women, avoids the same kind of critique by being less overtly political and, untraditionally in the Iranian context, more personal and emotional in her writing than other women writers.[4]

Choosing the life-writing genre to convey her feminist message allows Rachlin to be politically critical while masking her agenda as a personal story. Her text gives her claims special force as memoir offers a veneer of authenticity that Rachlin could not have obtained through a fictional account. Based on my readings of reviews by the general public, Rachlin's audience mentions most frequently that her vivid portrayal of Iranian culture fascinates them.[5] While these remarks suggest that readers are interested in exoticized depictions of foreign lands, hooking them to her narrative in such a way might make them more receptive to thinking about crucial issues, such as immigration by Muslim individuals to the United States and domestic violence. And, indeed, many readers express empathy for women's situation in Iran, even if few comment on Rachlin's sister, who features prominently and tragically in the book, or on the interconnectedness of Iranian women's lives—elements that function as a stronghold of the author's transnational and intersectional feminist message.

While the intimate moments Rachlin shares with her readers make her memoir stand out, her writing is similar to other Iranian (American) women's texts since "self-analysis is not the favored objective of the overwhelming majority of these works. Although they purport to be vehicles to allow the authors to speak for themselves, most of them actually incorporate multiple voices, especially that of a biographer" (Milani 223). This blurring of boundaries between autobiography and biography constitutes an important technique of Rachlin's collective memoir, which I see rooted in women's status in Iranian society. Rachlin is not the only protagonist in her book. While, in fact, most memoirs by Iranian women offer the biographies of a number of their family members, most importantly their mothers', most of these works limit these references to the beginning and never make the reader question who constitutes the singular focus of the story. *Persian Girls*, in contrast, depicts the lives of multiple women who are all in close emotional connection with Rachlin and comprise, I surmise, different versions of her. Rachlin tells her own life through the lives of others and the forms of oppression they experience to offer a platform for women's struggles globally.

Life-writing theory and especially feminist concepts prove valuable in discussing *Persian Girls* as collective memoir. For example, Leigh Gilmore's "autobiographics," which build on "resistance and contradiction as strategies of self-representation" (*Autobiographics* 42), present paradoxes in the representation of the "I" that go against the philosophical ideal of a unified, determined self. They are marked by experimental treatment of identity and offer a portrayal of the possibility of multiple forms of self and resulting shapes of agency. Autobiographics are helpful for my analysis of *Persian Girls* as Gilmore sees them "operating within texts that have not been seen as autobiographies" (42). In my interpretation, Rachlin's form of self-representation functions as a tool for resisting a socially imposed gender and national identity upon which both life writing and politics depend heavily. Because of its deviations from traditional demands for authenticity and self-reference, *Persian Girls* might well be regarded by some critics as not fitting the category of memoir. If read as autobiographic, however, working at the crossroads where women's life writing breaks with "regulatory laws of gender and genre" (45), it becomes clear that Rachlin's book challenges generic rules to portray how women defy gender norms.

Jeanne Perrault's concept of "autography" further helps theorize some aspects of *Persian Girls* as collective autobiography. Perrault defines "autography" as "a writing whose effect is to bring into being a 'self' that the writer names 'I;' but whose parameters and boundaries resist the monadic" (2). Rachlin, as I will demonstrate, presents her "I" as part of a feminist "we." Autography also "invites the reader to reconsider the imbrications of subjectivity, textuality, and community" (Perrault 2), which speaks to the systemic forces of oppression at work—regulating what female subjectivity and national community are allowed to look like—in Iranian women's lives. While these elements of "autography" certainly fit my reading of *Persian Girls*, the term does not succeed in capturing fully Rachlin's text as collective autobiography. Rachlin writes about another person biographically with the aim of establishing an auto/biography of herself in community with that person. Perrault discusses, for example, Audre Lorde's technique in *The Cancer Journals* of inserting her own diary entries in italics into her autobiography. This idea of different selves making up the autobiographical self, of course, matches Rachlin's conceptualization of herself as composed of multiple selves. But these identities are not confined to Rachlin alone; they also reside in other women close to her.

STORYTELLING AS PROTECTION AGAINST MISOGYNY

Beginning with the title of her memoir, Rachlin sets up the subject of her writing as a collective. The plural of *Persian Girls* indicates an intersubjective rather than an individual approach to telling the author's own life story. The title expresses how, according to Farzaneh Milani, "in Iran, where not only has art been mainly impersonal but also where an individual's identity is closely tied to the community and where use of the first-person-singular pronoun is still hard for people and is often diffused a bit by *we*, writing an *I*-book is not an easy task" (206; emphasis in original). Based in this explication of Iranian communal culture, it might seem natural that Rachlin would opt for plurality in her title.

Perhaps somewhat astounding to some readers might be her choice of "Persian" instead of "Iranian" as a description of her origin. It likely reflects Rachlin's intention to fight stereotypes about Iranians as part of an "axis of evil." In reminding her readers, through her title, of the magnificent cultured empire that Persia used to be instead of immediately making them think of the fundamentalist theocracy that the Islamic Republic of Iran is now, she appeals to her audience to face her story unbiased. Her deliberate attempt to avoid connection with the post-revolutionary Iranian regime is, of course, a very political choice. Azadeh Moaveni explains the preference for "Persian" further in her memoir, *Lipstick Jihad*: "Persian like a fluffy cat, a silky carpet—a vague Oriental notion belonging to history, untraceable on a map. It was the term we insisted on using at the time, embarrassed by any association with Iran, the modern country, the hostage-taking Death Star. Living a myth, a fantasy, made it easier being Iranian in America" (vii). Like Moaveni, Rachlin embraces her Persian ethnicity while distancing herself from her nationality. Her self-description supports my understanding of immigrant women's identity-construction as independent of citizenship. While the term "Persian" is complicated in that it conjures up Orientalist connotations, it is also likely to make Rachlin's readers more amenable to her account, which recalls Rosalina Rosay's technique of calling *Journey of Hope* a memoir instead of a testimonio, as discussed in chapter 1.

Persian Girls starts as a conventional, author-focused memoir, in telling the story of Rachlin's intrafamilial adoption negotiated between her mother and her aunt: "I was a gift to Maryam from her younger sister, Mohtaram. I was Mohtaram's seventh baby, her fifth living child . . . Maryam hadn't been able to get pregnant when she was married. Then she became a widow. She had begged Mohtaram to let her adopt one of her children. . . . I was that next child" (4).[6] Although Rachlin is I-centered in this description, the passage sets up the tight, communal nature of Iranian women's lives and begins to explain Rachlin's intricate connection with multiple women. Though Rachlin is taken from her aunt by her father when she turns nine years old—the age at which Iranian girls during the mid-1950s could get married—she continues to consider Maryam her mother and educates the readers about Maryam's life throughout the memoir.

The plural in the title designates an even wider communal subject than Rachlin's female family members by creating a female "us" that is united by class, gender, and religious expectations. Rachlin recounts some of the most eye-opening moments in her life as shared with other women in private settings: "Only in the public baths did I come to understand the difficulties of being a woman . . . [when] the women spoke of the unfairness of the system that gave women so much less power than men. . . . Didn't sons inherit twice as much as daughters. . . ? And weren't men allowed to marry more than one woman? Didn't fathers automatically get custody of the children in cases of divorce?" (19). At the bathhouse, Maryam and her friends share their life stories. Such reunions teach Rachlin about the power of storytelling, which allows even the mostly illiterate women in Maryam's social circle to pass on knowledge orally: "The sweet intimacy among the [women] and the support they gave to one another gradually relieved their pain" (20). Storytelling functions as a coping mechanism. Embracing this power, Rachlin refuses to describe merely one woman's exemplary life and to infer that her life story is special or worthier to tell than those of other ordinary Iranian women.

The practice of communal storytelling that pervades Rachlin's life inspires her to create fictional stories based on the real accounts she has heard from her adoptive mother and her friends. She includes a number of these stories in a smaller font than her nonfiction writing in her memoir. Some of these are just excerpted, but some the reader gets to read in full length, often taking up multiple pages. As one example, Rachlin writes a short story, "with some changes from real life" (150), about reading a long heroic tale to her family's illiterate servant, Ali. The tone of the story creates an atmosphere that resembles a mother-son relationship: "As I read, he would gasp or thrust his body forward at the hero's mishaps or smile triumphantly, revealing his small teeth, at the hero's good fortune" (150). Inspired by the tale, Ali's "face was very tense with thought, his gestures had acquired grandeur" (151). The narrative set-up risks insinuating an atmosphere that infantilizes Ali; yet, through Ali's reaction, Rachlin also points to literature's influence on people's self-perception and its ability to raise socioeconomic consciousness and empower the oppressed.

Such an overt hint at the strength inherent in literature comments on Iran's censoring and banning of books under the Shah as well as the Islamic regime. Rachlin underlines this connection when writing, "how strange that in our culture books were considered dangerous, that the written word was given so much power, that a person was thought of as a criminal for owning or reading certain books" (73). She links politics and nation to literature and connects control with cultural construction. She positions writing as having power, which underlines the autobiographical goal of regaining authority, especially for women and other minorities.

To buttress her social justice narrative, Rachlin intersperses *Persian Girls* with political and historical data. Those facts are rarely the main focus of the memoir, but they contextualize Rachlin's narrative and demonstrate that women's rights violations were a concern under the Shah as well as in the Republic. Rachlin cites the pillars of twentieth-century Iranian history such as the 1953 coup by Mossadegh, who nationalized Iranian oil, and "Operation Ajax," through which the CIA restored the Shah (42). Most of these examples remain uncommented, presumably as objective evidence that speaks for itself. Rachlin, however, combines those events that address women's rights directly with episodes from her own life. In 1962–1963, for example, as part of the Shah's "White Revolution," which also included land reform, Iranian women received the right to vote. In bringing this landmark change to her readers' attention, Rachlin recalls a conversation she had at the time with her father: " 'Father, do you like all the changes the Shah is making?' . . . [Father:] 'None of it should concern you.' [Rachlin:] 'Women can vote now.'. . . [Father:] 'Girls wouldn't know whom to vote for. . . . It's better if they didn't' " (125–126). Even though politics opened up spaces for women, patriarchal control—embodied by Rachlin's father—remained deeply entrenched in Iranian culture and continued to limit women's freedom.

As Rachlin's teacher, Mrs. Soleimani, explains, the new voting law was not enforced since "men told their wives, daughters, and sisters not to vote, or dictated to them whom to vote for" (128). Although the right to vote officially functions as a mark for women's liberation, behind the scenes, women are treated like puppets by the patriarchy. In an effort to keep young women in a state of ignorance, the regime forces Mrs. Soleimani to resign from her job for discussing women's rights in the classroom, which authorities considered "brainwashing the young girls" (Rachlin 129). This policing of knowledge has detrimental effects on women's self-perception as agents of social change.

Iranian women are silenced not only by their own political leaders and traditions, both under the Shah and the Islamic Republic, but also through the West's perceptions and treatment of them. Through Orientalist paradigms that have been used to bolster imperialist, nationalist, xenophobic, and anti-immigrant rhetorics, Middle Eastern women, and especially Muslim women, are perpetuated as passive, inferior beings. As Evelyn Shakir has established, the lives of Arab women have historically been documented by white male Westerners (5); and these Orientalist depictions, rooted in beliefs of racial superiority that buttress a "Western style for dominating, restructuring, and having authority over the Orient" (Said 3), painted Arab women as "fictions," "nonentities, so brain dead" (Shakir 8). Immigrant women's life writing, like *Persian Girls* and the oral histories Shakir collected in *Bint Arab* (1997), critique such sexist and racist Western ideologies. Life writing as political tool offers Muslim women the opportunity to push their audience to see the subject not through preconceived archetypes but personal experiences. As Fatemeh Keshavarz claims in her critique of Nafisi's *Reading Lolita in Tehran*, such an approach entails a holistic depiction of Iran that avoids focusing only on oppressive elements. Texts that portray Iran mostly negatively and aggressively, which Keshavarz terms "New Orientalist" writings (3), build on the victimization of Middle Eastern women and denigrate Iranian society and history by selectively limiting it.

Despite her refusal to paint a solely dark picture of Iran, Rachlin is forceful in her details about the injustices she sees perpetrated against women in a patriarchal society (under the Shah as well as under the Islamic regime). In a second fictional story that she includes in her memoir and that is inspired by a conversation she overheard, a woman leaves her blind daughter behind in the desert to die so that she herself can marry a man who would not have married her with a disabled child: "I picture Monir standing in the vast desert, listening to the vanishing echoes of her mother's footsteps. Then waiting desperately for her to appear again until other frightening images and echoes swept over her consciousness" (Rachlin 74). Although in the real-life version of the story, the mother only contemplates leaving the daughter behind, but does not go through with it, Rachlin takes the incident further and succeeds in capturing, as her teacher, Mrs. Soleimani, puts it, "the desperation of women all around us" (75). Rachlin uses a fictionalized real-life incident to depict the lives of many "Persian Girls," whose bodies and opportunities are controlled by men.

Iranian patriarchy—which limits women's social roles to those of mothers and wives, regulates their access to education, demands that women have male permission to marry and travel, and reduces the worth of a woman's testimony in court to a third of a man's—is not solely based on Islamic law but also culturally instituted, as seen in the oppression of women even in secular, Westernized families such as Rachlin's prior to the Islamic Revolution.[7] Rachlin describes how the sexism she experienced affected her as a child in her relationship with her family: "I wondered if Father and Mohtaram were evil. But my grandmother, whom I loved so much, had done the same to her daughters, had forced them to marry men she and my grandfather chose. They themselves were victims of the oppressive system that dictated to people how they should feel and live their lives" (69). Much like Rosay and Trenka defend their mothers' choices in their memoirs discussed in earlier chapters, Rachlin explains that she understands some women perpetuate other women's oppression because they were raised in a patriarchal system. In her anecdote, the abandonment of the blind girl parallels a metaphorical abandonment by Rachlin's mother in a culture that neglects its female citizens. The little girl's blindness connects to women's inability to be valued in any misogynistic society that locates a girl's personal worth in her bodily perfection, (sexual) virtue, and her ability to become a "good" wife and mother.

Rachlin offers a candid picture of her family to underline patriarchy's destructiveness: "My father was attentive, but I couldn't warm up to him. He had too much power over me. He had single-handedly changed the course of my life" (39). While her father "didn't criticize [her] brothers, at least not in front of [the] women," he "commanded and criticized" all women in the household, including his wife (47), which leads Rachlin to announce that "when it comes to Mother and us, he's a dictator" (67). Through her choice of the word "dictator," Rachlin describes her father as a symbol of oppressive, patriarchal, national power. Most times when she mentions him in her memoir, it is in connection with the control he exerts over other people. This establishes a community among the "dictator's" subjects and especially among the women in that group. At the same time, Rachlin keeps a personal connection with the men in her family and refrains from offering an abstract critique of all Muslim men as brute forces. In fact, the memoir portrays a number of male characters, such as Ali, the housekeeper, and Rachlin's brothers, as ordinary Iranian men with no interest in fanaticism or suppressing women. Importantly, Rachlin, later in her life, reconciles with her father, speaking to the possibility of change in a person and culture.

The oppression of women justified via a misinterpretation of religion and culture exists in patriarchal countries all over the world. But what exactly this oppression looks like varies depending on geographic location. As Sara Ahmed forcefully reminds us, oppression is not rooted in religion or culture but comes out of patriarchal forces abusing both. She deems counterproductive the call on women to abandon their culture and religion when they are working to reform them from within and compares the vilification of the veil in Islam to the physical harm that the corset caused without creating a global outcry to "liberate" Victorian women (244). Rachlin, in my opinion, does not set out to portray Iranian culture or Islam as fundamentally corrupt. Instead, she points out how patriarchal oppression is an issue worldwide that hinders girls' and women's self-actualization. Thus, her life writing creates a community among all women who experience oppression due to their gender and calls for social, cultural, and religious change in support of women's freedom.

Persian Girls establishes sympathy in her audience especially through the image of Rachlin as a courageous young girl unafraid of standing up to an oppressive system from a very young age. Rachlin befriends the owner of a bookstore, who regularly provides her with books that have been blacklisted by the Shah, such as Victor Hugo's *Les Misérables* (1862) (72). It is noteworthy that Rachlin mentions a European text to underline her rebelliousness. She references Hugo's work, it seems, not only because it is likely a novel that her Western audience will be familiar with, but because of the work's connection to oppression and political renewal. *Les Misérables* chronicles political injustices in the French past and calls for compassion and humanitarianism. Especially the figure of Fantine, an uneducated orphan, resonates with Rachlin's demands since the young woman's story stands as a strong condemnation of the subjection of women and a society that takes advantage of women by keeping them dependent and poor. Hugo's opus unabashedly demands a democratic future, social reforms, and a revolution. *Persian Girls* echoes this political stance in its insistence that cultural and social reforms in support of the empowerment of women—decidedly not steeped in cultural imperialism spreading Western ideology—constitute a global social justice issue.

Tellingly, it is Rachlin's writing that enables her to leave Iran to study in the United States. Her father, sole maker of this decision, sends her to "Lindengrove College" near St. Louis because he "was afraid of the kind of books [she] read, the stories [she] wrote, of the fact that [she] broke rules" (131). Rachlin's rule-breaking with regard to literature in her childhood comes to life again in the stylistic choices she made for her memoir as "the law of genre" stipulates that "genres are not to be mixed" (Derrida 55). Derrida's claim speaks to Western cultural expectations of purity. A genre, much like one's national allegiance, should be natural and easily defined via distinct codes and characteristics. *Persian Girls*' generic hybridity not only breaks with Western literary and cultural expectations, but also offers a venue for immigrant women to express an identity that is shaped by multiple nations, influenced by various cultures, and that demands a close connection with people necessarily left behind, often spanning continents.

PERSIAN GIRLS AS AUTO/BIOGRAPHY

A number of Western critics have investigated the mixing of fiction and life writing as a phenomenon that goes back to the late nineteenth century. Much of this criticism focuses on autobiographical fiction or the telling of lies in life-writing texts.[8] Rachlin's technique of incorporating fictional accounts into her own memoir is different from such approaches. While in these earlier texts, it is often impossible for the reader to distinguish between fiction and reality, Rachlin sets her stories clearly apart from her autobiographical writing. Through a smaller font and indented lines, she alerts her readers that what they are about to read diverts from the main body of her memoir. Much like Jane Jeong Trenka and Meri Nana-Ama Danquah, Rachlin does not meet the demands of Lejeune's autobiographical pact since her book is not only about herself—whole chapters of the memoir recount her sister's life, a person whose name is not mentioned as author. Derrida and Lejeune's theories involving the "law," "contract," and "propriety" rely heavily on masculine, authoritarian, nationalist Western concepts. In challenging these theories, Rachlin opens up a space for immigrant women's intersectional experiences.

While Rachlin includes much biographical information, especially about her sister Pari, she does not merely write a biography or an autobiography disguised as someone else's autobiography, such as Gertrude Stein's *The Autobiography of Alice B. Toklas* (1933). In her discussion of *The Autobiography*, Mary Mason identifies an "evolution and delineation of an identity by way of alterity," a "pattern of alterity-equality" (41). She sees a similar approach of "the pairing of one's own image with another, equal image" (41), in the writing of Margaret Cavendish, who "identifies herself most sharply when she is identifying [her husband] too" (23). Yet, Rachlin does not resort to ventriloquist techniques, mimicking someone else's voice and ideas, as, in my opinion, Pari's life completes her own. Rachlin's critique of life writing's reliance on nationalism would also be diminished if she had written one person's history in one geographic location alone. Hence *Persian Girls* constitutes a collective, hybrid text that, like the other memoirs I have discussed in this book, demonstrates immigrant women's intention to give a platform to those who are rarely heard.

To this end, Rachlin elaborates on some of the alternative ways in which the women in her life communicate their pain and desires. She mentions, for example, that the only way that her biological mother, Mohtaram, is "allowed to express herself" is in making tapestries (67). Art offers her the venue for voicing her feelings and desires, which she cannot articulate even when it comes to raising her own children. This specific instance of art offering a venue for those whose voices are repressed—very much mirroring Rachlin's social change agenda that she practices in her life writing—presents a striking resemblance to the Greek myth of Philomela and Procne.[9] Although Rachlin does not give detailed descriptions of her mother's craft, the reader can compare Philomela's cry for justice through her weaving with Mohtaram's attempt to express her experiences in her tapestries. Likewise, silenced Pari uses poetry as an outlet for her feelings. Via her writing, Rachlin takes revenge for these women by speaking up and making their oppression public. As with her insertion of the blind girl's story, Rachlin uses the absence of voice and sight as political metaphors demanding women's liberation.

For Rachlin, much as for Mexican immigrant Rosay, the most effective way to reach autonomy would be a higher level of education, but the "idea of Father sending me, a daughter, to America was ridiculous" (107). While her father lets his oldest sons attend college in the United States, he responds to her desire to leave Iran with "'you already know the answer. No!'" (Rachlin 110). His authority is overpowering in the limitations it sets on the intellectual development of the women in the family. When he finally allows her to go to the United States—for opportunistic reasons to avoid trouble for the family instead of seeing the value in educating his daughter—he tells her as a final goodbye: "'Go, go, you've been causing so much worry, trouble'" (Rachlin 135). Even though his "cold words hit [her] like pieces of hail" (135), Rachlin nevertheless feels for "the first time in years . . . lighthearted. A tightly sealed door had started to open and [she] was finally walking out" (135). For Rachlin, as for many immigrant women, self-authorization comes at the expense of family unity. While Rachlin reaches freedom, at least physically, in a new country, her older sister, Pari, is trapped in Iranian patriarchy. This circumstance doubles Rachlin's self and creates an intense sublevel of her relational identity.

As young girls, Pari and Rachlin decide to resist their father's efforts to marry them off and to follow their dreams of becoming an actress and a writer, respectively. They are extremely close, with similar character traits and ambitions. With their lives lined up to develop comparably, Pari ends up dead at a young age, while Rachlin is able to break out of the system and become an author. I see Rachlin regarding Pari's life as the existence she herself might have led if she had been forced to stay in Iran. Rachlin positions Pari as the sacrifice that enabled her to live as an autonomous woman. As a result of their intertwined existence, "the loss of Pari has left a hole in [her] existence" (Rachlin 287). Rachlin even takes up Pari's purpose in life after the latter's death, which is to find her son from whom she was separated after her divorce. Tellingly, the very last lines of Rachlin's memoir read as follows: "When I look at a photograph of Pari on my desk . . . images rush back: how my loneliness disappeared the moment she entered our house in Ahvaz . . . . Yes, dearest Pari, it is to bring you back to life that I write this book" (288). This (very much political) approach of amplifying the voice of the silenced and pushing for their humanity changes the form and purpose of immigrant life writing as well as, necessarily, our interpretation of it.

Once Pari moves out of her parents' house, readers learn of her life through letters that she sends Rachlin, who quotes them at length. Pari's writing, like the fictional pieces Rachlin works into her memoir, are visually set apart from her main narrative through italics, with longer sections indented. This should prevent the reader from confusing Pari's words with Rachlin's and, through the italics, also distinguishes Pari's writing from the short stories in the memoir. Rachlin essentially publishes someone else's epistolary autobiography in her own memoir, whereby she changes these letters' audience and turns them into a political tool. Rachlin establishes what Liz Stanley, Andrea Salter, and Helen Dampier call an epistolary pact, which is marked by referentiality: "Writing letters is not merely to 'write the self,' or even the self and the other, but concerns other people, events, and circumstances in a world shared in common, even if not every aspect of the meaning of this is agreed between signatory and addressee" (280). Building on this relational nature of letter writing and by means of the fragmented nature of letters, which captures only vignettes of a person's life at a time, Rachlin portrays women's fragmented identity and experiences with oppression worldwide.

In her letters, Pari makes clear how much she suffers in her marriage. An image that keeps coming up is that of Pari as prisoner: "*He's keeping me a virtual prisoner*" and "*When he's at work his sister comes to the house and watches over me like a prison guard*" (Rachlin 96).[10] When she speaks to her father in hopes that he might encourage her to come home, he instead demands she stay with her husband. While Taheri, Pari's husband, promises her that if she has a baby, things will get better, Pari insists on a visit home: "I don't want children, I don't want to become a baby machine like Mother. And I don't want a child from him" (103). Pari understands that having a baby would limit even further her chances of getting out of this marriage, but instances of domestic violence make it harder and harder for her to stay strong: "'Father is never *deliberately* cruel. Taheri is a sadist. He put a lit cigarette on my arm.' . . . . 'Taheri tortures me mentally, too. . . . He wants me to cook and iron his clothes in certain ways. . . . The slightest deviation throws him into a fit'" (103; emphasis in original). Pari's father, as a stand-in for Iranian patriarchal society, sanctions this marital abuse not only by simply ignoring Pari's pleas but by apologizing to his son-in-law for his daughter's behavior: "'I admit my daughter is spoiled. . . . Bear with her. She'll grow up'" (Rachlin 105). Even in the face of domestic abuse and the threat to his daughter's livelihood, Pari's father is trained to worry about the family's image and money. Rachlin presents Pari as trapped by social forces that infantilize and dehumanize her and rob her of agency.

Learning about her sister's oppression increases in Rachlin the wish to break out of the Iranian system and go to the United States for college. She wants Pari to get a divorce and join her. But whereas Rachlin "was getting out," Pari "was still in her prison" (134). Using the image of force and control with which Pari describes her experiences, Rachlin sets up specific parts of her memoir as a doubled life narrative, simultaneously depicting Pari's life in confinement and Rachlin's attempt at freeing herself from misogynistic forces in the United States. As soon as Rachlin arrives in the United States, Pari's letters become the sole means for Rachlin to narrate Pari's life. They present splinters of her life distorted by patriarchal forces that hold her captive in her role as wife and do not allow her to develop her other identities.

Rachlin's epistolary technique would certainly not be innovative if she was writing Pari's biography. What is unique about Rachlin's use of Pari's letters is that these letters give readers auto/biographical insight into her relational subjectivity. As Margaretta Jolly and Liz Stanley propose, "the 'truth' of the [letter] writing is in the relationship rather than in its subject" (93). Pari's writing is a (sometimes encrypted) performance in support of women limited by patriarchy that is geared particularly toward Rachlin as her audience but perhaps also intended to be spread among a wider sympathetic readership. As Pari is a prisoner in her marriage and likely dies from suicide because of the trauma her situation causes, her letters might be compared to those of death row prisoners, which Janet Maybin found to help prisoners establish supportive relationships and preserve a sense of self-knowledge and -worth. Likewise, this correspondence supported the letter readers in overcoming their own traumatic experiences. This reciprocal benefit seems to apply to Pari and Rachlin, as both attempt to work through separation, isolation, and fragmentation in their lives. As Pari's letters confirm Rachlin's life choices, it is important that Rachlin publishes the letters with the "inevitable ethical issues that come with reading another's correspondence" in mind (Jolly and Stanley 113). She honors them, I argue, in employing them as a key component of her social justice life writing intended to serve others in similar situations as Pari.

The letters Rachlin receives from Pari in the United States take a darker tone, but at least in the beginning are still a testament to Pari's will-power: "*There is a dark hollow space between me and my husband. I feel this is a good* time to get out of the marriage, before I have a child" (158). But without her parents' support, Pari cannot go through with her plans: "*Jobs wouldn't come easily to a young divorced woman here and the same with trying to rent a place and living alone, even if I could afford it. . . . A divorced woman living alone practically has the status of a prostitute*" (Rachlin 158–159). In Pari's Iran, a woman is considered a valuable part of society only if she is connected to a man. Sattareh Farman-Farmaian asserts in her memoir, *Daughter of Persia* (1992), that a "woman by herself was nothing, a nonentity, a creature who without a father, brother, husband, or son to guide her was incapable of making important decisions, looking after herself properly, or even leading a moral life" (78). Being independent of male power would label Pari as a prostitute—someone marked as indecent, immoral, and promiscuous. A few months later Pari sends a letter with a message that seems to seal her fate: "*I am pregnant*" (Rachlin 159).

This last letter also contains the poem "A Wind-up Doll" by Iranian poet Furugh Farrukhzad, which was attacked for its depictions of women's desires.[11] Citing this poem at full length serves as an additional form of auto/biographical writing that nourishes the readers' understanding of Pari's entrapment as Rachlin's doubled self. Certain lines warrant special attention: "*With stiff fingers you push aside the drapery on the window / you stand there motionless and like a wind-up doll, you see the world with glass eyes*" (qtd. in Rachlin 160). These verses speak to Pari's physical incarceration in her house and ideological confinement in her roles as wife and mother. Being thus trapped has made her go emotionally numb, and also physically paralyzed to a degree. Her limbs are "stiff," and only if the person in control of her allows her to move or "wind[s] her up" can Pari revive for a short while. Patriarchy has removed her autonomy over her own body.

Most of the poem elaborates on this state of many Iranian women, until the last section calls for action: "*Rise up and seek your freedom, my sister / Why are you quiet? / Seek your rights, my sister / You must tear apart from those who seat you in a corner of the house / so that your life will be free*" (qtd. in Rachlin 160). The words are direct: All women need to liberate themselves by speaking up about the injustices they experience. They must revolt against their oppressors. Only in physically distancing themselves from their tormentors will they gain freedom. These verses, although Pari does not comment on them or make a connection between the poem and her own life, make a strong impression on Rachlin. She has continuous dreams of Pari vanishing or being with a Pari who turns out to be an imposter (Rachlin 161). Rachlin comments that she "was haunted by Pari's state in life" (160), which underscores how entwined their lives are. When Rachlin cannot reach Pari on the phone, she considers visiting her, but for that to happen she would need a letter from her father to be able to return to the United States, and she is worried that he would force her to stay in Iran, where she would likely enter a life similar to Pari's. Pari, meanwhile, cannot come to the United States without consent from her husband, which he would never give. Patriarchy limits choices of mobility by women that could provide them life-sustaining relationships and opportunities. Because Rachlin and Pari are physically kept apart, they nourish their bond through writing.

After this last letter, *Persian Girls* offers long sections, such as one on Pari giving birth to her son, Bijan, in which Rachlin tells Pari's stories not through the latter's own words in her letters but as if Rachlin herself had been present at these events. In fact, chapter 23 is entirely on Pari's life. Even more clearly in those sections than before, Rachlin acts as a biographer of another person in her own memoir and establishes Pari's life as intrinsic to her own life story. While some readers might question the authenticity of Rachlin's detailed account—a supposed violation of the autobiographical pact—I see Rachlin effectively using this technique to reveal human rights violations.

In these biographical sections about Pari, the reader learns that she joined a group trying to improve laws for women in Iran. Her engagement with this group, presumably, encourages her to recite another poem by Farrukhzad at one of her group's meetings: "*More and more I am thinking that / I will suddenly spread my wings. / And fly out of this prison, laughing at my jailor!*" (qtd. in Rachlin 168). Rachlin does not specify how she learned of this poem. The means of transmission regarding news about Pari's life become more and more obscure in favor of the need to emphasize Rachlin's emotional relationality with Pari. The poem appears to show that Pari's intention to break out of her patriarchal prison has strengthened. Her determination only increases when she finds papers that prove Taheri had run over a woman with a motor scooter in his youth and was sentenced to ten years in prison, but that his father had bribed officials to let him out after one year. Pari hopes that the evidence of this crime might help her get a divorce without losing her child, which in Iran, at the time, is possible only if the husband can be found at fault of having deceived his wife.

But while the last poem Pari included in a letter to Rachlin is full of careful optimism and resolution, Pari's next poem by Farrukhzad reflects her despair over ever escaping her marriage. The two lines of the poem read: "*If one day I try to fly out of this prison, / how will I explain it to my weeping child?"* (qtd. in Rachlin 170). Pari appears to be contemplating the idea that she might have to abandon her son in order to escape confinement. The weighing of her own survival against her love as a mother intensifies once Pari realizes that her father will not support her in getting a divorce even when she makes it clear she is "'afraid of'" Taheri (Rachlin 171). Despite the fact that Pari's fear for her own livelihood also implies a lack of safety for Bijan, Pari's father insists that Bijan needs his father and that Pari should consider how a divorce would affect Taheri's reputation. Pari, in her main role as wife, must sacrifice herself to preserve her husband's social status. When Pari asks whether she herself is not "entitled to some individual happiness,'" her father replies that her idea is influenced by an American sense of individualism, which is purely "selfish;" he claims that what "we have is superior; each person should think of the happiness of the whole" (Rachlin 171). These words, insinuating a collectivism that primarily benefits men, stand as a powerful example for the widespread use of a dangerous, misogynistic rhetoric that justifies women's oppression and abuse. Despite her parents' disapproval and her longing for her son, Pari leaves her husband.[12] While she is granted visitation rights for her son, she is unable to enforce them.[13]

The patriarchal use of relationality subsumed in national ideologies stands in stark contrast to Rachlin's conceptualizing of the collective as a liberating and supportive space for women. According to her father's nationalistic understanding of community, women should stop thinking about their own well-being and surrender to the family and the state—a demand gendered to limit only women in their life choices. Through her collective memoir, Rachlin challenges literary and social discourse rooted in male nationalism that polices and confines women's identity. Without suggesting that Western cultures are entirely empowering to women or unproblematic in their treatment of minoritized groups, Rachlin politicizes her life writing to portray the need for change in any culture that oppresses women and necessitates their migration.

Rachlin's collective subjectivity is put to an intense test when she learns of Pari's death. A friend of Pari tells her on the phone that Pari "lost her balance and tripped down the stairway of their house. It was too late by the time she reached the hospital" (Rachlin 245). Rachlin immediately doubts that Pari's death was an accident: It "must have been intentional. Pari so closely identified with Furugh Farrukhzad, and she believed that the poet killed herself because she couldn't bear her situation in life. I'd seen Pari's perspective on her own life grow darker and darker. No hope. No escape. No passion" (245). The memoir, ultimately, never clarifies whether Pari died in a fatal accident or through suicide, although the latter option grasps Rachlin's imagination the most forcefully. In this feminist narration, it does not seem important how Pari died; what needs to come across is the notion that Pari had to die in a patriarchal world that denied her the means to live a fulfilling life. Rachlin imagines Pari's sense of desperation and her last thoughts, "*Jump and that will be the end of pain*" (245; emphasis in original). Because Pari represents Rachlin's double, her death puts in front of Rachlin's eyes what could have been her own end in Iran. Not only did misogyny necessitate Rachlin's emigration and prevent her return for many years, it also destroyed a part of her identity that she had to leave behind.

Rachlin makes a clear connection between Pari's depression and the lack of access to the world of imagination in a sexist culture that limits women's self-determination: "She wasn't allowed to give her dissatisfaction and disappointments, her losses, shape and meaning and so she became their prisoner" (246). Because for Pari, unlike Rachlin, it is not possible to work through her experiences and feelings—she had to die. When Rachlin travels to Tehran to investigate her sister's passing, she realizes that Pari had even lost her physical freedom as her second husband had committed her to a sanitarium. Upon visiting the institution, Rachlin learns that Pari should never have been admitted. As she leaves the sanitarium, women start shouting at her: "'Get me out of this cage. . . . What have I done to be punished like this?'" (Rachlin 262). These pleas for help confirm Rachlin's suspicion that some Iranian men abuse mental hospitals to have their wives physically contained and keep them from striving to change the status quo.

Rachlin's interpretation of the mental institution as a tool of patriarchal control recalls Michel Foucault's critical history of asylums in *Madness and Civilization* (1964). In the chapter "The Birth of the Asylum," Foucault illustrates how asylums were created to protect society from those who do not fit its norms by confining them. He considered this approach to "healing" a cruel form of control and punishment, an assessment that certainly also applies to the troubling history of patriarchal societies labeling women who break out of gender norms as "hysterical" and "crazy." Rachlin's visit to the sanitarium triggers in her "a strange daydream in which [she is] Pari," who confronts her first love interest, Majid, about his false intentions to leave his wife for her (266). In this time of great distress, Pari takes over Rachlin's identity as the culmination of *Persian Girls*' collectively constructed subject to declare the hindrance of women's physical and emotional development a human rights violation.

CONCLUSIONS

Consistent with her push for the liberation of women from oppressive, patriarchal forces, Rachlin ends her memoir with an epilogue that describes how the women in her family have succeeded in regaining agency in their lives. Maryam, Mohtaram, and Rachlin's younger sisters, Farzin and Manijeh, now live together independent of male control. The last letter that Rachlin includes in her memoir speaks to a deep sisterly support that shows Iranian women's wisdom and strength regarding the circumvention of patriarchal restrictions, notably without the need of an intervention on the part of Western ideals. Two sentences from said letter written by Mohtaram, her biological mother, to Maryam, her adoptive mother, stand out: "*I'm happy to give you one of my children. I know how sad you are that you don't have any of your own*" (Rachlin 279). These words lead Rachlin to forgive Mohtaram for giving her up, although she still sees Maryam as her real mother. Recalling Trenka's empathy for her birthmother's decisions (see chapter 2), Rachlin now better understands the reasons for biological mothers' choices: "I am . . . more aware than ever of how difficult her life was—married at the age of nine to a grown man, starting at the age of fourteen to give birth to ten children and then losing so many of them. I imagined her and Father together in bed on their wedding night, he experienced with women, and she completely innocent, no breasts, no pubic hair" (287).

Rachlin's image of her parents' wedding night sets the tone for all of Mohtaram's adult life: she is pregnant from the beginning of puberty until she is thirty-nine years old and silenced in her needs and desires by her husband who believes that "birth control is preventing life" (Rachlin 97). Mohtaram has no autonomy over her own body, and the physical and emotional burden this takes on her is enormous. Rachlin gives an impression of her mother's desperation when she describes how, upon giving birth to her last children, girl twins, she "squeezed [her] thighs, hoping the babies wouldn't come into this world. Didn't [she] have enough children already?" (99). To liberate her mother, at least fictionally, Rachlin imagines an affair for her with a jeweler whom she used to visit frequently when her husband was traveling (68). Rachlin, like Rosay, Danquah, and Trenka, understands her mother's oppression and the actions resulting from it. Through her collective memoir, she establishes a community among women whose intersectional lives are connected by the consequences of a nationally sanctioned misogyny.

Persian Girls does not stand alone in its generic freedoms among the memoirs by women of Iranian descent. In fact, digressions from life-writing traditions prevail in that demographic. For example, Nafisi's *Reading Lolita in Tehran*, mentioned earlier in the chapter, combines memoir, literary criticism, and social history. The Iranian migrant memoir I see as being the closest to *Persian Girls* in its portrayal of multiple voices is Marjane Satrapi's *Persepolis* (2003). As Amy Malek explains, "Satrapi's liminality allowed her to fuse Western genres of memoir and comics with Iranian history, culture, and her own mixed sensibilities to create a 'third space' environment from which to speak and tell her hybrid tale" (379). The visuals in Satrapi's graphic memoir enable an intense portrayal of violence—such as a cut-up human body or skulls floating in mid-air—emotions, and the loss of individuality that dress codes impose on girls and women. Additionally, the frames allow her to express her older autobiographical self in comment boxes, which contrasts her younger voice in thought bubbles. But even works like *Reading Lolita* and *Persepolis*, while bending the life-writing genre, do not go as far in their relational experimentation as Rachlin does in covering multiple lives as one subject in a memoir.

No matter their scope of generic deviation, what unites Iranian immigrant women's life writing texts is the authors' intention to do away with Western misperceptions about Iran. For most Westerners, for instance, the images they connect with Iran hail from popular culture elements like the movie adaption of Betty Mahmoody's *Not without My Daughter* (1987), a story despised by Iranians for its portrayal of them as uncivilized and dirty. In contrast to the film's plot, "people don't go crazy just because they come to Iran" (Bahrampour 238). But this imagery is not limited to only one production. Western media frequently portray Middle Eastern women solely as the docile, oppressed, muted, and passive victims that Western opinion makes Muslim women out to be: "In photographs, women across the Middle East illustrate a cultural landscape: They are portrayed as distant, shielded from direct view through the veil; as passive, reacting to events rather than actively participating in them; and as impersonal, warranting little identification through individual status" (Wilkins 60). Orientalist, nationalist rhetoric perpetuates the victimization of Middle Eastern women for political gain to justify military intervention without acknowledging these women's agency (Abu-Lughod).

The Iranian women's movement, unprecedented in strength in the Middle East, has been fighting the victimization of Iranian women for decades. Activists like Nobel Peace Prize winner Shirin Ebadi, the young women wearing lipstick in the streets of Tehran who inspired Moaveni's writing, as well as the many women taking selfies in public places and sharing them on the Facebook page "My Stealthy Freedom" challenge the Islamist regime on a daily basis.[14] Rachlin's memoir adds to this social legacy in pushing her readers to understand that the religious radicals governing the country at this moment in time do not represent all of Iran. This didactic goal strongly resembles Rosay's aim of proving that undocumented Mexican immigrants are not social parasites and Danquah's fight against misperceptions of people experiencing mental illness. Immigrant women's life writing functions as a tool to impel social justice for those oppressed groups denied the privilege to write their own stories, which is very much the case for the vast majority of women refugees and displaced women globally.

5
LIFE NARRATIVES AND THE SYRIAN REFUGEE CRISIS

The year 2019 propelled the numbers of displaced people to record heights. As "displaced people are seen as challenging and subverting [national] order . . . national and international bodies control and manage anyone who is perceived not to have territorial roots" (Dossa 4), which predominantly takes the form of silencing and othering refugees. Leigh Gilmore asserts that according to widespread public perception, "the refugee is the one who belongs elsewhere" ("Refugee" 674). Many displaced women have experienced intense deprivation and (sexual) violence in their home countries, on their journeys, and in foreign detention centers, but their stories rarely receive a platform.[1]

Gillian Whitlock stresses in *Soft Weapons* (2007) that much like refugees' bodies, their testimonies are "carefully controlled and contained" (18). Thus, Whitlock views refugee life writing as an effective political act, considering how "the extraordinary lengths that are taken to deny a face and history . . . to individual refugees indicate that attaching an autobiography to an individual can be a powerful act of resistance" (18). Aline Lo adds that such life narratives offer "more complex and nuanced understanding of refugees" (644), which might bring forth empathy. This chapter juxtaposes and dissects refugee texts as they add an essential focus on experiences of violently forced displacement to my investigation of immigrant women's life narratives. I am particularly invested in how authors use the perceptions of children and young adults to bring to life various horrors that rendered them displaced, and how these childlike visions likely affect their audiences' attitudes toward refugees. I share Vinh Nguyen's hope that "perhaps . . . refugee stories of survival and resilience [can] *teach* [people] to be more compassionate, to offset compassion fatigue" (Nguyen, Phu, and Troeung 444; emphasis in original).

In response to refugee life writing's potential social and political impact, those who want to curtail rights and support for displaced people restrict and fragment refugee testimony. Stories *about* refugees created by non-refugees are prolific and often describe them as violent masses of people who intentionally set out to change (read most often as Islamicize) other countries' cultures and to be burdens on the economies of countries of asylum. As part of a "resurgence of national self-determination in relation to immigration" (Woolley 13), such rhetoric—which is very similar to propaganda that vilifies undocumented migrants—has been successfully promulgated by right-wing politicians in European countries such as Italy and Hungary as well as the United States to justify the refusal to accept refugees and asylum seekers.[2]

Until recently, studies about refugees have been relegated to the social sciences (Woolley 7). But, as Agnes Woolley has discussed, "contemporary representations of asylum address the ethical, political and aesthetic questions that converge on the topic of forced migration" (4), which makes refugee life writing, particularly by women, a fruitful ground for analysis. In particular, Clare Brant, Tobias Heinrich, and Monica Soeting claim that life narratives' strength lies in "exposing the continuing and evolving forms of the colonial gaze that permeates the discourse of forced migration" (627). This gaze others and dehumanizes displaced people, makes them responsible for their own trauma, and presents them as a threat to Western civilization.

Refugee women, especially, are marked as passive victims, and their agency and courage in seeking a better life for themselves and their families are undermined. They are often isolated and traumatized. A significant number of them might be pregnant or might have just given birth on open waters. Their experiences are shocking and could provide vital insights into migration processes and how these women confront masculinist hegemonies.[3] One possible reason for the suppression of women's voices might be that their everyday experiences of abuse and poverty disrupt our standard narratives of war and migration and are hard to deal with emotionally. But such a male-centered approach to analyzing global issues invites stereotypes into the conversation without challenging them. Solely depicting women as vulnerable might have the intention of protecting them, but it also disempowers them and diminishes "the potential vulnerability of refugee men by stigmatising them as aggressive" (Parrs 196). It is vital to emphasize that refugee women's precariousness is not rooted in biology but in patriarchal structures and abuses of bodies and powers (Parrs 200). I, hence, strongly believe that offering displaced women alternative ways to participate and share their intersectional experiences, especially through life-writing forms, can be an influential social justice tool.

Gilmore addresses the current movement of displaced people in *Tainted Witness* (2017) when she writes that "the global crisis affecting immigrants, refugees, and asylum seekers brings urgency to a focus on testimony. . . . Witnesses will be bringing stories of harm with them as they flee. They will also be sending stories ahead of them, and these stories will mingle with precirculated stories about how they are, what they seek, and what they might do" (21). Gilmore expresses the importance of life narratives in creating understanding for human rights violations and shaping perception of refugees in receiving countries. Malala Yousafzai, in turn, sees the strength of refugee testimony in its ability to make "people understand the tangle of emotions that comes with leaving behind everything you know" (45).[4] Woolley agrees that refugee life writing is crucial because it offers impressions "of forced migration outside the prescriptive spaces of officialdom" (25). And Brant, Heinrich, and Soeting postulate that "life writing, with its focus on the singular, non-interchangeable nature of each person's history, not only serves as an act of reappropriation, but is also able to question the modes in which the debate as a whole is framed" (627). Life writing, I concur, individualizes people's experiences, returns power over their own stories to the authors, and can change the conversation about displacement as it creates visibility for refugees and amplifies their voices.

Many current refugee narratives are, at this point, oral or available on social media platforms. As is to be expected, not much traditional life writing has been published yet by people who have lived through the ongoing wave of displacement in the Middle East.[5] Online media have shown themselves more accessible to displaced people and their communication needs and, in many cases, have exposed their messages to a wider audience than print media might be able to. Working through trauma, securing survival, and adjusting to life in new countries and cultures certainly do not allow for much time to write. And online platforms are more amenable toward not fully formed and polished snippets of experiences or thoughts. In either format, however, refugee life narratives (especially by women) are a somewhat rare genre.

This dearth makes Thanhha Lai's *Inside Out and Back Again* (2011) stand out.[6] While the book is marketed as an autobiographical novel in verse,

Lai emphasizes in an "author's note" at the end of the book that everything that happened to the main character "also happened to me" (261). The book collects the innocent thoughts and impressions of seven-year-old Hà and chronicles her family's life, starting in war-torn Vietnam in 1975 through resettlement in Alabama in 1976. Lai brings to live the fears and hopes of Vietnamese refugees in the 1970s; yet, the experiences she describes assume a universal character that helps readers better understand the struggles of all displaced people.

Nguyen explains that the displacement of millions of Syrians has "thrust [Southeast Asian refugees] back into the public spotlight" with their "'successful' stories" (Nguyen, Phu, and Troeung 443). And indeed, many parallels exist between Lai's autobiographical account conveyed through the experiences of a child and the tweets of young Syrian refugee Bana al-Abed. With the help of her mother, Bana tweeted from the besieged city of Aleppo in Syria, starting in September 2016 when she was seven years old. Due to the visceral nature of her tweets, she soon gathered a large audience for her posts, and her book, *Dear World* (2017), has shared Bana's story of narrow survival with a global audience. Both printed texts help satisfy a "need for a flexible and holistic perspective toward our understanding of refugees worldwide" (Ezer 616). Only once knowledge about refugees' experiences becomes more widespread, can displacement and its oppressive consequences be tackled effectively.

DISPLACEMENT THROUGH THE EYES OF A CHILD

In their vivid descriptions of young women's lives during war and their push for social justice, the works I analyze in this chapter join such powerful life narratives as Anne Frank's *The Diary of a Young Girl* first published in 1952 and Zlata Filipović's *Zlata's Diary: A Child's Life in Sarajevo* (1993), which chronicles the siege of Sarajevo from 1991 to 1993 during the Bosnian war. Sidonie Smith, in her discussion of the latter memoir, argues that narratives by victimized girl children have a lasting impact due to their affective influence on the reader ("Narratives and Rights"). Similarly, Kate Douglas, in *Contesting Childhood* (2009), assesses as effective the consciousness-raising about human rights abuses in many African countries created by child soldier memoirs.

The very first words of *Inside Out and Back Again* transport the reader into the heart of besieged Saigon: "We pretend / the monsoon / has come early. // In the distance / bombs / explode like thunder, / slashes / lighten the sky, / gunfire / falls like rain. // Distant / yet within ears, / within eyes. // Not that far away / after all." These verses appear again later on in the text, but placed at the very beginning of the book, they create a powerful entry for the reader into the memories of a young child and the dangerous world she inhabits. The lines convey fear, hope, and a desperate attempt at preserving normalcy—likely with the intention to alleviate children's anxieties. These stanzas stand uncommented by the author and are followed by the book's standard title page. Two pages later, the author dedicates her work to "the millions of refugees in the world, may you each find a home." This dedication in connection with the first page sends a strong message of support to people fleeing their homes and a call for awareness and empathy geared at nondisplaced readers.

Inside Out offers a look at the everyday life of a refugee family through the emotions of a child and her detailed descriptions of smells and other senses, initially in Vietnam and then in the United States. Hà lives with her mother and three brothers. Her father, a soldier, is missing. While the family initially hopes to be able to stay in the country, Hà's mother and her older brothers eventually come to terms with the heartbreaking decision that, in order to survive, they will have to abandon their home. At that point, Hà's mother begins nerve-racking negotiations about how to flee as safely as possible. She makes clear that she "*will not risk / fleeing with [her] children / on a rickety boat*" (42; emphasis in original). These concerns become all too real when one considers that thousands of refugees have died in the Mediterranean since the onset of the largest movement of people since World War II in 2015. And the lines echo the widely shared sentiments in British-Somali poet Warsan Shire's poem "Home" (2015), which proclaims that "no one leaves home unless / home is the mouth of a shark;" "you only leave home / when home won't let you stay." The poem continues that "no one puts their children in a boat / unless the water is safer than the land." Shire and Lai's verses convey the dreadful decision parents must make to put their children into possible danger to protect them from a different kind of danger. And, too many times, these calculations end tragically, such as in the case of three-year-old Alan Kurdi, whose lifeless body was washed ashore in Turkey in September 2015. His family had paid smugglers thousands of dollars for spots on an overcrowded dinghy with useless life-jackets. *Inside Out* brings across that parents do not decide to send their children on this journey unless they absolutely have to. As Hà's mother exclaims, her children "*deserve to grow up / where* [they] *don't worry about / saving half a bite / of sweet potato"* (47; emphasis in original).

Children constitute a quarter of all refugees worldwide. In 2015, almost 200,000 refugee children made their way to Europe across the Balkan alone (von Welser 105–106). In addition, many female refugees—12 percent in fall 2015 according to UNICEF—make the dangerous journey while pregnant ("Number of Women"). This assessment was made while most families were still sending male relatives to Europe first. Beginning in 2016, a shift occurred as more and more families started sending women and children, hoping that their gender and age would make them more likely to receive protected status for themselves and their whole families (Freedman 126, 138). While the exact number of female refugees in the current crisis is unknown because data are often not aggregated by gender, studies show that women are at much higher risk than men of dying on their journey (Freedman 128). Maria von Welser's book, *Kein Schutz, Nirgends: Frauen und Kinder auf der Flucht (No Protection, Nowhere: Women and Children on the Run)* captures refugee women's power, resilience, and agency. A common conversation she had with refugee women living in camps revealed that, for these women, their children's lives were worth sacrificing everything. Many explained that they fled their homes only in an attempt to ensure survival and a better future for their children (von Welser 42, 193).

Although Hà's family does not end up on a plastic raft, conditions for them are abysmal. In fact, "everyone knows the ship / could sink" (Lai 63). Sugarcoating the danger is not an option. And so Hà's family goes from the traumatic experience of leaving their lives and cherished people and items behind—described in the entry titled "Left Behind" (Lai 57)—to an unknown journey "At Sea" (Lai 71), which starts part II of Lai's account. Lai's lines express the inhumane conditions on the boat: "Our ship creeps along / the river route / without light / without cooking / without bathroom. // We are told / to sip water / only when we must / so our bodies / can stop needing. // Mine won't listen" (73). The journey demands a life in darkness below deck in unsanitary conditions and, as such, brings to mind imagery of slave ships. This parallel is further solidified when one considers how during the Vietnam War, as well as during the present crisis, smugglers made/make millions in profit off the bodies of refugees in exploiting their desperation (von Welser 207). Lai especially hones in on children's experiences in this situation for whom it is impossible to adhere to the cruel demands set up to preserve the passengers' security—like complete stillness and rationing of water. It's a responsibility entirely too massive to shoulder for a young, confused child. Hà's experiences are not a singular occurrence, as Sabreen, a Yemeni refugee whom Yousafzai interviewed, reports being tricked into believing that she was purchasing a ticket from Egypt to Europe on a small, safe boat, but instead had to go without food, water, and any way to relieve herself (77ff).

The next step in Hà's journey also resembles that of many contemporary refugees. After being rescued by an American ship, Hà's family and the other passengers are brought to the island of Guam, where they become inhabitants of a "Tent City" (Lai 96). Lai describes this time in limbo as a "Life in Waiting" (98). Everyday camp life is made harsher by cheap canned food that "tast[es] like salty vomit" (Lai 96). But the problems go well beyond a lack of food quality. Hà's entries convey how deeply this time period is marked by gnawing uncertainty that puts psychological pressure on refugees—so much so that her younger brother "rarely speaks anymore" (Lai 99). This refusal to communicate captures many refugee children's trauma caused by forced relocation. It might further be influenced by linguistic confusion created by aid workers giving English lessons to the camp inhabitants. Especially for young children, life in such a situation can prove overwhelming, and shutting down verbally can be a natural reaction. English lessons in refugee camps are certainly a practical idea—especially for those refugees who will likely be relocated to an English-speaking country. But language lessons do not replace actual schooling, of which refugee children are often deprived, especially in camps. As a result, Syrian refugee children are currently at risk to become a "lost generation" despite attempts on the part of aid organizations to provide basic education ("Over 40 per cent"). For many people who might want to believe that such conditions were only possible in the past or in more remote geographical areas, the testimony of Analisa from Guatemala in *We Are Displaced* (2019) should serve as a wakeup call. Analisa describes the camps in which she was detained in the United States as an "ice box" and a "dog pound," respectively (Yousafzai 132). The terms viscerally purport the inhumane conditions under which refugees are currently held in the United States.

Analisa and Lai intentionally offer these details about camp to contradict common misconceptions about the treatment refugees receive and how they supposedly abuse international aid and purposefully leave their homes to live a plentiful life abroad. Such misunderstandings of the relocation process fuel dangerous stereotypes about refugees that can be rhetorically effective at turning populations against the idea of accepting refugees into their societies. In an interview with the publisher printed at the end of the book, Lai expresses hope that future refugees "would be greeted with more awareness and compassion than I was" ("Back again" 4). Like the immigrant women whose life-writing texts I have analyzed in previous chapters, Lai believes that her narrative can help rectify faulty information and educate her readers about refugees' experiences. Considering the current global conversations about refugees, this constitutes a powerful political act.

The next location on Hà's journey is another tent city, this time in Florida, where she and her family must wait for an American citizen to sponsor them in order to be able to leave. The family's uncertainty about their future is heightened by a system that makes them dependent on the goodwill of strangers and limits their agency. Lai's story, like other refugee narratives, points out the "paradoxes of contemporary globalizing trends which liberalize the flow of money, media and goods while reinforcing national borders against those experiencing the worst effects of uneven development" (Woolley 6). While policies have changed, refugees today still have no control over where they will be placed and depend on the arbitrary mercy of wealthy nations to accept a certain amount of refugees for relocation. Once they arrive in these nations, they are required to repay the government for their transportation costs—unless they decide to take matters into their own hands and start migrating without government sanction, which recalls Rosalina Rosay's experiences from chapter 1 of this book.

While other refugees in the camp eventually find sponsors, Hà and her family are left behind. Hà's mother initially reasons that a possible widow with four children is not a favored option (Lai 107), thereby underscoring the randomness of the selection and support system and her own inability to change the situation. Her feelings of paralysis change when she becomes suspicious that "sponsors prefer those / whose application say 'Christians'" (Lai 108). Without the ability to stand up for her religious rights and to push back against Americans' religious prejudices, Hà's mother decides to take back some power over her and her children's lives and, out of pure practicality, changes their faith statement on their application to say "Christian." She acts on Shire's desperate statement that "insults are easier to swallow / than rubble / than bone / than your child [sic] body / in pieces" . . . "forget pride / your survival is more important." This change makes possible the family's 'adoption' by a white man from Alabama and their ability to leave camp life behind; yet, it also foreshadows the racism and xenophobia they will have to endure for the foreseeable future in the U.S. South, which further contradicts the misperceptions that refugees enjoy a "free ride" after leaving their home and that they are completely safe once they escape war zones.

The book's part III, "ALABAMA," offers a recollection of the ostracization that Hà, her siblings, and mother endured after permanent resettlement in the United States. From the beginning, it becomes clear that the initial altruism that brought the family to Alabama does not emanate from everyone around them in their new living environments. The way Christian charity did not protect Jane Jeong Trenka from growing up in a racist society—as I elaborated on in chapter two—the good intentions on the part of Hà's family's sponsor do not create a welcoming atmosphere. Their sponsor, whom Hà calls their "cowboy" due to his clothes, is confused by the hard time Hà, her siblings, and mother have adjusting to American food. He asks, "why are *his* refugees so picky?" (120; emphasis mine). While this question might sound innocent on the surface, it does insinuate an attitude one might expect toward pets or a hobby that are/is supposed to offer entertainment without too much labor or annoyance. On an even more harmful scale, the sponsor's "wife insists / [Hà and her family] keep out of / her neighbors' eyes" (116). This woman's intolerance extends to not wanting to be associated with refugees in public. And the stereotypes that generate such reluctance—such as refugees being dangerous, dirty, heathens, lazy, and so on—persist today. In the case of Syrian refugees, a layer of Islamophobia is added that marks them wrongfully as terrorists and influences international policies, such as the Trump administration's 2017 travel ban restricting Muslim individuals' entry into the United States, that make it even harder for them to secure their survival.

Lai presents school as the setting where Hà experiences racism the most intensely. She is immediately marked as the other due to her appearance in a homogenous space because she is "the only / straight black hair / on olive skin" (Lai 142). This status of other comes with frequent incidents of bullying, such as when "*someone called [her] Ching Chong*" (Lai 152; emphasis in original), which echoes descriptions by young refugee women in Yousafzai's book who were targeted with calls of "'Jihad!,'" implying that they are dangerous and unwanted terrorists (84). Initially, Hà is overcome with fear and absorbs the hatred to the detriment of her self-esteem. But with the help of one of her brothers, she learns self-defense techniques that give her the strength to fight back against her abusers. However, it is not just the taunting by the other students that makes adjusting to her new life difficult for Hà. Expressing herself in English is one of the most difficult challenges for her to overcome. *Inside Out* consists of many entries that center on Hà's struggles with pronunciation or grammar rules. In the entry "First Rule," for example, Hà processes that you need to "add an *s* to nouns / to mean more than one / even if there's / already an *s* / sitting there. . . . All day / I practice / squeezing hisses / through my teeth" (118). She is frustrated that she lacks the ability to express the knowledge she already has gained and cannot yet communicate successfully: "I'm furious, / unable to explain / I already learned fractions / and how to purify / river water" (156–157). Her teacher and classmates infantilize her when praising her for being able to read her ABCs and count in English. This language barrier intensifies the bullying, scraping away at the thin layer of self-confidence Hà retains, to the point that she announces "so this is / what dumb / feels like" (157). Being ostracized for looking different is a harsh experience; to be made to feel as if you are not intelligent or hard working enough to fit in exacerbates these feelings of rejection and failure.

While Hà must come to terms with starting from scratch in school, her oldest brother, who has an engineering degree from a Vietnamese school, must start over his career as a car mechanic because his qualifications are not valued in his country of asylum. This necessity holds true for many refugees worldwide, whose work and educational experiences are denied and whose only option is to provide for their families through menial labor. *Inside Out* excels at portraying the "shock of immigration" ("Back again" 5), which Lai underwent herself and finds crucial for her readers to understand in order to better grasp refugees' experiences. Ultimately—reflecting Lai's own migration story—the kindness of an elderly woman who volunteers to teach Hà's family English renews their faith in the United States and gives them hope for a less painful future. Through the character of Mrs. Washington, whose son died fighting in Vietnam (200), Lai calls on her readers for empathy and acceptance toward refugees and offers suggestions for how to nourish lasting integration.

In addition to following the observations of a young displaced child, *Inside Out* puts special focus on the plight of Hà's mother. Women fleeing their home countries experience a high degree of sexual violence at the hands of their own family members, smugglers, military or government officials, other refugees, and NGO workers (Martin 45).While Lai does not disclose any sexual violence the mother might have endured, the latter clearly carries the immense burden of protecting her children in a foreign country whose language she does not speak. While many see displaced women as powerless victims, Lai emphasizes the mother's agency and ingenuity—such as when she changed their religion to secure sponsorship. To demonstrate her full humanity, Lai has Hà write about her mother's bloody fingers from working on a factory sewing machine that "sews so fast" (149). Despite her efforts to be strong for her children and make the best of their situation, she admits to herself that it's *"more difficult here / than [she] imagined"* (176; emphasis in original). Without the help of her husband or any support network, she feels an intense "loneliness" in the United States (Lai 122). She longs for meaningful connection and support instead of pity as "the pity giver / feels better / never the pity receiver" (Lai 133). Authentic integration starts with truly trying to get to know someone instead of reducing them to the worst elements in their lives.

Lai discusses how people projected the Vietnam War onto her and made it her defining characteristic when she tried to assert that she "was just a person, not a war" ("Back again" 4). In Hà's case, her teacher frequently shows images of emaciated Vietnamese children in class, condensing Vietnam—and by extension Hà—to mere violence and brutality. Hà resents that the beauty and heritage of her home country are ignored in favor of pushing a political message and painting the United States as a flawless savior nation. She announces fervently that she "would choose / wartime in Saigon / over / peacetime in Alabama" (Lai 195). Throughout the book, Lai uses the papaya as a symbol of the cultural and culinary richness of Vietnam. It also embodies the homesickness most displaced people feel, and thus recalls the comment made by Guatemalan refugee Maria, who says that "when I dream of home, I dream of mangoes" (Yousafzai 117). Toward the end of *Inside Out*, the reader finds Hà eating a soaked, dried piece of the fruit that functions as a sign of slow social adjustment; the dried papaya is "not the same, / but not bad / at all" (Lai 234). Lai ends her narrative on a decidedly optimistic note when Hà writes "our lives / will twist and twist, / intermingling the old and the new / until it doesn't matter / which is which" (257). Hà embraces adaptation and creating something new out of a horrible situation—a message that Lai uses effectively to push her readers to trust, believe, and invest in refugees.

TWEETS FROM ALEPPO AS LIFE-WRITING ACTIVISM

Like *Inside Out*, Bana al-Abed's tweets offer insight into a child's horrific experiences during war, which began when she was three years old and has shaped her life. For example, on November 24, 2016, Bana tweeted, "Good morning from #Aleppo. We are still alive" (al-Abed).[7] Similar to the way Lai starts her book with a focus on bombing and everyday dangers, Bana's online expressions convey a matter-of-factness about the life-threatening situation in which Bana, her family, and her community are trapped. Recalling Yousafzai's blogging about her experiences under the Taliban regime for BBC Urdu, Twitter as a platform for disseminating testimony of war and human rights abuse presents different possibilities for Bana as "new media does not merely reinforce existing cultural figures of the self; rather, it is a space that encourages practices that construct some new possibilities for political action" (Whitlock, *Soft Weapons* 24–25). In Bana's case, her tweets made it possible for her to gather 352,000 followers of her accounts. While many people tried to use social media to bring widespread attention to violence in Syria, Ana Belén Martínez García argues that it was Bana's "age and gender, coupled with her looks, [that rendered her] the perfect 'poster child' of a humanitarian campaign" (138), creating an "emotional link" that actually makes people care (136).[8]

Unlike Hà, who is able to flee the country before getting too close to physical harm, Bana is exposed to intense violence. We learn on November 27, 2016, that "tonight we have no house, it's bombed & I got in rubble. I saw deaths and I almost died. #Aleppo" (al-Abed). Coming from a child, the tweet conveys an urgency that might reach people differently than war-time journalistic reporting. Her anxiety and fear come through clearly without overelaboration of her feelings. Her tweets thus closely resemble the poetic effectiveness of Lai's verses.

Bana and her family were perilously evacuated to Turkey in December 2016, from where she continues to post, especially about the continued horrific situation for children in Syria.[9] On October 11, 2017, for example, she posts that "tonight I am thinking of my friends in Syria who cannot sleep, who cannot go to school. I am very sad. They just need peace" (al-Abed). Resembling the published texts I have analyzed in this book, Bana's online life writing pushes for justice for her community. Her tweets highlight the inhumane conditions under which children in Syria are growing up, lacking safety, shelter, and education. Demanding peace and protection, Bana uses her privilege of safety and her access to a public forum to push a clear political message. When read as life writing, Bana's "live update" tweets—in line with the other published texts in this book—support my suggestion that we are seeing a shift in purpose that moves the genre further away from self-analysis and self-creation toward an exposition of existential problems in the world and a demand for activism.

While there has been some discussion about how much control Bana's mother, Fatemah, has over the Twitter account, most of Bana's tweets are written in a childlike manner and broken English that suggest a young writer's mind. For example, on February 2, 2018, a tweet proudly proclaims "I got A+ in my exam" (al-Abed). This expression of pride and happiness hints at a certain level of adjustment that Bana has undergone since leaving Syria. Like at the end of *Inside Out*, the reader perceives a slow progression toward integration, which, importantly, keeps neither Hà nor Bana from speaking out against the injustice around them. These glimpses of positivity cut against the pressure put on refugees' life stories to be "appropriately horrific and devastating" in order to meet requirements for asylum (Lo 643), which creates the "passive victimization" of refugees (Lo 644). In their refusal to "just capture refugees' desperation" (Lo 645), Lai and Bana distill displaced people's complex humanity.

Bana's popularity gained through her tweets heightened in 2017 when Simon and Schuster offered her a book deal. The resulting text, *Dear World: A Syrian Girl's Story of War and Plea for Peace*, constitutes one of few published life narratives by a Syrian refugee. It is perhaps not surprising that a publisher chose a child's story to be printed in book form. As a profit-driven corporation, they are aware that audiences tend to emphasize more easily with children, which, of course, promises more sales. The book was blurbed by J. K. Rowling, who was touched by this "testimony of a child who has endured the unthinkable."

Similar to Lai, Bana dedicates her book "to every child suffering in a war. You are not alone." The urgency of these lines is emphasized with a quotation from Anne Frank on the next page that insists "where there's hope, there's life." By insinuating the well-known fate of Anne Frank, *Dear World* makes a clear connection between the Holocaust and people's suffering caused by the war in Syria and other global turmoil creating the displacement of millions. As an appeal to her readers' historical knowledge and investment in the prevention of genocide, the quotation accompanies Bana's author's note, in which she acknowledges that her mother and editor helped her with her English, but that "these are all my memories from the war. . . . I hope it makes you want to help people." Anticipating pushback against the authenticity of her writing and the truth it conveys—criticism to which all works in this study were exposed—Bana emphasizes that despite some deliberate challenges to the genre of memoir, her story is worth being heard. Her focus on social justice in trying to make her readers care about refugees and to actively support them is apparent.

Considering Bana's emphasis on the veracity of her own memories, it might seem odd that *Dear World* starts with Bana's mother's words. Yet, since Bana was only three years old when the war started, the reader needs

Fatemah to contextualize and offer an impression of Syria before the war. So she reminds the audience that *"Aleppo is one of the oldest continuously inhabited cities in the whole world"* and that, before the war, there were *"so many ordinary days"* (al-Abed 2, 3).[10] Fatemah's descriptions push back against common misconceptions about Syria as a dilapidated, cultureless country that has been sending off uneducated masses into the world—a rhetorical move on the part of right-wing, anti-refugee parties in many European countries. Like Lai's alter-ego Hà, who challenges conversations about Vietnam as only limited to violence and destruction, Fatemah reminds us that Syria *"was beautiful"* (al-Abed 9). To underline this message, *Dear World* contains photographs of pre-war Aleppo that display the city's former majestic atmosphere. Later in the book, these photos will be contrasted viscerally by images of destruction of architecture as well as human life. Resembling Rosay's technique of including images of her Mexican village and her family, discussed in chapter 1, Bana's memoir uses visuals as well as an oral and collaborative composition style to appeal to readers' pathos and create in them productive outrage against human rights violations.

Bana's own narrative, too, starts with memories and images of her carefree childhood. But after only eight pages, the reader receives a first glimpse into the horrors that loom with the announcement that "the bad times started. First they came to take Baba away" (al-Abed 18). Bana's father is taken by president al-Assad's secret police and only able to return home after two days. Shortly thereafter, in 2012, the bombing begins in retaliation to student protests against the regime the previous year. While Bana describes with childlike innocence that she "didn't know what it was when the first big bomb came" (al-Abed 21), that sense of wonderment switches radically into matter-of-fact descriptions such as a "chlorine bomb is the worst" (27). That a young child is able to distinguish different kinds of bombs and must "get used to the bombs" is heartbreaking to read (al-Abed 37). Bana supports this emotional social justice rhetoric that aims at moving her readers into political action by juxtaposing many moments spent in the family's dark and cold basement in fear with her disappointment of no longer being able to pursue normal activities for children, such as going to the park or swimming, which she had enjoyed immensely.

Like the other memoirs in *Lives beyond Borders*, *Dear World* points out larger systemic causes that endanger communities' survival instead of individual actions or choices. It soon becomes clear that the family has lost all control over their lives and safety due to no fault of their own. Bana repeatedly emphasizes the surreal nature of this fact in contrasting her innocence as a young child with the terror she experienced as a consequence of the war. One particular night, for example, Bana's family must yet again seek shelter in the basement. The situation is so dire that Bana has to leave her new Barbie boots at her bedside. Like any young girl in her case, Bana is inconsolable about possibly having lost them and "wish[es she] had slept in them" (al-Abed 39). This account might evoke a smile until readers recall the horror of the setting. This contrast in emotions—from amusement to shock—followed by clear statements such as there "was nowhere that was safe anymore" may serve as a wakeup call to readers (al-Abed 44). The lines echo Yousafzai's claim that what her family "and all these [displaced] people were doing wasn't a choice: It was survival" (17).

Lack of safety severely curtails Bana's opportunities. She writes that while she tried to be as brave as possible, she "did cry . . . when Baba [her father] and Mummy decided that [she] couldn't go to school anymore" (al-Abed 46). Similar to Rosay, Bana appeals to her audience by using education as a platform for justice. Her desperation over her lack of schooling is a clear hint at the predicament of Syrian children as a "lost" generation, as mentioned above. Yet, *Dear World* does not only focus on the plight of children but, through its inclusion of Fatemah's voice, also echoes *Inside Out*'s elaborations on the impossible choices that parents are forced to make regarding their children's fate. Perhaps envisioning criticism from the reader about choosing to remain in Syria for as long as they did, Bana's mother justifies that if she and her husband "*had understood from the beginning how things would end up in Aleppo or the horrors that awaited us, we would have left*" (al-Abed 54). Of course, no one can predict how long a period of violence might last, and desperate clinging to normalcy is a common human trait. But Bana's parents were also influenced in their decision-making process by "*terrible stories of isolation and poverty*" in "*countries that didn't want*" refugees (al-Abed 54); such life narratives were shared via phone calls, social media posts, texts, and WhatsApp messages by many of those who had left before them. Fatemah reminds her reader that it "*is a hard thing to leave your entire life and everything you've ever known and become a refugee*" (al-Abed 54). The identity category "refugee" is not voluntary but one imposed on people by governments. Receiving the designation has long-lasting implications. Bana's parents thus find themselves in a double bind of feeling guilty both for not having left soon enough and for leaving at all (al-Abed 56).

The decision to depart Aleppo is eventually made for the family when Bana's mother becomes unexpectedly pregnant with her third child (despite having struggled for years to conceive her first two children). Since the hospital in town had been destroyed and a horrible pattern of "babies [being] born sick because of the war" had emerged (al-Abed 66), Bana, her mother, and brother leave for Turkey. Bana's father is unable to join them because he has no passport. Thus, the family accepts separation and undergoes a dangerous car ride across the border to secure the well-being of a child. The emotional insights that *Dear World* offers into Bana's family's living conditions sharply contradict Western populist representations of refugees as opportunists and terrorists. Instead, Bana emphasizes her family's humanity and makes their choices relatable to a broad readership.

While to this point Bana's memoir remains somewhat optimistic, the narrative assumes a decidedly darker tone once Bana, her siblings, and mother return to a seemingly quieter Syria after months in Turkey. Bana focuses on the psychological toll the war has taken on her and her brothers. Although the active warfare has died down, her family still lives in constant fear because it is "hard for that feeling to go away, even when you are safe" (al-Abed 95). While Bana does not use the word herself, her elaborations on persistent anxiety and the fact that her younger brother, comparable to Hà's in *Inside Out*, refuses to speak suggest that the children were suffering from post-traumatic stress disorder (al-Abed 100). But instead of being able to start the recovery process, "everything became worse than ever" (al-Abed 103).

Bana meticulously chronicles her thoughts during this time and effectively recreates an environment of suffocation and death that supports her anti-war activism. She mentions that she "forgot what quiet even sounded like," referring to the consistent presence of bombs and gunshots, and offers the heart-breaking confession that she became obsessed with the question of "what does it feel like to die" (al-Abed 105, 109). This abstract question becomes horrifically real for Bana as her best friend, Yasmin, is killed when her apartment complex is destroyed (al-Abed 113). Bana's social justice message relies on her audience being mortified and outraged by children having to undergo such experiences and senselessly losing their lives. As Fatemah puts it, there "*are no children in Syria. You all were forced to become adults*" (al-Abed 122). While many narratives of war focus on the sacrifices of those fighting and most news reporting from war zones concentrates on political decision-makers, *Dear World* brings children to the center, values their awareness, and highlights their unjust suffering.

Tragically, Bana's life in Syria culminates in the height of the siege of Aleppo in the fall and winter of 2016. The narrative oscillates between assertions regarding a lack of food—only macaroni and rice were available, no fruit or vegetables—and explanations that the children "had to play, or it just felt like all [they] did was wait for the bombs to see who died," and candid descriptions of what a bombed body looks like (al-Abed 137, 147). The situation is forlorn and paralyzing until Bana regains agency through her first tweet after the siege had been going on for three months. Her tweet on September 24, 2016, captures the essence of Bana's activist efforts. It reads quite simply "I need peace" (al-Abed). In her memoir, Bana explains that she took to social media because she "wanted to do something" (al-Abed 142). Her hopes for what her tweets might achieve and how they might affect people strikes me as similar to her intentions with her writing published in book format. Ideally, both media formats will motivate her audiences to "please do something to stop the war" (al-Abed 143). Bana validates the explicitness of her posts, a technique that she also employs in her memoir, by explaining that she was "afraid people wouldn't believe us if they didn't see how bad it was, like all the dead bodies and crumbled buildings" (al-Abed 145). She is likely correct in her assessment that images of horror are more effective in getting people's attention, even if only briefly, as we have seen with Alan Kurdi, the drowned boy mentioned earlier. Her Twitter feed functions as a tool for her to feel proactive and to ensure that "people [would not] forget about us" during a time when she and her family "didn't have any more tears" (al-Abed 148, 154).

At her most desperate, when her family must run daily from government forces, lacks access to water, and is able to consume only one meal a day, Bana declares apathetically that she "was tired of fighting to stay alive" (al-Abed 171f). Hearing a child give up on life can have a moving effect on a reader, likely inciting indignation that a child could be put into such an appalling position. At the brink of death, the remaining civilian inhabitants of Aleppo are finally evacuated to a rural part of Syria after spending hours and hours on a bus without food, water, or the ability to relieve themselves in a dignified way (al-Abed 188). Among the life narratives I have discussed in this book, Bana's most directly reveals how for many women and children, and refugees in particular, survival is at stake in being able to migrate—not a narcissistic desire to become rich in a foreign country or vicious fanaticism to destroy Western societies.

Toward the end of the memoir, Fatemah explains that "connecting with other people and sharing our story made us feel better" (al-Abed 196). This focus on establishing community and generating agency is shared by the other women migrant writers in *Lives beyond Borders*. Disastrously, her online life writing put Bana into even further danger and necessitated her final migration to Turkey, as her mother suspects that the Syrian government specifically targeted Bana and bombed their home because of the attention her tweets garnered globally. Whether these apprehensions are warranted or not, feminist critics such as myself find it plausible that the power in the voice and life stories of a young girl would make a patriarchal government nervous to the point that it decides to eliminate the source. But the pushback comes not only from official sources. According to Fatemah, Bana has received many death threats on social media (al-Abed 196). While absolutely detestable, this resistance certifies the strength of Bana's social justice life-writing forms. Despite the threats, Bana persists and will not be silenced. Directly addressing people who refuse to welcome refugees in their countries, she writes "I wish . . . that you share with them and help them and try to understand what they have been through" (al-Abed 202). By letting them know that "you can help too" (al-Abed 204), which is the final sentence of *Dear World*, Bana ends her memoir with a forceful call for empathy and activism. Elsa Lechner emphasizes the positive impact life writing can have on its readership: "Narratives of refugees enable the empowerment or liberation of their narrators and public by . . . fostering awareness . . . in relation to the collective dimension of individual experiences" (642). This liberating potential of refugee voices certainly mattered more than ever when the Trump administration announced in late 2019 that it planned to cut the admission numbers of refugees in the United States to a historic annual low of 18,000 (U.S. Committee for Refugees and Immigrants).

EPILOGUE

THE POWER AND FUTURE OF IMMIGRANT WOMEN'S LIFE WRITING

Edwidge Danticat captures the essence of the migrant artist's work as follows: "There are many possible interpretations of what it means to create dangerously, and Albert Camus . . . suggests that it is creating as a revolt against silence, creating when both the creation and the reception, the writing and the reading, are dangerous undertakings, disobedience to a directive" (11). The women in this book and many other female migrants across the globe certainly create dangerously. They move and write for their own, their families', and their communities' survival. They offer a platform for voices and stories that those at the top of the political, social, economic, and other hierarchies do not want to recognize. Their disobedience changes lives.

In the late 1980s, Patricia Pessar observed a "frequent charge that U.S. borders are uncontrolled and perceptions of a heightened immigrant and refugee presence in the United States" (1). This rhetoric persists today when, in fact, the number of undocumented immigrants has decreased and refugees are the most controlled migrant population in the world (Krogstad, Passel, and Cohn). Carmen Pearson explains that when "Americans think of immigrants, we think of European families, piled up at Ellis Island; of pioneers traveling across the prairies, clutching their children to their sides on their bumpy Conestoga wagons; of war refugees; . . . of Mexican workers dodging Border Control near the Rio Grande during dark hours of the night. We are none of those" (46). In chronicling her Mexican grandmother's life story, Pearson, like the authors in my previous chapters, gives voice to migrant women whom U.S. history silences.

A project that offers a platform for the voices of female migrants is of absolute relevance given the ongoing debate about immigration reform or migration blockage in the United States, the rise of anti-immigration, right-wing parties and anti-refugee movements, and the dislocation of people globally due to war and famine. Debra Castillo and María Córdoba criticize how "whiteness is the unmarked racial category, just as maleness is the unmarked gender that delimits the proper subject of traditional autobiography and also sets up the terms against which contestatory autobiographical models create their dialogical response: non Eurocentric, not white, not male" (95). *Lives beyond Borders* has demonstrated that central critical paradigms of life-writing and immigration studies—such as concepts of the self, assimilation, and transnationalism—change and expand when the narratives of immigrant women are taken into account as a locus of immigrant history and cultural production.

My chapters outline how U.S. immigrant women adapt the conventions of life writing—through masking the genre of their texts, inserting unconventional stylistic and narrative elements, and writing for a collective self—to accommodate their experiences and their fluid conceptions of national identity. The works I have analyzed display creative and rhetorical patterns of pushing their audiences toward political action in favor of supporting justice for oppressed groups worldwide. So much is at stake for these women and their communities since, as Danticat powerfully recounts her own experiences, in "another country . . . the artist immigrant, or immigrant artist, inevitably ponders the deaths that brought her here, along with the deaths that keep her here, the deaths from hunger and executions and cataclysmic devastation at home, the deaths from paralyzing chagrin in exile, and the other small, daily deaths in between" (17). Life writing can function as a means to work through trauma and for survival. Immigrant women's works constitute political teaching tools, calling for understanding of and compassion for silenced communities, instead of venues to describe supposedly exemplary lives. These texts are not just read by a privileged audience in academia but by a much wider demographic due to their vividness and accessibility. Mary Antin's *The Promised Land* (1912), for example, which I mentioned earlier because of its insistence on assimilation as the solution to push back against immigrants, sold almost 85,000 copies, and the author campaigned for Theodore Roosevelt as he ran for presidency and cited Antin as a major influence on his thoughts on immigration laws (Nadell). While, realistically, few lawmakers will create policy based on immigrant women's written testimonies, their constituents might pick them up and uphold the democratic principle by demanding change.

Some critics might argue that the authors of such narratives are embellishing their lives for personal gain, such as receiving a green card. Of course, it is impossible to negate that ulterior motives might have been at play, but such concerns are outweighed by female immigrants' use of life writing as a feminist political strategy to change the common terms of immigrants' representations, to offer alternative sources of knowledge, and to present a strong voice for minorities' survival. Immigrant women's lives speak to the gendered nature of migration processes and question assumptions about nation, identity, memory, borders, and conventional understandings of the law as truth and of knowledge. Such writing, I argue, brings about interethnic and intercultural awareness by explaining traditions and cultures and changing readers' perceptions of minoritized groups. My reading of immigrant women's memoirs presents life writing as a potential means for many, especially non-Western, immigrants to promote their humanity and equal opportunities globally.

To conclude this book, I want to suggest that connecting life writing by immigrant women of color with political theories of immigration could prove beneficial to decision-making processes in social, economic, and political spheres. Migration theories are contested. Philip Yang points out, for example, that "no single, coherent, well-developed theory of Asian migration to the United States" exists (1). Theorists attempt to explain the reasons for and processes of migration in various ways: push-pull theories, which suggest that push factors—such as economic hardship or natural catastrophes—motivate to leave, and pull factors—such as economic prospects or political differences—entice migrants to come, provide some of the earliest modes of explanation (Yang 2). Economic models like the "equilibrium model," in which migration occurs to cure the imbalance between sending and receiving countries in terms of demand for labor and resulting differences in wages, and sociological models such as the "social network theory," which focuses on how interpersonal relationships and connections influence migration patterns, offer different perspectives on processes of migratory behavior (Yang 4, 8). Yet, none of these models provide complete insights, and gender is rarely built into any of them as a decisive factor.

Lives beyond Borders poses fresh ways to see how the reading of immigrant women's life writing can help with the analysis of migration and with the development of policies related to its causes and effects.

Immigrant women's life narratives can provide answers to essential queries about migration since they create insight into immigrant women's personal and family lives via political and sociocultural details:[1] *Due to which social, cultural, economic, environmental, political, and other reasons do people leave their countries of birth?* The works I analyze offer poverty, sexism, war, and political repression as motivating reasons for migrating. Specifics on the gendered nature of these issues can help refine the management of global human movements. *Which prospects pull migrants to other countries?* Female immigrants seek education, bodily safety, job opportunities and higher wages, and a life free of discrimination for girls and women abroad. Guaranteeing girls and women's survival—endangered by poverty and/or misogynistic social practices—constitutes the center of attraction for living abroad. *How is migration shaped by laws, policies, economics, and other institutions of power?* Immigrant women's memoirs explain, to list just a few examples, the necessity for illegally crossing borders, the effects of being declared an orphan to enable transnational adoption, and patriarchal family structures limiting women's movements. *Under what circumstances do migrants turn into settlers?* The works in this book demonstrate that receiving an education in the United States, finding permanent work, starting a family, and the lasting inability to return to one's home country can lead migrants to settle abroad. In contrast, racism, xenophobia, and forced assimilation can cause a migrant to return to their native country. *How are countries of origin affected by migration flows?* While studies emphasize that sending countries can experience an extensive loss of inhabitants and benefit from financial remittances, women migrants specifically criticize how forced migration can function as a quasi-release of these countries from any obligation to create social support systems or fight the root causes, such as sexism, for losing its population.

    I agree with Parin Dossa's assessment that "stories and narratives have the potential to effect social change provided they form part of the larger political, social, historical, cultural and literary landscapes of societies" (20). Information like the above can generate a better understanding of migrants' lives, which promises to help develop more effective policies and bring about meaningful immigration reform. Lawmakers could benefit, for example, from answers to the question of *which factors influence the acceptance and integration of migrants into their new places of residence?* Public perception, female immigrants make clear, affects immigrants' acceptance. Attitudes that see migrants as opportunists and that demand assimilation at all cost create discrimination. Thinking of migrants' cultures as enriching, on the other hand, can create intercultural appreciation. Such knowledge is vital for passing essential legislation such as a replacement for DACA.

I have proposed immigrant women's life writing as a meaningful political, sociocultural, and research issue. These women's stories give complex insights into experiences of nationality, race, ethnicity, gender, and culture and reconfigure silences and invisibility in "a world where most travel requires passports and visas [and a world that] is not ready for 'world citizenship'" (Wong, "Denationalization" 19). They destabilize the persistent binaries between academy and activism and perceptions, among others, of legal/illegal and black/white; and they demonstrate the influence that gender, race, class, ability, and religion exert on the concept of "the immigrant woman." The process of naming their experiences is political as they challenge dominant, mainstream versions of their lives and assimilationist narratives that portray immigration as free of any struggles. Immigrant women offer memoirs as epistemological spaces that introduce their readers to their social change agenda as they position them as witnesses to the injustices and dislocations that these women have experienced because "though [they] may not be creating as dangerously as [their] forebears—though [they] are not risking torture, beatings, execution, though exile does not threaten [them] into perpetual silence—still, while [they] are at work bodies are littering the streets somewhere" (Danticat 18). The urgency of immigrant women's life writing is palpable.

Future developments in life writing and specifically life writing by women of color and female immigrants promise to be dynamic. I concur with G. Thomas Couser's assessment that as "long as oppression and injustice endure, testimony will challenge and oppose them" ("The Future" 380). As more and more migrant women enter the United States, their writings will continue to shape theoretical conceptions of migration processes, national identity formation, and autobiography. Issues to consider will be demographic and generational developments, political decisions about immigration, borders and nations, and progress regarding gender equality. It is my hope that *Lives beyond Borders* has created a foundation on which to pursue further investigations into this paramount social justice issue. More stories need to be heard.

NOTES

INTRODUCTION

1. Even if some scholars use the term "immigrant" for first-generation residents *and* their children, I use "immigrant" strictly to denote people who undergo a journey from their country of birth to the United States.

2. I apply the term "oppression" in accordance with Marilyn Frye's definition: "The experiences of oppressed people is that the living of one's life is confined and shaped by forces and barriers which are not accidental or occasional and hence avoidable, but are systematically related to each other in such a way as to catch one between and among them and restrict or penalize motion in any direction. It is the experience of being caged in: all venues, in every direction, are blocked or booby trapped" (4).

3. "Life writing" serves as an overarching term that captures writing about someone's life, including, but not limited to, autobiography, memoir, and biography. "Life narratives" are not necessarily limited to traditional forms of writing.

4. I use the term "female" as an adjective to denote cisgender individuals assigned female sex at birth. I regret that this makes my work complicit in the perpetuation of the binary construction of biological sex. While my work does not speak to the experiences of intersex or transgender women migrants, I strongly emphasize that these experiences are valid and need to become the focus of more activist and academic work.

5. In fact, at 51.8 percent, foreign-born women outnumber foreign-born men in the United States according to data from 2018 ("Immigrant Women").

6. For example, while Patricia Pessar's collection *When Borders Don't Divide* (1988) was groundbreaking as the first "contemporary treatment of hemispheric migration/refuge trends and developments" (1), none of the individual studies focus on women, and gender is brought up only in short subsections or conclusions, stating that women migrate more and that they get jobs after migrating or briefly describing how women organize their households after husbands migrate. Women's voices are absent.

7. Importantly, Eakin also calls for an acknowledgment of men's life writing as relational, claiming that "we need to liberate men's autobiography from the inadequate model that guided our reading to date" (*How Our Lives* 49).

8. With their political activist agenda, immigrant women's memoirs complement a recent resurgence of the political novel in the United States, which "shatters isolationist myths [and] updates national narratives" (Irr 4).

9. See, for example, Eva C. Karpinski's "Multicultural 'Gift(s)': Immigrant Women's Life Writing and the Politics of Anthologizing Difference" (1998); Betty A. Bergland and Lori Ann Lahlum's *Norwegian American Women: Migration, Communities, and Identities* (2011); and Nima Naghibi's *Women Write Iran: Nostalgia and Human Rights from the Diaspora* (2016).

10. *A Memory of Solferino* comprises Swiss Henry Dunant's testimony of brutality in the Franco-Austrian War (1848–49). Dunant gives a vivid account of the horrors during the battle of Solferino, which left thirty-eight thousand wounded or dead, and its aftermath. In describing how he organized the civilian population to assist the injured, Dunant offers concrete actions that people were able to take to bring about positive change. *A Memory of Solferino* lays out human rights grievances, shows how dramatically they affect people's chances of survival, and emphasizes how people can come together to effect change. In 1901, Dunant was awarded the first-ever Nobel Peace Prize (together with French economist Frédéric Passy) for his role in founding the International Red Cross.

11. Problematically, Boelhower uses the words "ethnic" and "immigrant" interchangeably.

12. For example, with the exception of the Convention on the Rights of the Child and the Convention on the Protection of the Rights of All Migrant Workers and Members of Their Families, all other conventions use only the male pronoun and assume a heterosexual model of family that pushes women into limiting gender roles.

13. See, for example, Anna Mollow's "'When Black Women Start Going on Prozac': Race, Gender, and Mental Illness in Meri Nana-Ama Danquah's *Willow Weep for Me*" (2006).

14. The 1953 Refugee Relief Act made it possible for "eligible orphans" from countries that had already surpassed their immigration quota, which were abolished only with the 1965 Immigration Act, to enter the United States.

15. For the purpose of this study, I limit my analysis of adoption to the transfer of born children between strangers via proper authorities. I want to acknowledge, though, that issues concerning fostering, intra-family transfers, surrogacy, and the human trafficking of children deserve more attention as well, which, unfortunately, goes beyond the scope of this book. All the adoption cases I analyze here are both transnational *and* transracial. For conciseness, I will refer to them only as transnational, which, in my use of the term, implies a process of racialization that I will elaborate on in chapter 3. I do not intend to minimize the complexity of adoptions that are transnational yet *not* transracial.

CHAPTER 1

1. At the time of Rosay's migration and during her adolescence in the 1970s, migration from Mexico to the United States began to increase sharply. Until then, mostly young men had crossed the border with the intention to return home once they had earned enough money. With demand for low-skilled labor remaining high after the expiration of the Bracero Program in 1964, economic troubles persevering in Mexico, and the relaxation of U.S. immigration laws in 1965—which made it easier for women with their children to join husbands and fathers or other male family members in the U.S.—the number of Mexicans permanently settling in the United States reached 2.2 million by 1980 (up from 760,000 in 1970); half of these migrants were undocumented (Passel, Cohn, and Gonzalez-Barrera).

2. Oral history projects offer other sources of information about immigrant women, especially in the late nineteenth and early twentieth century. In *Songs My Mother Sang to Me: An Oral History of Mexican American Women* (1992), Patricia Martin recounts, for example, the story of Julia Yslas Vélez, who was born in Mexico in 1910 and eventually moved to Nogales, Arizona. When her father became dissatisfied with the United States and went back to Mexico, Julia supported herself and her mother with work after school. During the Depression, she moved to Tijuana only to return with her husband to care for her mother.

3. Other published memoirs that add invaluable insights are Rose Castillo Guilbault's *Farmworker's Daughter* (2005), which describes the author's departure from Mexico at the age of five with her divorced mother and their life on farms in the Salinas valley; Reyna Grande's *The Distance between Us* (2012), which focuses on the experiences of children left behind by their parents who seek work in the United States; and Julissa Arce's *My (Underground) American Dream* (2016), which chronicles Arce's journey from undocumented immigrant to Wall Street executive.

4. According to their website, AR Publishing has released only two publications besides Rosay's memoir: a bike repair manual and a book on the use of Microsoft PowerPoint. There has been no apparent site activity since February 2011. The website's administrator seems to be Rosay's husband, whom she names and thanks in her acknowledgments.

5. For a detailed sociological study of the influence gender has on Mexican migration, see Pierrette Hondagneu Sotelo's *Gendered Transitions: Mexican Experiences of Immigration* (1994).

6. Tayler J. Mathews and Glenn S. Johnson's "Skin Complexion in the Twenty-First Century: The Impact of Colorism on African American Women" (2015) as well as the documentary *Dark Girls* (2011) offer an insightful discussion of colorism and discrimination based on skin complexion.

7. "I argued. I talked back. I was quite a bigmouth. I was indifferent to many of my culture's values. I did not let the men push me around. I was not good or obedient" (translated by Saldívar-Hull 71–72).

8. Kathryn Blackmer Reyes and Julia E. Curry Rodríguez's article "*Testimonio*: Origins, Terms, and Resources" (2012) presents an informative list of scholarly materials on the origins and characteristics of the testimonio.

9. Unless otherwise marked, Beverley's quotations are taken from his essay "The Margin at the Center."

10. Menchú did not write down her story herself but related it in a series of interviews to anthropologist Elisabeth Burgos-Debray, who then published the book. This is a traditional characteristic of testimonios, which makes the genre problematic as issues with transcribing and translating may occur.

11. See my 2015 article, "A Genre for Justice: Life Writing and Undocumented Immigration in Rosalina Rosay's *Journey of Hope*," published in *Life Writing*.

12. Examples of writings that fit this category are Ernesto Galarza's *Barrio Boy* (1971) and Richard Rodriguez's *Hunger of Memory: The Education of Richard Rodriguez* (1981).

13. A 2015 study by the Public Religion Research Institute shows that white Americans are most likely to think of themselves as "typical" Americans. Interestingly, the results also suggest that a majority of survey participants (54%) think of immigration as beneficial for the United States, while only 33 percent deem it as dangerous for American values.

14. For a detailed account of the history of DACA, the DREAM (Development, Relief and Education for Alien Minors) Act, and the undocumented rights movement, see Ina Batzke's *Undocumented Migrants in the United States* (2019).

15. As a result of several lawsuits filed against the Trump administration, people who received DACA before the administration's termination announcement were able to renew their deferred action, and the U.S. Supreme Court overturned the policy termination in June 2020. On August 31, 2018, United States Citizenship and Immigration Services estimated that 699,350 DACA recipients lived in the United States. Of these, 255,290 are twenty-one to twenty-five-year-olds.

16. As of August 2017, students of Hispanic heritage constituted 22.7 percent of all people enrolled at any level of education in the United States, which indicates a doubling of numbers since 1996. In 2016, 19.1 percent of college and university students identified as Hispanic, with almost half of these students attending two-year colleges. Despite advancements in education for Hispanic students, they still fall behind non-Hispanic students in both high school and college graduation rates and time (Bauman).

17. Rosay became a legal resident in 1986 with the Amnesty Act and a naturalized citizen in 1996. During the entire time her memoir captures she was considered an undocumented immigrant. The fact that Rosay's citizenship status turned her writing into a lower-threat project does, in my opinion, not discredit her objectives.

18. I have analyzed twelve reviews on *Journey of Hope's* Amazon.com page, which provides the only available reader comments on the book. Three of the twelve reviewers gave the book less than three (out of five) stars.

CHAPTER 2

1. Danquah's edited collections include *Becoming American: Personal Essays by First Generation Immigrant Women* (2000), *Shaking the Tree: New Fiction and Memoir by Black Women* (2004), and *The Black Body* (2009).

2. Between 1960 and 2009, the number of Black foreign migrants increased from roughly 35,000 (0.4% of all immigrants) to 1.5 million (3.9% of all migrants). One-third of all African migrants are from West Africa, with more migrants from Nigeria than any other African country (Halter and Johnson 14).

3. For the sake of avoiding repetition, quotations from Danquah's memoir will be denoted only with Danquah's last name. Citations from her other works will be followed by a shortened version of the respective title.

4. It is distinctly not my intention here to imply that Ghanaian and Nigerian culture are interchangeable. I suggest that because female migrants from Ghana and Nigeria are racialized and minoritized in similar ways in the United States and the United Kingdom, a comparative investigation of Danquah and Adichie's texts can serve as a productive means to analyze African immigrant women's experiences. For a discussion of the utility of conceptualizing *an* "African culture," see Gabriel E. Idang's "African Culture and Values" (2015).

5. For a detailed sketch of different models of disability as well as current movements within feminist disability studies, consult Gomes et al.'s "New Dialogues in Feminist Disability Studies" (2019).

6. Members of the Deaf community, for example, are powerfully pushing back against the medical industrial complex imposing cochlear implants on deaf children.

7. One notable work that started to rectify these omissions is Dolores Mortimer and Roy S. Bryce-Laporte's *Female Immigrants to the United States: Caribbean, Latin American, and African Experiences* (1981).

CHAPTER 3

1. A note on terminology: I always use "Korea" to refer to South Korea, which is geographically the only part of Korea from which U.S. citizens adopted children. It is the term that Korean adoptees use when referring to the country of their birth.

2. Trenka was adopted from Korea in 1972 at the age of six months. Together with her sister, four and a half years old at the time, she moved to their adoptive parents' home in rural Minnesota. Apart from Trenka's struggles with her identity, *The Language of Blood* recounts her experiences as a stalking victim in college. In 1995, after graduating college, Trenka visited for the first time her biological mother, whom she had been in contact with for many years and whom she eventually lost to cancer. Since 2004 Trenka has been living in Seoul where she is an activist and writer.

3. For a detailed history of adoption practices, procedures, and laws, as well as the adoption rights movement in the United States, starting in colonial times, I recommend Wayne Carp's *Family Matters: Secrecy and Disclosure in the History of Adoption* (1998).

4. The 2009 United Nations Department of Economic and Social Affairs' report on *Child Adoption: Trends and Policies* offers detailed statistics on the global decline of domestic adoption in many industrialized countries.

5. Arguably, a similar situation occurred at the U.S.-Mexico border where, in 2019, Central and South American asylum seekers fleeing deprivation, corruption, and violence (to which U.S. military intervention contributed) in their home countries were separated from their children. According to the American Civil Liberties Union (ACLU), separation guidelines went into effect in April 2018, with separations likely having taken place before then. After much public outcry, the policy was suspended in June 2018. That same month, in response to an ACLU class action lawsuit, a judge ordered all 2,654 children (the majority of them under the age of ten) to be reunited with their guardians, which revealed an irresponsible lack of information about where children had been sent ("Family Separation").

In April 2021, 445 children were still separated from their families (Alvarez). This raises the concern that many of them might end up in the foster care system. As the ACLU explains, termination of parental rights is possible if a child is considered "abandoned" for fifteen months within the last twenty-three months, and adoption becomes possible. This scenario is not unlikely for parents who are detained or deported. In many cases, parents also signed paperwork in custody insinuating that they would be willing to have their child be released from the care of the Office of Refugee Settlement (ORR) to live with a sponsor, which might be interpreted as parents indicating "an intent not to reunify" when advocates suggest that these parents possibly did not understand what they consented to or hoped that a sponsor will secure asylum for the whole family ("Family Separation").

For some, the current situation might also recall the New Life Children's Refuge case, which dealt with a group of U.S. Baptist missionaries attempting to kidnap thirty-three Haitian children in the aftermath of the devasting earthquake in 2010. The missionaries claimed they were trying to cross the border to bring the children to an orphanage. They did not have proper authorization and, in fact, most of the children were not orphans and still had family members able to care for them ("Profile"). In all these cases, imperialist histories and a willfulness to create abandoned children feeds the transnational adoption system.

6. Unless otherwise specified, all quotations from Trenka are taken from *The Language of Blood*.

7. For a detailed discussion of Trenka's blog as activist life writing, see my article "Adoptee Life Writing 2.0: Transnationality and Social Justice Online" (2019). While Trenka's call for the end of transnational adoption might seem radical, others

have made similar demands. For example, the signees of the "Declaration Calling for an Immediate End to the Industrial International Adoption System from South Korea," which was generated at a conference in California in 2017, "ask the Moon Jae-in administration to immediately terminate overseas adoption from South Korea. Although South Korea has addressed many of the root causes of overseas adoption over the past decade by introducing legislation to support single mothers and prioritize family preservation, we believe that South Korea, now more than ever, can end the needless separation of children from their mothers and families" (Kim and Lee 280).

8. In January 2015, the *New York Times Magazine* published an article on transnational adoptees returning in considerable numbers to Korea to bond with their birth families and culture. Author Maggie Jones interviewed Trenka, who now lives in Seoul with her husband (also an adoptee) and daughter, about her anti-adoption activism. Together with many other adoptee advocates, Trenka succeeded in 2012 "in enacting an amendment to the adoption law, implementing curbs on adoption that would have seemed unthinkable decades ago. Women must now receive counseling and wait seven days before placing a child for adoption" (Jones). Stricter qualifications and mandatory training for prospective adoptive parents are now also enforced (Bae 307–308).

9. It is conventionally accepted that the origins of transnational adoption lie in altruistic humanitarianism and narratives of Christian love and divine planning. Critics of the system point out that these assumptions often create an atmosphere that puts the adoptive parents in a position of power and allows them complete legal and cultural control over adoptees' bodies and identity, such as changing birth names and denying past experiences (Kim 43).

10. While Trenka should not have had to wait five years to be naturalized and this time frame likely reflects her adoptive parents' choice, adoptees in the late 1970s arrived on immigrant visas and adoptive parents had to apply for permanent residency with the Immigration and Naturalization Service, which could take several years. With the passing of the Child Citizenship Act in 2000, adoptees under the age of eighteen entering the United States became automatic citizens. But because many adoptive parents did not realize they had to apply for naturalization of their child, data from the Adoptee Rights Campaign suggests that between 2015 and 2033, 32,000 to 64,000 adoptees will have undocumented status in the United States (Martin-Montgomery et al.). Already, deportations among transnational adoptees whose naturalization was never completed are becoming more frequent, which insinuates that the urge to Americanize adoptees applies only as long as they are young children and a rescue narrative can be associated with them. As McKee claims, to "care for adoptees only when they are children highlights how their value is linked to their youth and perceived innocence" (*Disrupting* 50). With the Trump administration's 2019 creation of a new office within United States Citizenship and

Immigration Services charged with reviewing naturalization cases for inconsistencies in applications, concerns rose that more and more adoptees who have no connection to their country of birth would be deported. McKee observes that while there are clear similarities between adult adoptees and children brought to the United States as undocumented migrants (mostly from South and Central America), the adoptee rights community exerts efforts to keep themselves separate from migrants under DACA and their activism efforts, further feeding the good immigrant (adoptee) versus bad immigrant (DACA recipient) narrative (*Disrupting* 57–58).

11. Brian gives as an example of this problematic attitude an information meeting on transnational adoption during which "white privilege" was defined merely as "easiness to blend in" (41).

12. The supply for such adoption manuals seems overwhelming. Mostly, however, these books are geared toward couples considering or preparing for adoption. A number of children's books are available for young adopted children and nonadopted children awaiting the arrival of their adopted sibling. Most of these books support adoption to the point where any claims that might be seen as critical of adoption are left out, and very few self-help books exist that speak to adult transracial adoptees.

13. Religious communities continue to encourage their members to adopt "poor" children. Starting in the early 2000s, adoptions of numerous children by evangelical Christians as a missionizing practice have "become a movement that launched major conferences, spawned a small library of books on 'adoption theology,' and changed the complexion of many conservative U.S. churches" (Joyce). At the peak of the movement, "any child of an impoverished parent was viewed as the equivalent of an 'orphan'" who needed to be "redeemed" (Joyce). This led to the creation of "super-sized families with sometimes tragic results" as children were abused or even killed (Joyce). Many adopted children, especially from countries like Ethiopia, have since been revealed as still having extended family that wanted to care for them (Joyce). For further information about this topic, see the work of David Smolin, law professor and Christian advocate for adoption reform, such as "The One Hundred Thousand Dollar Baby: The Ideological Roots of a New American Export" (2019).

14. Some adoptive parents' unsuitability has led to a dangerous "re-homing" movement of domestic and transnational adoptees. As a 2013 Reuters investigation revealed, potentially thousands of legally adopted children (the majority of them foreign-born) were offered online to be given away without the children's consent nor the knowledge of the proper authorities. Many of these children ended up in abusive and exploitative situations. Since 2014, states have begun passing laws against this practice (Twohey). In addition, according to a 2018 report, the United States Department of State is "very concerned about efforts by adoptive parents to permanently return adopted children to countries of origin" (2). One such case received international attention in 2010: a Tennessee woman put her seven-year-old

adoptive son, Artyom Savelyev, on a plane to Russia, his country of birth, with a note that she no longer wanted him due to psychological concerns with the boy ("In Contentious System"). The incident led Russia to temporarily suspend adoptions to the United States.

15. This terminology is not unique to a transnational context as the quantity of books on all forms of adoption whose titles contain variations of "Chosen Child" confirms.

16. In *Fugitive Visions*, Trenka describes her move to Seoul as part of a large community of returning adoptees and elaborates on their lives in Korea and the surprisingly high suicide rate among that demographic. In this context, Eleana Kim offers an insightful discussion of how in South Korea the "commodification of human life [in the form of transnational adoption] is increasingly justified post facto via ideologies of upward mobility and opportunity," which adoptees are said to have benefited from due to their geographical movement ("Human Capital" 307).

17. Laurel Kendall's essay "Birth Mothers and Imaginary Lives" (2005) debunks the "rescue myth" by offering stories of orphans and abandoned children who stayed in Korea and led fulfilling, meaningful lives.

18. For a detailed analysis of adoptees' experiences specifically in Minnesota, the state with the largest per capita adoptee population in the United States, see Kim Park Nelson's collection of oral histories in *Invisible Asians* (2015).

19. The term "Twinkie" refers to an American snack food consisting of yellow cake and sweet, white filling. It represents the idea of being "yellow on the outside and white on the inside." An Asian American Twinkie is supposedly so assimilated and Americanized that they no longer have a connection to Asian values.

20. For a thorough discussion of how literature in all its forms has used adoption as a trope to "dramatize cultural tensions about definitions of family and the importance of heredity" (6), consult Marianne Novy's *Reading Adoption: Family and Difference in Fiction and Drama* (2005).

21. Trenka uses pseudonyms for her family members in her writing.

22. The widespread practice by adoption agencies of placing pictures of adorable young Asian girls on their brochures to attract readers' interest seems to be a symptom of this connection.

23. *I Wish for You a Beautiful Life*, a collection of letters by Korean mothers to their children who were adopted into families overseas, constitutes another example of the efforts undertaken to break the powers that silence birthmothers. In their letters, women write about the pain of having to give up a child: "Whenever I see children on the street, I go crazy. . . . it hurts that I could not peacefully hold you nor lie next to you" (Dorow 1999, 29). For more insight into the struggles of Korean birthmothers, see also the documentaries *Resilience* (2010) by Tammy Chu and *First Person Plural* (2000) and *In the Matter of Cha Jung Hee* (2010) by Deann Borshay Liem.

24. Lifton recalls a very similar reaction by one of her interviewees who was denied to have his records opened despite having three children with complicated medical problems: "'I am being treated like a fifty-year-old infant who lacks the good sense or sensitivity to handle his own affairs or those of others'" (*Lost and Found* 88).

CHAPTER 4

1. After much debate with her father, Rachlin was allowed to come to the United States on a student visa in 1962. She first attended Lindenwood University in Missouri (from where she received a BA in psychology) with the permission of her father, but then moved to New York City for graduate school without her family's knowledge. She married an American citizen and was naturalized in 1969. In addition to her memoir, Rachlin has published four novels and a collection of short stories. She currently teaches creative writing at the New School University (*Nahid Rachlin*).

2. Ten memoirs by women of Iranian descent were published in the United States between 1999 and 2005. Examples include Firoozeh Dumas's *Funny in Farsi: A Memoir of Growing up Iranian in America* (2003), Azadeh Moaveni's *Lipstick Jihad: A Memoir of Growing up Iranian in America and American in Iran* (2005), and Azar Nafisi's *Reading Lolita in Tehran: A Memoir in Books* (2003).

3. Roya Hakakian's *Journey from the Land of No* (2004) also depicts pre-revolution life in Iran but from the perspective of a Jewish girl living in a Muslim country. Hakakian's memoir ends with her family's plan to move to the United States. Farideh Goldin's memoir, *Wedding Song* (2003), resembles Hakakian's story in that she, too, is a Persian Jew; she, however, is able to leave Iran for college in the United States before the Revolution. Sattareh Farman-Farmaian was possibly the first woman to leave Iran for the United States to study. In *Daughter of Persia* (1992), she recounts her life under both Shahs, her studies in the United States, and her return to Iran to open its first School of Social Work. After the Islamic Revolution, she had to flee Iran and settled again in the United States. Lastly, in *Persia Is My Heart* (1953), Najmeh Najafi depicts her life as a successful business woman under the Shah and her decision to study business in the United States in order to build factories in Iran's poor villages.

4. Deviating from the content of the memoir, however, I see the book's cover attempting to attract the reader through an exoticized image of two "mysterious" women wearing *chadors* (black, full-body coverings) and through Oriental design patterns as the backdrop for the title.

5. Of fifty-one reviews on Amazon.com, only one reader gave the book the lowest rating of one star. They entitled their review "Eastern Openion" [*sic*] and

accuse Rachlin of spreading lies about Iranian culture. One other reviewer assigned the memoir only two stars, explaining they found the story "boring."

6. If not otherwise marked, all quotations by Rachlin are taken from *Persian Girls*.

7. Consult Sara Ahmed's seminal *Gender and Islam* (1992) for an extensive historicization of women's roles in Islam and Islamic societies.

8. See, for example, Françoise Lionnet's essay "Of Mangoes and Maroons" (1992) or Max Saunders' *Self Impression: Life-Writing, Autobiografiction, and the Forms of Modern Literature* (2010). Michael Lackey also discusses "biofiction—literature that names its protagonist after an actual biographical figure" (3), which is difficult to differentiate from biography and the historical novel and plays with "the competing and sometimes contradictory demands of biography (representation) and fiction (creation)" (6). Other authors, notably Charles Dickens, Maxine Hong Kingston, Philip Roth, and Jonathan Safran Foer, have engaged in autofiction that features fictional characters who have the authors' names. For a theorization of autofiction, see Arnauld Schmitt.

9. In the Greek myth, Procne's husband, Tereus, rapes her sister, Philomela, cuts out her tongue, and jails her so that she cannot tell of her suffering. Philomela manages to weave her story into a beautiful cloth and has a guard deliver it to her sister, who realizes her husband's crime. Together, the sisters take revenge by killing Procne's own son and feeding him to Tereus.

10. When citing Pari's letters, all emphases occur in the original text.

11. Farrukhzad (1935–1967) was one of Iran's most important modernist poets of the twentieth century.

12. Many recent memoirs by women of Iranian descent, such as Nafisi's *Reading Lolita*, make reference to the custom of taking children away from their mothers in a divorce as one of the most horrendous practices of Iranian patriarchy. Rachlin herself creates another account of a woman losing her children and of domestic abuse in the short story "Fatemeh," which is published in *Veils* (1992).

13. During its last years, the Shah regime passed several laws that, superficially, improved women's lives. While the minimum marriage age for women was raised to eighteen, this was often not enforced, especially in rural areas. The 1975 revised Family Protection Act (FPA) allowed women to include the right to a divorce in their marriage contracts and made divorce harder for men since they needed to involve the courts. A woman now also had to consent, in addition to the courts, to her husband taking a second wife. The FPA also gave wives the right to forbid men to work jobs that might affect the family's reputation, a right that Iranian husbands already held. The Shah legalized abortion, but wives needed their husbands' permission for the procedure. In 1976, a husband's permission for his wife to travel outside of Iran was declared valid for six years, which did not eliminate the control men had over women's movements. Finally, the last Shah left unchanged the laws

that women could inherit only half of their male relatives' shares and that a widow could inherit only an eighth of her husband's property (Moghissi).

14. "My Stealthy Freedom" was created by Iranian-born journalist Masih Alinejad in 2014. It now has over one million followers. The page also contains submissions by women who cover their heads, speaking out against the compulsory hijab.

CHAPTER 5

1. A May 2015 Amnesty International Report entitled "'Libya Is Full of Cruelty': Stories of Abduction, Sexual Violence and Abuse from Migrants and Refugees" collected chilling testimonies of violence against female migrants.

2. After fiscal year 2018, the Trump administration sharply decreased the number of resettled refugees in the United States. In fact, the administration failed to meet its own low benchmarks with all geographical groups except refugees from Europe, specifically white evangelical Christians from the former Soviet Union, who exceeded the limit set for them in 2018 (Lind). These data have led critics to claim that racial discrimination plays a significant role in U.S. refugee politics (as a subcategory of broader U.S. immigration policies).

3. See my article "Female Refugees in Rural Germany: A Local Aid Agency's Efforts to Build on Women and Children's Experiences and Needs" (2019) for conversations with refugee women about their agency and resilience.

4. In *We Are Displaced* (2019), Yousafzai collects the stories of nine female refugees from Yemen, Syria, Iraq, Colombia, Guatemala, the Congo, Myanmar, and Uganda. All proceeds of the book support refugees.

5. In this context, Ozlem Ezer's *Syrian Women Refugees* (2019) makes important contributions in collecting the life stories of nine Syrian women refugees. While not chronicling the author's experiences as a refugee, per se, Samar Yazbek's *A Woman in the Crossfire: Diaries of the Syrian Revolution* (2012) about the Syrian uprising attests to Yazbek's firm belief in testimonies of "courage" (88) and that "those who remain silent are accomplices to the crime" (134). The book also details the process of "Syrians being transformed into refugees" (131) and ends with the author being forced to make the difficult decision of leaving her country to live in hiding.

6. Equally noteworthy, Thi Bui's graphic memoir *The Best We Could Do* (2018) uses the power of illustrations to convey her family's pains and hopes as they escape Vietnam in the 1970s.

7. Quotations from Bana al-Abed's tweets are marked with a reference to her last name. Quotations from her memoir are followed by her last name and page numbers.

8. Yenal Göksun demonstrates Syrian bloggers' importance in creating awareness and influencing local and global opinion about the ongoing political upheaval.

9. For an insightful discussion of changes in tone and political stance in Bana's tweets after her evacuation, such as her call for violent restitution, see Ana Belén Martínez García.

10. All of Fatemah's words in the memoir are printed in italics.

EPILOGUE

1. My connections between life writing and policies are shaped by Stephen Castles and Mark Miller's analysis of migration patterns in *The Age of Migration: International Population Movements and the Modern World* (1993).

WORKS CITED

Abrams L. S., K. Dornig, and L. Curran. "Barriers to Service Use for Postpartum Depression Symptoms among Low-Income Ethnic Minority Mothers in the United States." *Qualitative Health Research* 19, no. 4 (2009): 535–551.
Abu-Lughod, Lila. *Do Muslim Women Need Saving?* Cambridge, MA: Harvard University Press, 2013.
Adichie, Chimamanda Ngozi. *Americanah. A Novel.* New York: Anchor Books, 2013.
al-Abed, Bana. *Dear World: A Syrian Girl's Story of War and Plea for Peace.* New York: Simon & Schuster, 2017.
Ahmed, Leila. *Women and Gender in Islam: Historical Roots of a Modern Debate.* New Haven, CT: Yale University Press, 1992.
@AlabedBana. twitter.com/AlabedBana?ref_src=twsrc%5Egoogle%7Ctwcamp%5Eserp%7Ctwgr%5Eauthor
Alcoff, Linda. "The Problem of Speaking for Others." *Just Methods. An Interdisciplinary Feminist Reader*, edited by Alison M. Jaggar. Boulder, CO: Paradigm, 2008, 484–495.
Alcoff, Linda, and Laura Gray-Rosedale. "Survivor Discourse." *Getting a Life: Everyday Uses of Autobiography*, edited by Sidonie Smith and Julia Watson. Minneapolis: University of Minnesota Press, 1996, 198–225.
Alinejad, Masih. "My Stealthy Freedom." *Facebook*. www.facebook.com/StealthyFreedom
Allen, Paula Gunn. "'Border' Studies: The Intersection of Gender and Color." *Introduction to Scholarship in Modern Languages and Literatures*, edited by Joseph Gibaldi. New York: Modern Language Association, 1992, 303–319.
Alvarez, Priscilla. "Parents of 445 Migrant Children Separated at Border under Trump Still Have Not Been Found, Court Filing Says." *CNN*, April 7, 2021. www.cnn.com/2021/04/07/politics/family-separation-court-filing/index.html
Anderson, Benedict. *Imagined Communities: Reflections on the Origin and Spread of Nationalism.* New York: Verso, 1992.
Angelou, Maya. *I Know Why the Caged Bird Sings.* New York: Random House, 1969.
Antin, Mary. *The Promised Land.* New York: Houghton Mifflin Company, 1912.

WORKS CITED

Anzaldúa, Gloria. *Borderlands/La Frontera*. 2nd ed. San Francisco: Aunt Lute Books, 1999.

———. "La Prieta." In *This Bridge Called My Back: Writings by Radical Women of Color*, 2nd ed., edited by Cherrie Moraga and Gloria Anzaldúa. Latham, NY: Kitchen Table, Women of Color Press, 1983, 198–209.

Arce, Julissa. *My (Underground) American Dream: My True Story as an Undocumented Immigrant Who Became a Wall Street Executive*. New York: Center Street, 2016.

Arendt, Hannah. *The Origins of Totalitarianism*. New York: Harcourt, Brace & World, 1966.

Arthur, John A. *African Diaspora Identities. Negotiating Culture in Transnational Migration*. Washington, DC: Lexington Books, 2010.

"Back Again: An Interview with Thanhha Lai." In Thanhha Lai, *Inside Out and Back Again*. New York: Harper, 2011, 3–6.

Baden, Amanda L. "Culture Camp, Ethnic Identity, and Adoption Socialization for Korean Adoptees: A Pretest and Posttest Study." *New Directions for Child and Adolescent Development* 150 (2015): 19–31.

Bae, Shannon. "Radical Imagination and the Solidarity Movement between Transnational Korean Adoptees and Unwed Mothers in South Korea." *Adoption & Culture* 6, no. 2 (2018): 300–315.

Bahrampour, Tara. *To See and See Again. A Life in Iran and America*. New York: Farrar, Strauss and Giroux, 1999.

Baker, Bryan, and Nancy Rytina. United States Department of Homeland Security. Office of Immigration Statistics. *Estimates of the Unauthorized Immigrant Population Residing in the United States: January 2012*. Washington, DC: Government Printing Office, 2013.

Balogun, F. Odun. "Self, Place, and Identity in Two Generations of West African Immigrant Women Memoirs: Emcheta's *Head above Water* and Danquah's *Willow Weep for Me*." In *The New African Diaspora*, edited by Isidore Okpewho and Nkiru Nzegwu. Bloomington: Indiana University Press, 2009, 442–458.

Batzke, Ina. *Undocumented Migrants in the United States: Life Narratives and Self-representations*. New York: Routledge, 2019.

Bauman, Kurt. "School Enrollment of the Hispanic Population: Two Decades of Growth." *census.gov*, 28 Aug. 2017. www.census.gov/newsroom/blogs/random-samplings/2017/08/school_enrollmentof.html

Beauboeuf-Lafontant, Tamara. "Strong and Large Black Women? Exploring Relationships between Deviant Womanhood and Weight." *Gender and Society* 17, no. 1 (2003): 111–121.

Bergland, Betty A., and Lori Ann Lahlum. *Norwegian American Women: Migration, Communities, and Identities*. St. Paul: Minnesota Historical Society Press, 2011.

Bertrand, Marianne, and Sendhil Mullainathan. "Are Emily and Greg More Employable than Lakisha and Jamal? A Field Experiment on Labor Market Discrimination." *National Bureau of Economic Research*, Working Paper 9873, 2003. doi:10.3386/w9873

Beverley, John. "The Margin at the Center: On Testimonio." In *The Real Thing: Testimonial Discourse and Latin America*, edited by George M. Gugelberger. Durham, NC: Duke University Press, 1996, 23–41.

———. "The Real Thing." In *The Real Thing: Testimonial Discourse and Latin America*, edited by George M. Gugelberger. Durham, NC: Duke University Press, 1996, 266–286.

Bishoff, Tonya. "Unnamed Blood." In *Seeds from a Silent Tree. An Anthology by Korean Adoptees*, edited by Tonya Bishoff and Jo Rankin. Glendale, CA: Pandal Press, 1997, 37–38.

Bloch, Katrina, and Tiffany Taylor. "Welfare Queens and Anchor Babies: A Comparative Study of Stigmatized Mothers in the United States." In *Mothering in the Age of Neoliberalism*, edited by Melinda Vandenbeld Giles. Ontario: Demeter Press, 2014, 199–210.

Boelhower, William. *Immigrant Autobiography in the United States: Four Versions of the Italian Self*. Rome: Essedue Edizioni, 1982.

———. "The Making of Ethnic Autobiography in the United States." In *American Autobiography: Retrospect and Prospect*, edited by Paul John Eakin. Madison: University of Wisconsin Press, 1992, 123–141.

Bok, Edward William. *The Americanization of Edward Bok. The Autobiography of a Dutch Boy Fifty Years After*. New York: C. Scribner's Sons, 1922.

Bozorgmehr, Mehdi, and Georges Sabagh. "High Status Immigrants: A Statistical Profile of Iranians in the United States." *Iranian Studies* 21, no. 3–4 (1988): 5–36.

Brant, Clare, Tobias Heinrich, and Monica Soeting. "The Placing of Displaced Lives: Refugee Narratives." *a/b: Auto/Biography Studies* 32, no. 3 (2017): 625–628.

Brian, Kristi. *Reframing Transracial Adoption. Adopted Koreans, White Parents, and the Politics of Kinship*. Philadelphia: Temple University Press, 2012.

Briggs, Laura. *Somebody's Children. The Politics of Transracial and Transnational Adoption*. Durham, NC: Duke University Press, 2012.

Bui, Thi. *The Best We Could Do*. New York: Abrams ComicArts, 2018.

Buss, Helen. *Repossessing the World: Reading Memoirs by Contemporary Women*. Waterloo, ON: Wilfrid Laurier Press, 2002.

Carp, Wayne E. *Family Matters: Secrecy and Disclosure in the History of Adoption*. Cambridge, MA: Harvard University Press, 1998.

Caruth, Cathy. *Unclaimed Experience: Trauma, Narrative, and History*. Baltimore, MD: Johns Hopkins University Press, 1996.

Castillo, Debra A., and María Socorro Tabuenca Córdoba. *Border Women. Writing from la frontera*. Minneapolis: University of Minnesota Press, 2002.

Castles, Stephen, and Mark J. Miller. *The Age of Migration. International Population Movements and the Modern World*. New York: Guilford Press, 1993.

Chansky, Ricia Anne. "Reading beyond Borders: Movement and Belonging in the Americas." *Auto /Biography across the Americas: Transnational Themes in Life Writing*, edited by Ricia Anne Chansky. New York: Routledge, 2016, 1–19.

Charlesworth, Hilary, and Christine Chinkin. *The Boundaries of International Law. A Feminist Analysis*. Manchester, UK: Manchester University Press, 2000.

Chu, Tammy (director). *Resilience*. Film. KoRoot, 2010.

Chua, Steven. "There Isn't a Word for Depression: Immigrants and Mental Health. Immigrants Are Less Than Half as Likely to Get Professional Help for Depression." *CBC News*, 10 Sept. 2013. www.cbc.ca/news/canada/british-columbia/there-isn-t-a-word-for-depression-immigrants-and-mental-health-1.1702475

Cisneros, Natalie. "'Alien' Sexuality: Race, Maternity, and Citizenship." *Hypatia* 28, no. 2 (2013): 290–306.

Cockcroft, James D. *Outlaws in the Promised Land. Mexican Immigrant Workers and America's Future*. New York: Grove Press, 1986.

Combahee River Collective. "A Black Feminist Statement." In *The Essential Feminist Reader*, edited by Estelle B. Freedman. New York: Modern Library, 2007, 325–330.

Condit-Shrestha, Kelly. "South Korea and Adoption's Ends: Reexamining the Numbers and Historicizing Market Economies." *Adoption & Culture* 6, no. 2 (2018): 364–400.

Cooper, Pauline. "Writing for Depression in Health Care." *British Journal of Occupational Therapy* 76, no. 4 (2013): 186–193.

Couser, G. Thomas. "Conflicting Paradigms: The Rhetorics of Disability Memoir." In *Embodied Rhetorics: Disability in Language and Culture*, edited by James C. Wilson and Cynthia Lewiecki-Wilson. Carbondale: Southern Illinois University Press, 2001, 78–91.

———. "The Future of Life Writing: Body Stories." *a/b: Auto/Biography Studies* 32, no. 2 (2017): 379–381.

———. *Memoir: An Introduction*. Oxford: Oxford University Press, 2012.

———. *Signifying Bodies: Disability in Contemporary Life Writing*. Ann Arbor: University of Michigan Press, 2009.

Crenshaw, Kimberlé Williams. "Mapping the Margins: Intersectionality, Identity Politics, and Violence against Women of Color." *Stanford Law Review* 43, no. 6 (1991): 1241–1299.

Cubilié, Anne. *Women Witnessing Terror: Testimony and the Cultural Politics of Human Rights*. New York: Fordham University Press, 2005.

Cutter, Martha J. *Lost and Found in Translation: Contemporary Ethnic American Writing and the Politics of Language Diversity*. Chapel Hill: University of North Carolina Press, 2005.

Dann, Patty. Review of Nahid Rachlin's *Persian Girls. A Memoir*. www.nahidrachlin.com/works.htm

Danquah, Meri Nana-Ama, editor. "A Conversation with Meri Nana-Ama Danquah." In *Willow Weep for Me*, edited by Meri Nana-Ama Danquah. London: One World, 1999, 275–282.

——— (ed.). *Becoming American: Personal Essays by First Generation Immigrant Women*. Westport, CT: Hyperion, 2000.
——— (ed.). *The Black Body*. New York: Seven Stories Press, 2009.
———. "Break Skin, Break Spirit." In *The Black Body*, edited by Meri Nana-Ama Danquah. New York: Seven Stories Press, 2009, 229–244.
———. "I am What I Am." *Joy Online*, 22 November 2013. www.myjoyonline.com/opinion/i-am-what-i-am-by-meri-nana-ama-danquah
———. Introduction. In *The Black Body*, edited by Meri Nana-Ama Danquah. New York: Seven Stories Press, 2009, 13–30.
———. Introduction. In *Becoming American*, edited by Meri Nana-Ama Danquah. Westport, CT: Hyperion, 2000, xiii–xviii.
——— (ed.). *Shaking the Tree: New Fiction and Memoir by Black Women*. New York: Norton, 2004.
——— (ed.). *Willow Weep for Me. A Black Woman's Journey through Depression*. London: One World, 1999.
Danticat, Edwidge. *Create Dangerously: The Immigrant Artist at Work*. Princeton, NJ: Princeton University Press, 2010.
Davies, Carole Boyce, "Private Selves and Public Spaces: Autobiography and the African Woman Writer." *Neohelicon* 17, no. 2 (1991): 183–210.
Davis, Rocío G. *Begin Here: Reading Asian North American Autobiographies of Childhood*. Honolulu: University of Hawai'i Press, 2007.
Davis, Rocío G., Jaume Aurell, and Ana Delago. "Introduction: Ethnic Life Writing and Historical Mediation: Approaches and Interventions." In *Ethnic Life Writing and Histories: Genres, Performance, and Culture*, edited by Rocío G. Davis, Jaume Aurell, and Ana Delago. Münster, Germany: Lit. Verlag, 2007, 9–21.
Deans, Jill R. "The Birth of Contemporary Adoption Autobiography: Florence Fisher and Betty Jean Lifton." *a/b: Auto/Biography Studies* 18, no. 2 (2003): 239–258.
Delale-O'Connor, Lori. "Learning to Be Me: The Role of Adoptee Culture Camps in Teaching Adopted Children Their Birth Culture." *Adoption & Culture* 2 (2009): 203–225.
Derr, Amelia Seraphia. "Mental Health Service Use among Immigrants in the United States: A Systematic Review." *Psychiatric Services* 67, no. 3 (2016): 265–274.
Derrida, Jacques. "The Law of Genre." Translated by Avital Ronell, *Critical Inquiry* 7, no. 1 (1980): 55–81.
Diallo, Kadiatou. *My Heart Will Cross This Ocean. My Story, My Son, Amadou*. New York: Ballantine Books, 2003.
Di Blasio, Paola, Elena Camisasca, Simona Carla Silvia Caravita, Chiara Ionio, Luca Milani, and Giovanni Giulio Valtolina. "The Effects of Expressive Writing on Postpartum Depression and Posttraumatic Stress Symptoms." *Psychological Reports* 117, no. 3 (2015): 856–882.

Dorow, Sara K. (ed.). *I Wish for You a Beautiful Life: Letters from Korean Birth Mothers of Ae Ran Won to Their Children*. South Korea: Yeong and Yeong, 1999.

———. *Transnational Adoption: A Cultural Economy of Race, Gender, and Kinship*. New York: New York University Press, 2006.

———. "Producing Kinship through the Marketplaces of Transnational Adoption." In *Baby Markets: Money and the New Politics of Creating Families*, edited by Michele Bratcher Goodwin. Cambridge: Cambridge University Press, 2010, 69–83.

Dossa, Parin. *Politics and Poetics of Migration: Narratives of Iranian Women from the Diaspora*. Toronto: Canadian Scholars' Press, 2004.

Douglas, Kate. *Contesting Childhood: Autobiography, Trauma, and Memory*. New Brunswick, NJ: Rutgers University Press, 2009.

Duke, Bill, and D. Channsin Berry (directors). *Dark Girls*. Film. Duke Media, 2011.

Dumas, Firoozeh. *Funny in Farsi: A Memoir of Growing up Iranian in America*. New York: Villard, 2003.

Dunant, Henry. *A Memory of Solferino*. Washington, DC: American National Red Cross, 1939. (First published in 1859.)

Eakin, Paul John (ed.). *American Autobiography: Retrospect and Prospect*. Madison: University of Wisconsin Press, 1992.

———. *How Our Lives Become Stories: Making Selves*. Ithaca, NY: Cornell University Press, 1999.

Elahi, Babak. "Fake Farsi: Formulaic Flexibility in Iranian American Women's Memoir." *MELUS* 33, no. 2 (Summer 2008): 37–54.

Ellerby, Janet Mason. *Following the Tambourine Man: A Birthmother's Memoir*. Syracuse, NY: Syracuse University Press, 2007.

Ezer, Ozlem. "Drawing a Narrative Landscape with Women Refugees." *a/b: Auto/Biography Studies* 33, no. 3 (2018): 610–617.

———. *Syrian Women Refugees: Personal Accounts of Transition*. Jefferson, NC: McFarland, 2019.

"Family Separation by the Numbers." *ACLU.org*, 2 October 2018. www.aclu.org/issues/family-separation

Farman-Farmaian, Sattareh. *Daughter of Persia: A Woman's Journey from Her Father's Harem through the Islamic Revolution*. New York: Crown Publishers, 1992.

Filipović, Zlata. *Zlata's Diary: A Child's Life in Sarajevo*. 1993. Translated by Christina Pribichevich-Zorić. New York: Penguin, 2006.

Fisher, Florence. *The Search for Anna Fisher*. New York: Arthur Fields, 1973.

Flores, René D., and Ariela Schachter. "Examining Americans' Stereotypes about Immigrant Illegality." *Contexts* 18, no. 2 (2019): 36–41.

Fogg-Davis, Hawley. *The Ethics of Transracial Adoption*. Ithaca, NY: Cornell University Press, 2002.

Foucault, Michel. *Madness and Civilization: A History of Insanity in the Age of Reason*. New York: Vintage Books, 1988.

Frank, Anne. *The Diary of a Young Girl*. New York: Doubleday & Company, 1952.
Frank, Arthur. *The Wounded Story Teller: Body, Illness, and Ethics*. Chicago: University of Chicago Press, 1995.
Freedman, Jane. "Women's Experience of Forced Migration: Gender-based Forms of Insecurity and the Uses of 'Vulnerability.'" In *A Gendered Approach to the Syrian Refugee Crisis*, edited by Jane Freedman, Zeynep Kivilcim, and Nurcan Özgür Baklacioğlu. New York: Routledge, 2017, 125–141.
Fricker, Miranda. *Epistemic Injustice: Power and the Ethics of Knowing*. Oxford: Oxford University Press, 2007.
Friedan, Betty. *The Feminine Mystique*. New York: Norton, 1963.
Friedman, Susan Stanford. *Mappings: Feminism and the Cultural Geographies of Encounter*. Princeton, NJ: Princeton University Press, 1998.
———. "Women's Autobiographical Selves: Theory and Practice." In *The Private Self: Theory and Practice of Women's Autobiographical Writings*, edited by Shari Benstock. Chapel, Hill: University of North Carolina Press, 1988, 34–62.
Frye, Marilyn. *The Politics of Reality: Essays in Feminist Theory*. Berkeley, CA: The Crossing Press, 1983.
Gabaccia, Donna. *From the Other Side: Women, Gender, and Immigrant Life in the U.S., 1820–1990*. Bloomington: Indiana University Press, 1994.
Gadsby, Meredith M. *Sucking Salt: Caribbean Women Writers, Migration, and Survival*. Columbia: University of Missouri Press, 2006.
Galarza, Ernesto. *Barrio Boy*. South Bend, IN: University of Notre Dame Press, 1971.
García, Ana Belén Martínez. "Bana Alabed: Using Twitter to Draw Attention to Human Rights Violations." *Prose Studies* 39, no. 2–3 (2017): 132–149.
Gberie, Lansana. "Mental illness: Invisible but Devastating. Superstition [sic] often Blamed for Acute Mental Health Diseases." *Africa Renewal*, December 2016–March 2017. www.un.org/africarenewal/magazine/december-2016-march-2017/mental-illness-invisible-devastating
Gerhards, Jürgen, and Silke Hans. "From Hasan to Herbert: Name-Giving Patterns of Immigrant Parents between Acculturation and Ethnic Maintenance." *American Journal of Sociology* 114, no. 4 (2009): 1102–1128.
Gilbert, Brian (director). *Not without My Daughter*. Film. MGM, 1990.
Gilmore, Leigh. *Autobiographics: A Feminist Theory of Women's Self-Representation*. Ithaca, NY: Cornell University Press, 1994.
———. "Refugee/Citizen: Mediating Testimony through Image and Word in the Wake of Hurricane Katrina." *a/b: Auto/Biography Studies* 32, no. 3 (2017): 673–681.
———. *Tainted Witness: Why We Doubt What Women Say about Their Lives*. New York: Columbia University Press, 2017.
Göksun, Yenal. "Cyberactivism in Syria's War: How Syrian Bloggers Use the Internet for Political Activism." In *New Media Politics: Rethinking Activism and*

National Security in Cyberspace, edited by Banu Baybars-Hawks. Cambridge: Cambridge Scholars, 2015, 39–64.

Goldin, Farideh. *Wedding Song. Memoirs of an Iranian Jewish Woman*. Waltham, MA: Brandeis University Press, 2003.

Goldman, Anne E. *Take My Word: Autobiographical Innovations of Ethnic American Working Women*. Berkeley: University of California Press, 1996.

Gomes, Ruthie Bonan, et al. "New Dialogues in Feminist Disability Studies." *Estudos Feministas* 27, no. 1 (2019): 1–13.

Gomez, Alan. "ICE Sets Record for Arrests of Undocumented Immigrants with no Criminal Record." *USA Today*, 21 March 2019. www.usatoday.com/story/news/politics/2019/03/21/ice-sets-record-arrests-undocumented-immigrants-no-criminal-record/3232476002

Graham, Akuyoe. "The Remembering." In *Becoming American: Personal Essays by First Generation Immigrant Women*, edited by Meri Nana-Ama Danquah. Westport, CT: Hyperion, 2000, 68–75.

Grande, Reyna. *The Distance between Us: A Memoir*. New York: Atria Books, 2012.

Grewal, Inderpal, and Caren Kaplan. "Introduction: Transnational Feminist Practices and Questions of Postmodernity." In *Scattered Hegemonies: Postmodernity and Transnational Feminist Practices*, edited by Inderpal Grewal and Caren Kaplan. Minneapolis: University of Minnesota Press, 1994, 1–33.

Grice, Helena. *Asian American Fiction, History and Life Writing: International Encounters*. New York: Routledge, 2009.

Gugelberger, Georg M. (ed.). *The Real Thing: Testimonial Discourse and Latin America*. Durham, NC: Duke University Press, 1996.

Guilbault, Rose Castillo. *Farmworker's Daughter: Growing up Mexican in America*. Berkeley, CA: Heyday Books, 2005.

Gusdorf, Georges. "Conditions and Limits of Autobiography." In *Autobiography: Essays Theoretical and Critical*, edited by James Olney. Princeton, NJ: Princeton University Press, 1980, 28–48. (First published in 1956.)

Guzmán, Isabel Molina, and Angharad N. Valdivia. "Disciplining the Ethnic Body. Latinidad, Hybridized Bodies and Transnational Identities." In *Governing the Female Body. Gender, Health, and Networks of Power*, edited by Lori Reed and Paula Saukko. Albany, NY: SUNY Press, 2010, 206–229.

Hakakian, Roya. *Journey from the Land of No: A Girlhood Caught in Revolutionary Iran*. New York: Three Rivers Press, 2004.

Halter, Marilyn, and Violet Showers Johnson. *African & American: West-Africans in Post–Civil Rights America*. New York: New York University Press, 2014.

Hannon, Lance, Robert DeFina, and Sarah Bruch. "The Relationship Between Skin Tone and School Suspension for African Americans." *Race and Social Problems* 5, no. 4 (2013): 281–295.

Harding, Sandra. "Rethinking Standpoint Epistemology: What is Strong Objectivity?" In *Feminist Epistemologies*, edited by Linda Alcoff and Elizabeth Potter. New York: Routledge, 1993, 49–82.

Haslanger, Sally. "Gender and Race: (What) Are They? (What) Do We Want Them to Be?" *Noûs* 34, no. 1 (2000): 31–55.

Henke, Suzette. *Shattered Subjects: Trauma and Testimony in Women's Life-Writing.* New York: Saint Martin's Press, 1998.

Hesford, Wendy S., and Theresa A. Kulpaga. "Labored Realisms: Geopolitical Rhetoric and Asian American and Asian (Im)migrant Women's (Auto)biography." In *Western Subjects: Autobiographical Writing in the North American West*, edited by Kethleen A. Boardman and Gioia Woods. Salt Lake City: University of Utah Press, 2004, 302–337.

Hintzen, Percy Claude, and Jean Muteba Rahier. "Introduction. From Structural Politics to the Politics of Deconstruction: Self-Ethnographies Problematizing Blackness." In *Problematizing Blackness: Self-Ethnographies by Black Immigrants to the United States*, edited by Percy Claude Hintzen and Jean Muteba Rahier. New York: Routledge, 2003, 1–20.

Hipchen, Emily. "Adoption Geometries." *Adoption & Culture* 6, no. 1 (2018): 229–247.

———. *Coming Apart Together: Fragments from an Adoption*. Pendleton, SC: Literate Chigger Press, 2005.

———. "Images of the Family Body in the Adoptee Search Narrative." In *New Essays on Life Writing and the Body*, edited by Christopher Stuart and Stephanie Todd. Cambridge: Cambridge Scholars Publishing, 2009, 168–189.

Hipchen, Emily, and Jill R. Deans. "Introduction: Adoption Life Writing. Origins and Other Ghosts." *a/b: Auto/Biography Studies* 18, no. 2 (2003): 163–170.

Holland, Ariel T., and Latha P. Palaniappan. "Problems with the Collection and Interpretation of Asian-American Health Data: Omission, Aggregation, and Extrapolation." *Annals of Epidemiology* 22, no. 6 (2012): 397–405.

Homans, Margaret. "Adoption Narratives, Trauma, and Origins." *Narrative* 14, no. 1 (2006): 4–26.

———. " 'The Mother Who Isn't One': New Stories by Birthmothers." *Adoption & Culture* 2 (2009): 35–63.

Hondagneu-Sotelo, Pierette (ed.). *Gender and U.S. Immigration: Contemporary Trends.* Berkeley: University of California Press, 2003.

———. *Gendered Transitions: Mexican Experiences of Immigration*. Berkeley: University of California Press, 1994.

hooks, bell. "Homeplace: A Site of Resistance." In *Available Means: An Anthology of Women's Rhetoric(s)*, edited by Joy Ritchie and Kate Ronald. Pittsburgh, PA: University of Pittsburgh Press, 2001, 382–390.

"How the United States Immigration System Works." *American Immigration Council*, 10 October 2019. www.americanimmigrationcouncil.org/research/how-united-states-immigration-system-works

Huff, Cynthia. "Towards a Geography of Women's Life Writing and Imagined Communities: An Introductory Essay." In *Women's Life Writing and Imagined Communities*, edited by Cynthia Huff. New York: Routledge, 2005, 1–16.

Hugo, Victor. *Les Misérables*. Paris: Le Livre de Poche, 1985.
Hunsaker, Steven V. *Autobiography and National Identity in the Americas*. Charlottesville: University Press of Virginia, 1999.
Idang, Gabriel E. "African Culture and Values." *Phronimon* 16, no. 2 (2015): 97–111.
"Immigrant Women and Girls in the United States: A Portrait of Demographic Diversity." *American Immigration Council*. September 24, 2020. www.americanimmigrationcouncil.org/research/immigrant-women-and-girls-united-states
"In Contentious System, Hope for A Russian Orphan." *npr.org*, 25 March 2012. www.npr.org/2012/03/25/149319484/in-contentious-system-hope-for-a-russian-orphan
"Interview: Ghana's literary icon–Nana-Ama Danquah." *Kent's Diaries: From Everything to Anything Readable*, 15 April 2011. kentgh.wordpress.com/2011/04/15/interview-ghanas-literary-icon-%E2%80%93-nana-ama-danquah
Irr, Caren. *Toward the Geopolitical Novel: U.S. Fiction in the Twenty-First Century*. New York: Columbia University Press, 2014.
Jacobson, Heather. *Culture Keeping: White Mothers, International Adoption, and the Negotiation of Family Difference*. Nashville, TN: Vanderbilt University Press, 2008.
Jelinek, Estelle C. *The Tradition of Women's Autobiography: From Antiquity to the Present*. Woodbridge, CT: Twayne Publishers, 1986.
Jerng, Mark. *Claiming Others: Transracial Adoption and National Belonging*. Minneapolis: University of Minnesota Press, 2010.
Jolly, Margaretta. "Introduction: Life/Rights Narrative in Action." *We Shall Bear Witness: Life Narratives and Human Rights*, edited by Meg Jensen and Margaretta Jolly. Madison: University of Wisconsin Press, 2014, 3–22.
Jolly, Margaretta, and Liz Stanley. "Letters as / not a Genre." *Life Writing* 2, no. 2 (2005): 91–118.
Jones, Maggie. "Why a Generation of Adoptees Is Returning to South Korea." *New York Times Magazine*, 14 January 2015. www.nytimes.com/2015/01/18/magazine/why-a-generation-of-adoptees-is-returning-to-south-korea.html
Joyce, Kathryn. "The Trouble with the Christian Adoption Movement." *New Republic*, 11 January 2016. newrepublic.com/article/127311/trouble-christian-adoption-movement
Kaplan, Caren. "Resisting Autobiography: Out-Law Genres and Transnational Feminist Subjects." In *De/Colonizing the Subject: The Politics of Gender in Women's Autobiography*, edited by Sidonie Smith and Julia Watson. Minneapolis: University of Minnesota Press, 1992, 115–138.
Karpinski, Eva C. *Borrowed Tongues: Life writing, Migration, and Translation*. Waterloo, ON: Wilfrid Laurier University Press, 2012.
———. "Migrations and Metamorphoses." *a/b: Auto/Biography Studies* 32, no. 2 (2017): 171–173.

———. "Multicultural 'Gift(s)': Immigrant Women's Life Writing and the Politics of Anthologizing Difference." In *Literary Pluralities*, edited by Christl Verduyn. Peterborough, ON: Broadview Press, 1998, 111–124.

Karpinski, Eva C., and Ricia Anne Chansky. "Finding Fragments: The Intersections of Gender and Genre in Life Narratives." *a/b: Auto/Biography Studies* 33, no. 3 (2018): 505–515.

Kawai, Yuko. "Stereotyping Asian Americans: The Dialectic of the Model Minority and the Yellow Peril." *Howard Journal of Communications* 16, no. 2 (2005): 109–130.

Keefe, R. H., C. Brownstein-Evans, and R. S. Rouland Polmanteer. "Having Our Say: African-American and Latina Mothers Provide Recommendations to Health and Mental Health Providers Working with New Mothers Living with Postpartum Depression." *Social Work in Mental Health* 14, no. 5 (2016): 497–508.

Kendall, Laurel. "Birth Mothers and Imaginary Lives." In *Cultures of Transnational Adoption*, edited by Toby Alice Volkman. Durham, NC: Duke University Press, 2005, 162–181.

Keshavarz, Fatemeh. *Jasmine and Stars: Reading More than Lolita in Tehran*. Chapel Hill: University of North Carolina Press, 2007.

Kim, Eleana. *Adopted Territory: Transnational Korean Adoptees and the Politics of Belonging*. Durham, NC: Duke University Press, 2010.

Kim, Eleana, and James Kyung-Jin Lee. "Introducing the Ends of Adoption." *Adoption & Culture* 6, no. 2 (2018): 278–281.

Kim, Hosu. "Reparation Acts: Korean Birth Mothers Travel the Road from Reunion to Redress." *Adoption & Culture* 6, no. 2 (2018): 316–335.

Kim, Hyunil, et al. "Lifetime Prevalence of Investigating Child Maltreatment Among US Children." *American Journal of Public Health* 107, no. 2 (2016): 274–280.

Kingston, Maxine Hong. *The Woman Warrior: Memoirs of a Girlhood among Ghosts*. New York: Knopf, 1976.

Krogstad, Jens Manuel, and Ana Gonzalez-Barrera. "Key Facts about U.S. Immigration Policies and Proposed Changes." *Pew Research Center*, 17 May 2019. www.pewresearch.org/fact-tank/2019/05/17/key-facts-about-u-s-immigration-policies-and-proposed-changes

Krogstad, Jens Manuel, Jeffrey S. Passel, and D'Vera Cohn. "5 Facts about Illegal Immigration in the U.S." *Pew Research Center*, 12 June 2019. www.pewresearch.org/fact-tank/2019/06/12/5-facts-about-illegal-immigration-in-the-u-s

Kruger, Sasha, and Syantani DasGupta. "Embodiment in [Critical] Auto/Biography Studies." *a/b: Auto/Biography Studies* 33, no. 2 (2018): 483–487.

Krupat, Arnold. *Ethnocentricism: Ethnography, History, Literature*. Berkeley: University of California Press, 1992.

Kurz, Katja. *Narrating Contested Lives: The Aesthetics of Life Writing in Human Rights Campaigns*. Heidelberg: Universitätsverlag C. Winter, 2015.

Kusek, Robert. *Through the Looking Glass: Writers' Memoirs at the Turn of the 21st Century*. Poland: Jagiellonian University Press, 2018. (Distributed by Columbia University Press, New York)

Lackey, Michael. "Locating and Defining the Bio in Biofiction." *a/b: Auto/Biography Studies* 31, no. 1 (2016): 3–10.

Lai, Thanhha. *Inside Out and Back Again*. New York: Harper, 2011.

Larson, Thomas. *The Memoir and the Memoirist: Reading and Writing Personal Narrative*. Athens: Ohio University Press, 2007.

Lechner, Elsa. "Narratives in/with and beyond Borders: Constraints and Potentialities of Biographical Research with Refugees." *a/b: Auto/Biography Studies* 32, no. 3 (2017): 637–643.

Lejeune, Philippe. "The Autobiographical Pact." Translated by Katherine Leary. In *On Autobiography*, edited by Paul John Eakin. Minneapolis: University of Minnesota Press, 1989, 119–137.

Liem, Deann Borshay (director). *First Person Plural*. Film. MU Films, 2000.

——— (director). *In the Matter of Cha Jung Hee*. Film. MU Films, 2010.

Lifton, Betty Jean. *Lost and Found: The Adoption Experience*. New York: Harper and Row, 1988.

———. Lifton, Betty Jean. *Twice Born: Memoirs of an Adopted Daughter*. New York: McGraw-Hill, 1975.

Ling, Huping. *Voices of the Heart: Asian American Women on Immigration, Work, and Family*. Kirksville, MO: Truman State University Press, 2007.

Lionnet, Françoise. *Autobiographical Voices: Race, Gender, Self-Portraiture*. Ithaca, NY: Cornell University Press, 1989.

———. "Of Mangoes and Maroons: Language, History, and the Multicultural Subject of Michelle Cliff's Abeng." In *De/Colonizing the Subject: The Politics of Gender in Women's Autobiography*, edited by Sidonie Smith and Julia Watson. Minneapolis: University of Minnesota Press, 1992, 321–345.

Lind, Dara. "Under Trump, Refugee Admissions Are Falling Way Short—Except for Europeans." *Vox.com*, 17 September 2018. www.vox.com/2018/9/17/17832912/trump-refugee-news-statistics

Lo, Aline. "Fanciful Flights: Reimagining Refugee Narratives of Escape in Kao Kalia Yang's *The Latehomecomer: A Hmong Family Memoir*." *a/b: Auto/Biography Studies* 32, no. 3 (2017): 643–648.

Lorde, Audre. *The Cancer Journals*. Glenwood Springs, CO: Argyle, 1980.

———. 'The Master's Tools Will Never Dismantle the Master's House.' *Sister Outsider: Essays and Speeches*. Berkeley, CA: Crossing Press, 1984, 110–113.

———. *Zami: A New Spelling of My Name*. Berkeley, CA: Crossing Press, 1982.

Lowe, Lisa. *Immigrant Acts: On Asian American Cultural Politics*. Durham, NC: Duke University Press, 1991.

"'Libya Is Full of Cruelty': Stories of Abduction, Sexual Violence and Abuse from Migrants and Refugees." *Amnesty International*, 11 May 2015. www.amnesty.org/en/documents/mde19/1578/2015/en

Lyons, Scott. "Rhetorical Sovereignty: What Do American Indians Want from Writing?" *College Composition and Communication* 51, no. 3 (2000): 447–468.

Mahmoody, Betty. *Not without My Daughter*. New York: St. Martin's Press, 1987.

Malek, Amy. "Memoir as Iranian Exile Cultural Production: A Case Study of Marjane Satrapi's *Persepolis* Series." *Iranian Studies* 39, no. 3 (2006): 352–380.

Martin, Biddy, and Chandra Talpade Mohanty. "Feminist Politics: What's Home Got to Do with It?" In *Feminisms: An Anthology of Literary Theory and Criticism*, edited by Robyn R. Warhol and Diane Price Herndl. New Brunswick, NJ: Rutgers University Press, 1997, 293–310.

Martin, Patricia Preciado. *Songs My Mother Sang to Me: An Oral History of Mexican American Women*. Tucson: University of Arizona Press, 1992.

Martin, Susan Forbes. *Refugee Women*. 2nd ed. Washington, DC: Lexington Books, 2004.

Martin-Montgomery, Anne, et al. "U.S. Adoptees Without Citizenship: National and State-by-State Estimates." *Adoptee Rights Campaign*, March 2018.

Mason, Mary G. "The Other Voice: Autobiographies of Women Writers." *Life/Lines: Theorizing Women's Autobiography*, edited by Bella Brodzki and Celeste Schenck. Ithaca, NY: Cornell University Press, 1988, 19–44.

Mathews, Tayler J., and Glenn S. Johnson. "Skin Complexion in the Twenty-First Century: The Impact of Colorism on African American Women." *Race, Gender & Class* 22, no. 1–2 (2015): 248–274.

Maybin, Janet. "Death Row Penfriends: Some Effects of Letter Writing on Identity and Relationships." In *Letter Writing as a Social Practice*, edited by David Barton and Nigel Hall. Amsterdam: John Benjamins, 2000, 151–178.

McElmurray, Karen Salyer. *Surrendered Child: A Birth Mother's Journey*. Athens: University of Georgia Press, 2004.

McFadden, Cynthia, Sarah Fitzpatrick, Tracy Connor, and Anna Schecter. "Birth Tourism Brings Russian Baby Boom to Miami." *nbcnews*, 9 Jan. 2018. www.nbcnews.com/news/us-news/birth-tourism-brings-russian-baby-boom-miami-n836121

McKee, Kimberly Devon. "Adoption as a Reproductive Justice Issue." *Adoption & Culture* 6, no. 1 (2018): 74–93.

———. *Disrupting Kinship: Transnational Politics of Korean Adoption in the United States*. Champaign-Urbana: University of Illinois Press, 2019.

———. *The Transnational Adoption Industrial Complex: An Analysis of Nation, Citizenship, and the Korean Diaspora*. 2013. Unpublished PhD dissertation, The Ohio State University, Columbus, Ohio.

McKinley, Catherine E. *The Book of Sarahs: A Family in Parts*. Berkeley, CA: Counterpoint, 2002. (Distributed by Penguin Random House)

McLeod, John. "Adoption Studies and Postcolonial Inquiry." *Adoption & Culture* 6, no. 1 (2018): 206–228.

Melosh, Barbara. *Strangers and Kin: The American Way of Adoption*. Cambridge, MA: Harvard University Press, 2002.

Menchú, Rigoberta. *I, Rigoberta Menchú: An Indian Woman in Guatemala*. Translated by Ann Wright. Edited by Elisabeth Burgos-Debray. New York: Verso, 1984.

Milani, Farzaneh. *Veils and Words: The Emerging Voices of Iranian Women Writers*. Syracuse, NY: Syracuse University Press, 1992.

Min, Eun Kyung. "The Daughter's Exchange in Jane Jeong Trenka's *The Language of Blood*." *Social Text* 26, no. 1 (2008): 115–133.

Mintz, Susannah B. *Unruly Bodies: Life Writing by Women with Disabilities*. Chapel Hill: University of North Carolina Press, 2007.

Moaveni, Azadeh. *Lipstick Jihad: A Memoir of Growing up Iranian in America and American in Iran*. New York: PublicAffairs, 2005.

Moghissi, Haideh. *Feminism and Islamic Fundamentalism: The Limits of Postmodern Analysis*. London: Zed Books, 1999.

Mollow, Anna. "'When Black Women Start Going on Prozac': Race, Gender, and Mental Illness in Meri Nana-Ama Danquah's *Willow Weep for Me*." *MELUS* 31, no. 3 (2006): 67–99.

Moorman, Margaret. *Waiting to Forget: A Motherhood Lost and Found*. New York: W. W. Norton & Company, 1996.

Moraga, Cherríe. *Loving in the War Years. Lo que nunca pasó por sus labios*. 1983. Boston: South End Press, 2000.

Moraga, Cherríe, and Gloria Anzaldúa (eds.). *This Bridge Called My Back: Writings by Radical Women of Color*. 2nd ed. Latham, NY: Kitchen Table, Women of Color Press, 1983.

Mortimer, Dolores, and Roy S. Bryce-Laporte. *Female Immigrants to the United States: Caribbean, Latin American, and African Experiences*. Washington, DC: Research Institute on Immigration and Ethnic Studies, Smithsonian Institution, 1981.

Nadell, Pamela S. "Mary Antin." *Jewish Women's Archive*, 27 February 2009. https://jwa.org/encyclopedia/article/antin-mary

Naff, Alixa. *Becoming American: The Early Arab Immigrant Experience*. Carbondale: Southern Illinois University Press, 1993.

Nafisi, Azar. *Things I've Been Silent about: Memories*. New York: Random House, 2008.

——— . *Reading Lolita in Tehran: A Memoir in Books*. New York: Random House, 2003.

Naghibi, Nima. "Revolution, Trauma, and Nostalgia in Diasporic Iranian Women's Autobiographies." *Radical History Review* 105 (2009): 79–91.

——— . *Women Write Iran: Nostalgia and Human Rights from the Diaspora*. Minneapolis: University of Minnesota Press, 2016.

Najafi, Najmeh, with Helen Hinckley. *Persia Is My Heart*. New York: Harper & Brothers, 1953.

Narayan, Uma. "Essence of Culture and a Sense of History: A Feminist Critique of Cultural Essentialism." *Hypatia* 13, no. 2 (1998): 86–106.

Ngai, Mae M. "Transnationalism and the Transformation of the 'Other': Response to the Presidential Address." *American Quarterly* 57, no. 1 (2005): 59–65.

Nguyen, Vinh, Thy Phu, and Y-Dang Troeung. "Refugee Compassion and the Politics of Embodied Storytelling: A Critical Conversation." *a/b: Auto/Biography Studies* 33, no. 2 (2018): 441–445.
Novy, Marianne. *Reading Adoption: Family and Difference in Fiction and Drama.* Ann Arbor: University of Michigan Press, 2005.
"Number of Women and Children Passing through the Former Yugoslav Republic of Macedonia to Seek Refuge in Europe Triples in Three Months." *UNICEF*, 1 Sept. 2015. www.unicef.org/turkey/en/press-releases/number-women-and-children-passing-through-former-yugoslav-republic-macedonia-seek
Ofori-Atta, Angela, et al. "Common Understandings of Women's Mental Illness in Ghana: Results from a Qualitative Study." *International Review of Psychiatry* 22, no. 6 (2010): 589–598.
Ong, Aihwa. *Flexible Citizenship: The Cultural Logics of Transnationality.* Durham, NC: Duke University Press, 1999.
"Over 40 per cent of Syrian Refugee Children in Turkey Missing out on Education, despite Massive Increase in Enrollment Rates." *UNICEF*, 19. January 2017. www.unicef.org/press-releases/over-40-cent-syrian-refugee-children-turkey-missing-out-education-despite-massive
Padilla, Genaro M. *My History, Not Yours: The Formation of Mexican American Autobiography.* Madison: University of Wisconsin Press, 1993.
Park, Heui-Yung. *Korean and Korean American Life Writing in Hawai'i: From the Land of the Morning Calm to Hawai'i Nei.* Washington, DC: Lexington Books, 2015.
Park, Pauline. "Homeward Bound: The Journey of a Transgendered Korean Adoptee." In *Homelands: Women's Journey's across Race, Place, and Time*, edited by Patricia Justine Tumang and Jenesha de Rivera. Emeryville: Seal, 2006, 125–134.
Park Nelson, Kim. *Invisible Asians: Korean American Adoptees, Asian American Experiences, and Racial Exceptionalism.* New Brunswick, NJ: Rutgers University Press, 2015.
Parrs, Alexandra. "The Vulnerable Refugee Woman, from Damascus to Brussels." In *Gender and Migration: A Gender-Sensitive Approach to Migration Dynamics*, edited by Christiane Timmerman, Maria Lucinda Fonseca, Lore Van Praag, and Sónia Pereira. Belgium: Leuven University Press, 2018, 195–215.
Passel, Jeffrey S., D'Vera Cohn, and Ana Gonzalez-Barrera. "Net Migration from Mexico Falls to Zero—and Perhaps Less." *Pew Research.* 23 April 2012. www.pewresearch.org/hispanic/2012/04/23/net-migration-from-mexico-falls-to-zero-and-perhaps-less
Paul, Heike. *Mapping Migration: Women's Writing and the American Immigrant Experience from the 1950s to the 1990s.* Heidelberg: Universitätsverlag C. Winter, 1999.
Pearce, Susan C., Elizabeth J. Clifford, and Reena Tandon. *Immigration and Women: Understanding the American Experience.* New York: New York University Press, 2011.

Pearson, Carmen. "My Name Is Carmen but This Story Is Not Mine. An Introduction to
" 'Searching for Carmen': A Mexican-American Odyssey." In *Ethnic Life Writing and Histories: Genres, Performance, and Culture*, edited by Rocío G. Davis, Jaume Aurell, and Ana Delago. Münster, Germany: Lit. Verlag, 2007.
Pérez, Ramón. *Diary of an Undocumented Immigrant.* Translated by Dick. J. Reavis. Houston, TX: Arte Publico Press, 1991.
Perrault, Jeanne. *Writing Selves: Contemporary Feminist Autography.* Minneapolis: University of Minnesota Press, 1995.
Pessar, Patricia R. "Introduction: Migration Myths and New Realities." *When Borders Don't Divide: Labor Migration and Refugee Movements in the Americas*, edited by Patricia R. Pessar. Washington, DC: Center for Migration Studies, 1988, 1–7.
Pitzer, Andrea. "Trump's 'Migrant Protection Protocols' Hurt the People They're Supposed to Help." *The Washington Post*, 18 July 2019. www.washingtonpost.com/outlook/2019/07/18/trumps-migrant-protection-protocols-hurt-people-theyre-supposed-help
Ponte, Iris Chin, Leslie Kim Wang, and Serena Pen-Shian Fan. "Returning to China: The Experience of Adopted Chinese Children and Their Parents." *Adoption Quarterly* 13, no. 2 (2010): 100–124.
Potochnick, Stephanie R., and Krista M. Perreira. "Depression and Anxiety Among First-Generation Immigrant Latino Youth. Key Correlates and Implications for Future Research." *Journal of Nervous and Mental Disease* 198, no. 7 (2010): 470–477.
"Profile: New Life Children's Refuge." *British Broadcasting Corporation*, 5 February 2010. news.bbc.co.uk/2/hi/americas/8490843.stm
Rachlin, Nahid. *Nahid Rachlin.* www.nahidrachlin.com
———. *Persian Girls: A Memoir.* Los Angeles: Tarcher, 2006.
———. *Veils: Short Stories.* San Fransicso: City Lights, 1992.
Radford, Jynnah. "Key Findings about U.S. Immigrants." *Pew Research Center*, 17 June 2019. www.pewresearch.org/fact-tank/2020/08/20/key-findings-about-u-s-immigrants
Rak, Julie. "Are Memoirs Autobiography? A Consideration of Genre and Public Identity." *Genre* 37, no. 3–4 (2004): 305–326.
———. *Boom! Manufacturing Memoir for the Popular Market.* Waterloo, ON: Wilfrid Laurier University Press, 2013.
Ramos, Blanca M., Bonnie E. Carlson, and Louise-Anne McNutt. "Lifetime Abuse, Mental Health, and African American Women." *Journal of Family Violence* 19, no. 3 (2004): 153–164.
Rees, Matt Beynon. Review of *Persian Girls. A Memoir*, by Nahid Rachlin. "Works." *Nahid Rachlin.* www.nahidrachlin.com/works.htm
Reyes, Kathryn Blackmer, and Julia E. Curry Rodríguez. "Testimonio: Origins, Terms, and Resources." *Equity and Excellence in Education* 45, no. 3 (2012): 525–538.

Robinson, Katy. *A Single Square Picture: A Korean Adoptee's Search for Her Roots.* New York: Berkley Books, 2002.

Rodriguez, Richard. *Hunger of Memory: The Education of Richard Rodriguez.* Boston: D.R. Godine, 1981.

Rogers, Katie, and Nicholas Fandos. "Trump Tells Congresswomen to 'Go Back' to the Countries They Came From." *New York Times,* 14 July 2019. www.nytimes.com/2019/07/14/us/politics/trump-twitter-squad-congress.html

Rosay, Rosalina. *Journey of Hope: Memoirs of a Mexican Girl.* New York: AR Publishing Company, 2007.

Rosenthal, Norman E. *Winter Blues: Seasonal Affective Disorder. What It Is and How to Overcome It.* New York: Guilford Press, 1993.

Rubin, Gayle. "The Traffic in Women: Notes on the 'Political Economy' of Sex." *Toward an Anthropology of Women,* edited by Rayna R. Reiter. New York: Monthly Review Press, 1975, 157–210.

Said, Edward. *Orientalism.* New York: Vintage Books, 1978.

Saldívar-Hull, Sonia. *Feminism on the Border: Chicana Gender Politics and Literature.* Berkeley: University of California Press, 2000.

Samuels, Gina Miranda. "'Being Raised by White People': Navigating Racial Difference among Adopted Multiracial Adults." *Journal of Marriage and Family* 71 (2009): 80–94.

Satrapi, Marjane. *Persepolis: The Story of a Childhood.* New York: Pantheon, 2003.

Saunders, Max. *Self Impression: Life-Writing, Autobiografiction, and the Forms of Modern Literature.* New York: Oxford University Press, 2010.

Saussure, Ferdinand de. *Course in General Linguistics.* Translated by Roy Harris, edited by Charles Bally and Albert Sechehaye, Open Court, 1983. (First published in 1916.)

Schaffer, Kay, and Sidonie Smith. *Human Rights and Narrated Lives: The Ethics of Recognition.* New York: Palgrave, 2004.

Schmitt, Arnaud. "Making the Case for Self-narration against Autofiction." *a/b: Auto/Biography Studies* 25, no. 1 (2010): 122–137.

Seethaler, Ina. "Adoptee Life Writing 2.0: Transnationality and Social Justice Online." *Interactions: Studies in Communication and Culture* 9, no. 2 (2018): 155–168.

———. "Female Refugees in Rural Germany: A Local Aid Agency's Efforts to Build on Women and Children's Experiences and Needs." *Frontiers: A Journal of Women's Studies* 40, no. 2 (2019): 167–192.

———. "A Genre for Justice: Life Writing and Undocumented Immigration in Rosalina Rosay's *Journey of Hope.*" *Life Writing,* 6 July 2015. doi:10.1080/14484528.2015.1053026

Shakespeare, William. *Othello.* Penguin Classics, 2015. (First published in 1622.)

Shakir, Evelyn. *Bint Arab: Arab and Arab American Women in the United States.* Westport, CT: Praeger, 1997.

Shire, Warsan. "Home." *Facinghistory*, 2015. www.facinghistory.org/standing-up-hatred-intolerance/warsan-shire-home
Silliman, Jael, Marlene Gerber Fried, Loretta Ross, and Elena R. Gutiérrez. "Founding the National Black Women's Health Project: A New Concept in Health." *Undivided Rights: Women of Color Organize for Reproductive Justice*, edited by Jael Silliman, Marlene Gerber Fried, Loretta Ross, and Elena R. Gutiérrez. Boston: South End Press, 2004, 63–85.
Singley, Carol J. *Adopting America: Childhood, Kinship, and National Identity in Literature*. Oxford: Oxford University Press, 2011.
Slaughter, Joseph R. *Human Rights, Inc.: The World Novel, Narrative Form, and International Law*. New York: Fordham University Press, 2007.
Smith, Jeanne Rosier. *Writing Tricksters: Mythic Gambols in American Ethnic Literature*. Berkeley: University of California Press, 1997.
Smith, Sidonie. "Narratives and Rights: Zlata's Diary and the Circulation of Stories of Suffering Ethnicity." *WSQ: Women's Studies Quarterly* 34, no. 1–2 (200): 133–152.
———. *A Poetics of Women's Autobiography: Marginality and the Fictions of Self*-Representation. Bloomington: Indiana University Press, 1987.
———. *Subjectivity, Identity, and the Body: Women's Autobiographical Practices in the Twentieth Century*. Bloomington: Indiana University Press, 1993.
Smith, Sidonie, and Julia Watson. "Introduction: De/Colonization and the Politics of Discourse in Women's Autobiographical Practices." In *De/Colonizing the Subject: The Politics of Gender in Women's Autobiography*, edited by Sidonie Smith and Julia Watson. Minneapolis: University of Minnesota Press, 1992, xiii–xxxi.
———. "Introduction: Situating Subjectivity in Women's Autobiographical Practices." In *Women, Autobiography, Theory: A Reader*, edited by Sidonie Smith and Julia Watson. Madison: University of Wisconsin Press, 1998, 3–52.
———. *Reading Autobiography: A Guide of Interpreting Life Narratives*. 2nd ed. Minneapolis: University of Minnesota Press, 2010.
Sommer, Doris. "'Not Just a Personal Story': Women's *Testimonios* and the Plural Self.' In *Life/Lines: Theorizing Women's Autobiography*, edited by Bella Brodzki and Celeste Schenck. Ithaca, NY: Cornell University Press, 1988, 107–130.
SooHoo, Jill Kim. "Home, Adopted." In *Homelands: Women's Journeys across Race, Place, and Time*, edited by Patricia Justine Tumang and Jenesha de Rivera. Emeryville: Seal, 2006, 247–256.
Smolin, David M. "The One Hundred Thousand Dollar Baby: The Ideological Roots of a New American Export." *Cumberland Law Review* 49, no. 1 (2019): 1–54.
Stanley, Liz, Andrea Salter, and Helen Dampier. "The Epistolary Pact, Letterness, and the Schreiner Epistolarium." *a/b: Auto/Biography Studies* 27, no. 2 (2012): 262–293.
Stanton, Domna. *The Female Autograph*. New York: New York Literary Forum, 1984.
Stein, Gertrude. *The Autobiography of Alice B. Toklas*. New York: Harcourt, Brace and Co, 1933.

Steinberg, Gail, and Beth Hall. *Inside Transracial Adoption*. Mulgrave, Victoria, Australia: Perspectives Press, 2000. www.oregon.gov/gov/policy/Documents/LRCD/Meeting2_112315/Data_on_DHS_outcomes/NCJFCJ_Disproportionality.pdf

Summers, Alicia. "Disproportionality Rates for Children of Color in Foster Care." Washington, DC: National Council of Juvenile and Family Court Judges, 2015.

"Survey: Most Americans Believe Protests Make the Country Better; Support Decreases Dramatically among Whites If Protesters Are Identified as Black." *Public Religion Research Institute*, 23 June 2015. www.prri.org/research/survey-americans-believe-protests-make-country-better-support-decreases-dramatically-protesters-identified-black

Timmerman, Christiane, Maria Lucinda Fonseca, Lore Van Praag, and Sónia Pereira (eds.). *Gender and Migration: A Gender-Sensitive Approach to Migration Dynamics*. Belgium: Leuven University Press, 2018.

Torres-Saillant, Silvio. "The Latino Autobiography." In *Latino and Latina Writers, I: Introductory Essays, Chicano and Chicana Authors*, edited by Alan West-Duran, Maria Herrera-Sobek, and Cesar A. Salgado. New York: Scribner's, 2004, 61–79.

Trenka, Jane Jeong. *The Language of Blood: A Memoir*. Minneapolis: Graywolf Press, 2003.

———. *Fugitive Visions: An Adoptee's Return to Korea*. Minneapolis: Graywolf Press, 2009.

———. *Jane's Blog. Bitter Angry Ajumma*. [Currently inactive]

Trenka, Jane Jeong, Julia Chinyere Oparah, and Sun Yung Shin. Introduction. In *Outsiders within: Writing on Transracial Adoption*, edited by Jane Jeong Trenka, Julia Chinyere Oparah, and Sun Yung Shin. Boston: South End Press, 2006, 1–15.

Trotta, Daniel, and Mica Rosenberg. "New Trump Rule Targets Poor and Could Cut Legal Immigration in Half, Advocates Say." *Reuters*, 12 August 2019. www.reuters.com/article/us-usa-immigration-benefits/new-trump-rule-targets-poor-and-could-cut-legal-immigration-in-half-advocates-say-idUSKCN1V219N

Tumang, Patricia Justine, and Jenesha de Rivera (eds.). *Homelands: Women's Journeys across Race, Place, and Time*. Emeryville: Seal, 2006.

Twohey, Megan. "Americans Use the Internet to Abandon Children Adopted from Overseas." *Reuters*, 9 September 2013. www.reuters.com/investigates/adoption/#article/part1

United Nations, Department of Economic and Social Affairs. *Child Adoption: Trends and Policies*. 2009. hwww.un.org/en/development/desa/population/publications/pdf/policy/child-adoption.pdf

———. *International Migration Report 2017: Highlights*. 2017. www.un.org/en/development/desa/population/migration/publications/migrationreport/docs/MigrationReport2017_Highlights.pdf

United Nations, General Assembly. *Convention on the Elimination of All Forms of Discrimination against Women*. 1979. U.N. Women. www.un.org/womenwatch/daw/cedaw/cedaw.htm

———. *Convention on the Protection of the Rights of All Migrant Workers and Members of Their Families.* 1990. Office of the United States High Commissioner for Human Rights. www.ohchr.org/en/professionalinterest/pages/cmw.aspx

———. *Convention on the Rights of the Child.* 1990. Office of the United States High Commissioner for Human Rights. www.ohchr.org/en/professionalinterest/pages/crc.aspx

———. *Universal Declaration of Human Rights.* 10 December 1948, 217 A (III). United Nations. www.un.org/en/universal-declaration-human-rights

United States Citizenship and Immigration Services. "DACA Population Data. August 31, 2018." USCIS.gov.

United States Committee for Refugees and Immigrants. "Statement of the U.S. Committee for Refugees and Immigrants (USCRI) on the Presidential Determination of Refugee Admissions for Fiscal Year 2020." *Reliefweb*, 27 September 2019. https://reliefweb.int/report/united-states-america/statement-us-committee-refugees-and-immigrants-uscri-presidential

United States Department of State's Office of Children's Issues. "Annual Report on Intercountry Adoption." *Bureau of Consular Affairs.* https://travel.state.gov/content/dam/NEWadoptionassets/pdfs/Tab%201%20Annual%20Report%20on%20Intercountry%20Adoptions.pdf

Verrier, Nancy Newton. *The Primal Wound: Understanding the Adopted Child.* Louisville, KY: Gateway Press, 1993.

Viglione, Jill, Lance Hannon, and Robert DeFina. "The Impact of Light Skin on Prison Time for Black Female Offenders." *The Social Science Journal* 48, no. 1 (2011): 250–258.

Volkman, Toby Alice, editor. *Cultures of Transnational Adoption.* Durham, NC: Duke University Press, 2005.

von Welser, Maria. *Kein Schutz—Nirgends: Frauen und Kinder auf der Flucht.* Wiesbaden, Germany: Ludwig Verlag, 2016.

Wallace-Sanders, Kimberly. *Mammy: A Century of Race, Gender, and Southern Memory.* Ann Arbor: University of Michigan Press, 2008.

Wendell, Susan. "Toward a Feminist Theory of Disability." *Hypatia* 4, no. 2 (1989): 104–124.

Whitlock, Gillian. *Postcolonial Life Narratives: Testimonial Transactions.* Oxford: Oxford University Press, 2015.

———. *Soft Weapons: Autobiography in Transit.* Chicago: University of Chicago Press, 2007.

Wills, Jenny. *Aporetic Origins: Narratives of Transnational, Transracial Asian Adoption in a North American Context.* 2013. Unpublished PhD dissertation, Wilfrid Laurier University, Waterloo, Ontario, Canada.

———. "Claiming America by Claiming Others: Asian-American Adoptive Parenthood in *A Gesture Life* and *Digging to America*." *Americana: The Journal of American Popular Culture (1900–present)* 10, no. 1 (2011). americanpopularculture.com/journal/articles/spring_2011/wills.htm

Wilkins, Karin Gwinn. "Middle Eastern Women in Western Eyes: A Study of U.S. Press Photographs of Middle Eastern Women." In *The U.S. Media and the Middle East: Image and Perception*, edited by Yahya R. Kamalipour. Santa Barbara, CA: Greenwood Press, 1995, 50–61.

Winterson, Jeanette. *Why Be Happy When You Could Be Normal?* New York: Grove Press, 2011.

Wong, Sau-Ling Cynthia. "Denationalization Reconsidered: Asian American Cultural Criticism at a Theoretical Crossroads." *Amerasia Journal* 21, no. 1 (1995): 1–27.

———. "Immigrant Autobiography: Some Questions of Definition and Approach." In *American Autobiography: Retrospect and Prospect*, edited by Paul John Eakin. Madison: University of Wisconsin Press, 1992, 142–170.

Woolley, Agnes. *Contemporary Asylum Narratives: Representing Refugees in the Twenty-First Century*. New York: Palgrave, 2014.

Yagoda, Ben. *Memoir: A History*. New York: Riverhead Books, 2009.

Yamamoto, Traise. *Masking Selves, Making Subjects: Japanese American Women, Identity, and the Body*. Berkeley: University of California Press, 1999.

Yang, Philip Q. "A Theory of Asian Immigration to the United States." *Journal of AsianAmerican Studies* 13, no. 1 (2010): 1–34.

Yazbek, Samar. *A Woman in the Crossfire: Diaries of the Syrian Revolution*. Translated by Max Weiss. London: Haus Publishing, 2012.

Yousafzai, Malala. *We Are Displaced: My Journey and Stories from Refugee Girls around the World*. New York: Little, Brown and Company, 2019.

Zhao, Xian, and Monica Biernat. "'Welcome to the U.S.' but 'Change Your Name'? Adopting Anglo Names and Discrimination." *Journal of Experimental Social Psychology* 70 (2017): 59–68.

INDEX

9/11. *See* September 11, 2001

abuse: child, 72, 100, 178n13–14; domestic, 36, 100, 138–139, 181n12; sexual, 60–61, 71, 72
Adichie, Chimamanda Ngozi, 67–68, 175n4
adoptees: assimilation, 95–97, 103, 113–114, 116; birthmother, reunite with, 119, 120–121, 175n2 (chap. 3); commodification of, 31, 89, 97–98, 116, 179n16; country of birth, return to, 97, 120–121, 178n14; culture camps, 96–97; identity formation, 89, 90–91, 92–94, 95–96, 101, 113–115, 121–122; life writing, 19, 30–31, 88, 90, 91, 92, 103–105, 113–114, 121; mental illness and, 88, 96, 99, 112; objectification of, 101, 107–108, 111, 113, 179n22; sexism, 109–110, 116–117; transnational, 30–31, 87, 88, 98–99, 106, 172n15, 176n5; transracial, 31, 89, 91, 92, 101, 108, 114, 115, 178n12; undocumented, 177n10
Adopting America (Singley), 90
adoption: closed, 87–88, 90, 122–123, 180n24; criticism of, 91–92, 110, 123, 177n8–10, 178n11–14; definition of, 172n15; domestic, 73, 88, 110, 176n4; female, gendered as, 87, 116–117; intrafamilial, 130; religion, 78n13, 96, 177n9; reproductive justice, 117–118; rescue narrative, 31, 93, 98–99, 118, 179n17; root causes of, 99–100, 119, 121; transnational, 30–31, 88–89, 92, 99–100, 110, 123, 172n15, 176n7; transracial, 92, 117, 172n15; trauma, 88, 106–107, 112, 115, 120. *See also under* intersectionality; oppression; patriarchy; United States
Adoption Rights Movement, 122–123
adoptive parents. *See* parents, adoptive
African American women: intersectionality, 30, 59, 68; life writing, 76–77; mental illness, 30, 59, 63–64, 66, 67, 81. *See also* Black women
"African Culture and Values" (Idang), 175n4
African immigrants. *See under* immigrant
"A Genre for Justice" (Seethaler), 174n11
Ahmed, Sara, 134, 181n7
al-Abed, Bana, 33, 150, 157–164, 182n7, 183n9
Alcoff, Linda, 22, 77
alien, 12, 27, 59, 62, 174n14

alienation, 72, 106
Alinejad, Masih, 182n14
Amadou (son of Diallo), 82
American: becoming, 16–17, 27, 58, 93, 108–109; culture, 6; Dream, 81, 90; identity, 18, 28, 51, 62, 174n13. *See also* United States
Americanah (Adichie), 67
Analisa (Guatemalan refugee), 153
anchor babies. *See* children, of immigrants
Antin, Mary, 6, 166
Anzaldúa, Gloria, 36, 37, 39, 40, 42, 43, 52
appearance, physical, 40–41, 75, 101, 108–109, 155–156. *See also* colorism
Arab immigrants. *See under* immigrant
Arce, Julissa, 173n3
AR Publishing, 173n4
arranged marriage. *See* marriage: arranged
art: self-expression through, 136–137
Asian Americans, 19, 109. 179n19
Asian immigrants. *See under* immigrant
assault, sexual, 71–72
assimilation: costs of, 6, 75, 103, 113–114; forced, 96, 106–107, 116, 168; goal of immigration, as, 6, 50; immigration, and, 6, 27, 43, 50; life writing, and, 6, 27; Twinkie, 102, 116, 179n19. *See also under* adoptees; men, immigrant; women, immigrant
asylum. *See* institution, mental
audience. *See* readers
Aurell, Jaume, 15–16
autobiographical pact, 113, 136, 141
Autobiographical Voices (Lionnet), 55
autobiographics, 128–129
autobiography: analysis of, 10–11, 13–14; definition, 3, 11, 113; individual, focus on the, 126, 147; male, gendered, 166, 172n7; nontraditional, 2, 4, 7, 10, 12, 13, 57; readers, aimed at Western, 19, 27, 60; role of, 2, 14–15, 17. *See also* genre; life writing
Autobiography and National Identity in the Americas (Hunsacker), 20
autofiction, 181n8
autography, 129
A Woman in the Crossfire (Yazbek), 182n5

Baden, Amanda, 96
Balogun, Odun, 78
Barrio Boy (Galarza), 174n12
Batzke, Ina, 174n14
Beauboeuf-Lafontant, Tamara, 68
Becoming American (Naff), 15
belonging, 17, 18, 20, 21, 27–28, 90, 101, 106
Bergland, Betty A., 172n9
Beverley, John, 43–44, 58, 174n9
Bijan (Pari's son), 137, 141, 142
bildungsroman. *See under* genre
biography, 128, 129, 136, 181n8
biological parents. *See* birthmother; parents, biological
birth country. *See* country, of birth
birth identity. *See under* identity
birthmother, 99–100; child, reunite with, 119, 120–121, 175n2 (chap. 3); intersectionality, 117–119; life writing, 118; oppression, 117, 120, 121, 133–134, 179n23; rights, 121, 142; stigmatization of, 31, 32, 94, 99–100, 117; story of, 122, 144. *See also* parents, biological
"Birth Mothers and Imaginary Lives" (Kendall), 179n17
birth parents. *See* parents, biological
birth tourism. *See under* citizenship
Bishoff, Tonya, 93

Blackness, 59, 61, 65, 67, 68
Black women: depression, 30, 59, 66, 81; expectations, societal, 70–71, 73; health care, access to, 24, 68–69, 72–73. *See also* African American women
Bledsoe, Patricia, 80–81
blog. *See under* social media
Boelhower, William, 14, 27, 172n11
Book of Sarahs, The (McKinley), 114
books, banning of, 131, 135
border: crossing, 46; effects of, 37
Borderlands/La Frontera (Anzaldúa), 36
border wall, 29
Brant, Clare, 148, 149
Brian, Kristi, 91, 95, 99, 100, 123, 178n11
Bryce-Laporte, Roy S., 15, 175n7
Bui, Thi, 182n6
bullying. *See under* children

camps: U.S. detention, 5. *See also under* refugees
capitalism, 10, 12
Caribbean immigrants. *See under* immigrant
Carlson, Bonnie, 72
Carol (Trenka's sister), 97, 106, 107
Carp, Wayne, 176n3
Carter administration, 29
Castillo, Debra, 166
Castles, Stephen, 183n1
Chansky, Ricia Anne, 8, 17
child abuse. *See under* abuse
Child Adoption: Trends and Policies (UN), 176n3
Child Citizenship Act (2000), 177n10
children: bullying, 65–66, 155–156; foster care, 73, 176n5; immigrants, of, 47, 53; life writing, 12, 147–148, 150–151, 157–158, 159, 160, 162; refugees, 151–152, 153, 162, 176n5; trauma, 72, 153, 162. *See also* adoptees
Chinese immigrants. *See under* immigrant
Chu, Tammy, 179n23
citizenship: birth tourism, 47; concept of, 9, 17, 18, 45, 52–53, 130; U.S., obtaining, 4, 53, 93, 174n17
class, socioeconomic, 8, 38, 40
clinical depression. *See* depression
collectivism, cultural, 60–61, 72, 142
colorblindness. *See under* parents, adoptive; racism
colorism, 40, 65, 173n6. *See also* appearance, physical
communal identity. *See under* identity
community: collective narrative, 12, 18, 23, 32, 57, 61, 80, 128
conditions. *See under* refugees
conflation, 19, 109
construct, social. *See* social construct
Contesting Childhood (Douglas), 150
Convention on the Elimination of All Forms of Discrimination against Women (CEDAW), 21, 28
Córdoba, María, 166
country, of birth: leave one's, 2, 53; mental health, impact on, 64–65; return to, 47–48, 67, 97, 120–121, 143, 168, 177n8, 179n16
Couser, G. Thomas, 3, 60, 169
Cubilié, Anne, 22, 25
cultural collectivism. *See* collectivism
cultural divide. *See* divide
cultural relativism. *See* relativism
cultural sentivity. *See* sensitivity
culture: food, 51; loss of, 6, 106–107, 116; traditions, 22, 51
culture camps. *See under* adoptees
Cutter, Martha, 15

Dampier, Helen, 138

Dann, Patty, 125
Danquah, Meri Nana-Ama, 24, 30, 59–86, 118, 172n13, 175n1
Danticat, Edwidge, 165, 166
Dark Girls (Duke and Berry), 173n6
DasGupta, Syantani, 12–13
Daughter of Persia (Farman-Farmaian), 1, 140, 180n3
daughters: relationship with mothers, 39–40, 133–134, 144
Davis, Rocío G., 15–16, 92
Deans, Jill, 94, 103–104
Dear World (al-Abed), 33, 150, 159–160, 162, 164
death threats, 164
Deferred Action for Childhood Arrivals Program (DACA), 5, 29, 53, 174n14–15, 177n10
dehumanization, 22, 68, 74, 111, 148
Delago, Ana, 15–16
Delale-O'Connor, Lori, 96–97
deportation, 29, 52, 53, 176n5, 177n10
depression: Caucasian illness, as a, 63, 65, 67, 71, 78, 83; immigration status, and, 63, 65, 67; postpartum, 72–73; Seasonal Affective Disorder (SAD), 80–81; treatment for, 80–81, 83, 84; writing, and, 77. *See also* African American women; Black women; mental illness
Derr, Amelia, 65
Derrida, Jacques, 135–136
Desdemona, 79
Development, Relief and Education for Alien Minors Act (DREAM), 174n14
Diallo, Kadiatou, 82–83
disability: identity marker, 12; life writing, 60; mental, 30, 70; physical, 69–70, 175n5–6. *See also under* social construct

Distance between Us, The (Grande), 173n3
divide, cultural, 7, 19
domestic abuse. *See under* abuse
domestic violence. *See under* violence
Dossa, Parin, 26, 64, 66, 83, 168
Douglas, Kate, 150
Dumas, Firoozeh, 180n2
Dunant, Henry, 172n10

Eakin, Paul John, 11, 125–126, 172n7
East, the: inferior, as, 127, 132–133; uncivilized, as, 98–99, 107
education, 32, 38, 42, 52, 55, 137, 161, 174n16
embodiment, 12, 13, 104
emotional violence. *See under* violence
epistemic injustice. *See under* injustice
Epistemic Injustice (Fricker), 26
equilibrium model, 167
ethical witnessing. *See* witnessing, ethical
ethnicity, 15; migration experience, 8
Ethnic Life Writing and Histories (Davis, Aurell, and Delago), 15–16
European immigrants. *See under* immigrant
Ezer, Ozlem, 182n5

facial features. *See* appearance, physical
family: domestic violence, 38–39; human rights violations, 29; patriarchy, 39, 42, 100, 133–134; separation, 176n5; trauma, 11, 81, 119. *See also* birthmother; parents, adoptive; parents, biological
Family Matters (Carp), 176n3
Family Protection Act (FPA), 181n13
Farman-Farmaian, Sattareh, 1–2, 140, 180n3
Farmworker's Daughter (Guilbault), 173n3

INDEX

Farrukhzad, Furugh, 140, 141, 142, 181n11
Fatemah (al-Abed's mother), 158, 159–160, 161–162, 163–164
"Fatemeh" (Rachlin), 181n12
female: definition, 171n4
Female Autograph, The (Stanton), 10
Female Immigrants to the United States (Bryce-Laporte and Mortimer), 15, 175n7
"Female Refugees in Rural Germany" (Seethaler), 182n3
fiction. *See also* autofiction; genre
First Person Plural (Liem), 114, 179n23
Fisher, Florence, 104
Flores, René, 56
formation, identity. *See* identity formation
foster care, 73, 176n5. *See also* adoptees; adoption
Foucault, Michel, 143
fragmentation, 93, 105, 139
fragmented identity. *See under* identity
Frank, Anne, 150, 159
Frank, Arthur, 60, 105
Fricker, Miranda, 26, 111–112
From the Other Side (Gabaccia), 6
Frye, Marilyn, 171n2
Fugitive Visions (Trenka), 99, 111, 123, 179n16
Funny in Farsi (Dumas), 180n2

Gabaccia, Donna, 5, 6, 47
Gadalla, Tahany, 65
Gadsby, Meredith, 15
Galarza, Ernesto, 174n12
García, Ana Belén Martínez, 158, 183n9
gender: global human movements, role in, 6, 37; identity marker, 12; immigration experience, 7, 8, 14, 32, 49, 173n5; mental illness, 66, 68–69, 143; oppression, 9, 29–30, 38, 39–40, 100, 117–119, 133–134, 142–143; roles, 20, 36, 38, 41, 120, 130–131, 172n12. *See also under* hierarchy; identity; immigrant; immigrants, undocumented
Gender and Islam (Ahmed), 181n7
Gendered Transitions (Sotelo), 173n5
genderless. *See under* immigrant
Geneva Convention, 23
genre: adoptee, 104–105, 113, 114, 122; autobiographic, 128–129; autography, 129; bildungsroman, 24–25, 49; collective memoir, 16, 32, 57, 125, 126, 128, 136, 142, 144–145; cookbook, 12; crossword puzzle, 114–115; epistolary, 138, 139–140; fairy tale, 32, 105–106; fiction, 24–25, 122, 131, 133, 135–136, 181n8; fragmented, 105; graphic, 145, 182n6; hybrid, 60, 72, 76, 78–79, 105–106, 135, 136; "I," 7, 10, 26, 37, 126; métis, 43, 55; mixing of, 30, 32, 35; neoliberal, 18; oral, 15, 51, 122, 131, 132, 173n2; out-law, 12, 13, 28; play, 32, 106–107; self-help, 76, 78–79; testimonio, 12, 30, 37, 42, 43–45, 48, 57, 58, 174n8, 174n10; trickster text, 30, 35–36, 45–46, 48, 52. *See also* autobiography; biography; life writing
Ghana, 61, 63, 175n4
Gilmore, Leigh, 17, 18, 44–45, 80, 128, 147, 149
Göksun, Yenal, 182n8
Goldin, Farideh, 180n3
Goldman, Anne, 12
Gomes, Ruthie Bonan, 175n5
Grande, Reyna, 173n3
Grewal, Inderpal, 7–8

Guilbault, Rose Castillo, 173n3
Gusdorf, Georges, 11

Hà (child refugee), 150, 151–153, 154, 155–156, 157
Hakakian, Roya, 180n3
Hall, Beth, 95
Haslanger, Sally, 101
health care: barriers to access, 24, 68–69, 72–73
Heinrich, Tobias, 148, 149
hermeneutical injustice. *See under* injustice
hierarchy: gender, 20, 108; patriarchal, 4, 50; power, 22, 90, 99; racial, 55–56, 61, 108, 110, 117, 122, 132, 166; social, 45, 51, 101–102
Hipchen, Emily, 94, 104, 105
history, oral, 15, 122, 131, 132, 173n2, 179n18
Homans, Margaret, 88, 94, 99–100, 105
home: concept of, 19–20, 48, 151, 157
"Home" (Shire), 151
hooks, bell, 20
How Our Lives (Eakin), 11, 125–126, 172n7
Huff, Cynthia, 7, 11, 18
Hugo, Victor, 135
human rights: life writing, effect on, 22, 23, 24; literacy, 24–25; violations, 23, 29, 143, 149, 172n10
Human Rights, Inc. (Slaughter), 24
Human Rights and Narrated Lives (Schaffer and Smith), 23
Hunger of Memory (Rodriguez), 174n12
Hunsacker, Steven, 3, 20
hybridity, 16, 43, 89, 90, 103, 116, 135. *See also under* genre

"I." *See under* genre

Idang, Gabriel E., 175n4
identity: birth, 6, 62, 90, 92, 93, 113–114, 121–122; communal, 11–12, 16, 20–21, 32, 43–44, 128; exile, as, 115; fragmented, 91, 94, 113–114, 129, 138; gender, 16, 128; individual, 13, 27, 42, 74, 113–114; loss of, 6, 27, 62, 93, 94, 99, 106–107, 143; national, 12, 16, 17, 20, 28, 62–63, 74–75, 103–104; transnational, 105, 115–116, 121–122, 135. *See also* American; self
identity formation: factors influencing, 9, 14, 20, 62–63, 114–115, 130. *See also under* adoptees
identity markers, 6, 8, 12, 16, 26, 40, 59
Ifemelu, 67, 68
"illegal" immigrant. *See under* immigrant
images, use of, 53–54, 160, 163, 180n4, 182n6
immigrant: African, 30, 61, 62, 82–83, 175n2; Arab, 15; Asian, 15, 16; Caribbean, 15; Chinese, 14, 47; definition, 171n1; European, 6, 20, 48, 165; genderless, as, 6, 12–13; "illegal," 36, 46, 50, 51, 54, 56; Iranian, 32, 126; Latin American, 35, 37, 42–43; Mexican, 14, 29, 35–58, 173n1, 173n3, 173n5
Immigrant Autobiography in the United States (Boelhower), 14
immigrant men. *See* men, immigrant
immigrants, undocumented: adoptees, 177n10; children of, 47, 53; gender, and, 38–42; life writing, 35, 37, 43, 44, 50, 58; refugees, economic, 30, 54; response to, 29, 43, 46–47, 51–52, 55–56

immigrant women. *See* women, immigrant
immigration: male phenomenon, as a, 25–26, 172n12; patterns, 9, 61; reasons for, 7, 17, 30, 32, 36, 53, 54, 82, 168; right to, 2; risks of, 6, 151, 152–153; theories, 167; two-worldliness, 1, 15, 62–63, 91–92, 102–103; view of, Americans', 46–47, 167, 174n13. *See also under* intersectionality
Immigration Act (1965), 172n14
Immigration and Nationality Act, 4
imperialism, 12, 123, 135
injustice: epistemic, 26, 50, 111–112; hermeneutical, 26
Inside Out and Back Again (Lai), 33, 149, 150–151, 155, 156, 157, 161
Inside Transracial Adoption (Steinberg and Hall), 95
institution, mental, 64, 143
integration, 15, 156, 157, 159, 168
International Red Cross, 172n10
intersectionality: adoption, 88, 91, 94, 101, 107, 109–110; immigration, 36, 38, 44, 169; life writing, 2, 27, 44, 169; motherhood, 73–74, 117–118. *See also under* African American women; birthmother; mental illness; women, immigrant
In the Matter of Cha Jung Hee (Liem), 179n23
invisibility, social, 6, 30, 109–110
Invisible Asians (Park Nelson), 179n18
Iran: culture, 126, 127, 129; history, 131–132; religion, 134; women, 32, 130–131, 132, 133, 141–142. *See also* Persia
Iranian-American women: life writing, 126, 127, 128, 180n2-3
Iranian immigrants. *See under* immigrant

Islam, 127, 134, 181n7
Islamic regime: challenge to, by women, 145–146; rights, of women, 132, 133, 140, 141, 143, 181n13
Islamic Revolution, 32, 126, 127, 133, 180n3
I Wish for You a Beautiful Life (Dorow), 179n23

Jade (friend of Danquah), 81–82
Jane's Blog. Bitter Angry Ajumma (Trenka), 90, 91
Jelinek, Estelle, 10
Jerng, Mark, 104–105
Johnson, Glenn S., 173n6
Jolly, Margaretta, 139
Jones, Maggie, 177n8
Journey from the Land of No (Hakakian), 180n3
Journey of Hope (Rosay): immigrants, undocumented, 35, 36, 52, 55; intersectionality, 38, 40; reviews of, 57, 174n18; testimonio, 30, 35–36, 43–45, 50, 57; trickster text, 48, 54
justice, reproductive, 117–118
justice, social. *See under* social

Kaplan, Caren, 7–8, 12
Karpinski, Eva, 2, 8, 26, 172n9
Kein Schutz, Nirgends: Frauen und Kinder auf der Flucht (Welser), 152
Kendall, Laurel, 179n17
Keshavarz, Fatemeh, 133
Kim, Eleana, 179n16
Kingston, Maxine Hong, 106, 181n8
Korea. *See* South Korea
Kruger, Sasha, 12–13
Krupat, Arnold, 11
Kurdi, Alan, 151, 163
Kurz, Katja, 22

INDEX

Lackey, Michael, 181n8
Lahlum, Lori Ann, 172n9
Lai, Thanhha, 33, 149–150, 152–154, 156, 157
language: barrier, 36, 106, 153, 155–156
Language of Blood, The (Trenka): adoption, criticism of, 91, 92, 107; identity, self, 1, 31–32, 113, 115, 121; life writing, adoptee, 30, 87, 89, 90, 98, 122; violence, 175n2
Larson, Thomas, 22–23
Latin American immigrants. *See under* immigrant
laws: immigration, U.S., 4–5, 154; life writing, impact on, 2, 23, 24, 166–167, 168
Lechner, Elsa, 2, 164
Lejeune, Philippe, 113, 136
letters. *see* genre: epistolary
"Libya Is Full of Cruelty" (UN), 182n1
Liem, Deann Borshay, 114, 179n23
life narrative: children, 147, 150, 159, 163; collective identity, 16, 139; female, gendered as, 8, 10, 13; forms of, 32–33, 149, 161, 171n3; response to, ethical, 21, 23, 147
life writing: analysis of, 10–13; criticism of, 10, 18, 57–58, 127, 133, 135–136, 167; definition of, 2–3, 171n3; relational, as, 11, 125–126, 172n7; social justice, and, 21–25, 28, 42, 50, 76, 82, 117, 134–135; theories on, 11, 13–17; tool for change, as a, 1, 2, 13, 14, 23, 25, 37, 45. *See also* genre; individual groups
Lifton, Betty Jean, 88, 97, 105, 180n24
Ling, Huping, 15
Lionnet, Françoise, 55, 181n8

Lipstick Jihad (Moaveni), 130, 180n2
Lo, Aline, 147
Lost and Found (Lifton), 88, 97, 180n24
Lost and Found in Translation (Cutter), 15
Loving in the War Years (Moraga), 39

Madness and Civilization (Foucault), 143
Malek, Amy, 145
Malinche, 41
Mapping Migration (Paul), 15
Maria (Guatemalan refugee), 157
markers, identity. *See* identity markers
marriage: arranged, 32, 125, 138, 141–142, 144
Martin, Patricia, 173n2
Maryam (Rachlin's foster mother), 130, 131, 144
Mason, Mary, 11, 136
Mathews, Tayler J., 173n6
Maybin, Janet, 139
McKee, Kimberly, 31, 89, 116, 117, 120, 177n10
McKinley, Catherine, 114
McLeod, John, 89
McNutt, Louise-Anne, 72
media, social: blogs, 158, 176n7, 182n8 (chap. 5), 182n14 (chap. 4); life writing, 149, 150, 161; Twitter, 33, 157–159, 163, 164, 183n9
Melosh, Barbara, 88, 89
memoir: appeal of, 18, 21; criticism of, 10, 18, 26; definition of, 3, 17; tool, political, 3, 13, 23, 27–29. *See also* autobiography; genre; life writing
Memory of Solferino, A (Dunant), 23, 172n10
men, immigrant: assimilation, 16; life writing, 6, 49, 52, 172n7; portrayal of, 6; statistics, 171n5

INDEX 215

Menchú, Rigoberta, 44, 174n10
mental hospital. *See* institution, mental
mental illness: factors contributing to, 64, 65, 66, 72, 81, 88; intersectionality, 30, 60–61, 63–64, 69, 70, 79, 80–81; men, and, 70; racism and, 63–64, 65, 67–68, 74, 78, 81, 83; stigma, 30, 59, 63, 70–71, 78; treatment, barriers to, 65, 67, 68–69, 72–73, 80–81, 83; writing, and, 77; xenophobia and, 63, 64–65, 81. *See also under* adoptees
métis. *See under* genre
Mexican immigrants. *See under* immigrant
Mexico: culture, 51. *See also under* United States
Middle East: life writing, lack of, 149
migrant men. *See* men, immigrant
migrants, undocumented. *See* immigrants, undocumented
migrant women. *See* women, immigrant
migration: patterns, 9, 37, 61, 183n1; reasons for, 26, 30, 36, 167, 168; right to, 2; theories, 61, 167. *See also* immigration
Milani, Farzaneh, 129
Miller, Mark, 183n1
Min, Eun Kyung, 98
Mintz, Susannah, 69–70
Misérables, Les (Hugo), 135
Moaveni, Azadeh, 130, 180n2
models, migration, 167
Mohammed, Prophet, 2
Mohtaram (Rachlin's mother), 130, 136–137, 144
Mollow, Anna, 63–64, 172n13
monarch butterfly, 1
Moraga, Cherríe, 39, 40
Mortimer, Dolores, 15, 175n7

mother: depression, 72–73; relationship with daughters, 39–40, 133–134, 144. *See also* birthmother; parents, adoptive; parents, biological
motherhood: perceptions of, 74, 120
Muslim men, 134
Muslim travel ban, 32, 125, 155
Muslim women, 132–133, 145
My Heart Will Cross This Ocean: My story, My Son, Amadou (Diallo), 82
mysogeny, 38, 99–100, 130–135, 141–142, 144, 181n12
"My Stealthy Freedom" (Alinejad), 182n14

Naff, Alixa, 15
Nafisi, Azar, 127, 133, 145, 180n2, 181n12
Naghibi, Nima, 127
Najafi, Najmeh, 180n3
name: choosing one's, 75–76, 94; losing one's, 93, 94
Narayan, Uma, 22
Narrating Contested Lives (Kurz), 22
narrative, life. *See* life narrative
nation: definition of, 3
national identity. *See under* identity
nationality: concept of, 45, 50; life writing, and, 17–21, 28; migration experience, 8
native country. *See* country, of birth
Nepantla, 43
"New Dialogues in Feminist Disability Studies" (Gomes et al.), 175n5
Nguyen, Vinh, 148, 150
Nigeria, 67, 175n2, 175n4
Novy, Marianne, 179n20

Obama administration, 29
objectification, 111, 112–113. *See also under* adoptees

"Of Mangoes and Maroons" (Lionnet), 181n8
oppression: adoption, 91, 100, 117; counter histories of, 21–22; definition, 171n2; internalization of, 39, 41, 60, 74, 101, 108, 133–134; multilayered, 1, 9, 10, 22, 39. *See also under* birthmother; gender; patriarchy; race
oral history. *See* history, oral
Orientalism, 98–99, 101, 109–110, 111, 117, 130, 132, 145
Orientalism (Said), 99
Other: adoptees as, 101, 103, 104, 108, 111, 116; immigrants as, 3, 17, 24, 41, 75, 78; proximate, 125–126; refugees as, 147, 148, 155
othering, 13, 22, 69–70, 101
Outsiders within: Writing on Transracial Adoption (Trenka, Oparah, and Shin), 92

pact, autobiographical. *See* autobiographical pact
Padila, Genaro, 46, 51
parents, adoptive: colorblindness, 101–102; education, about adoptees, 96, 97, 178n12; ignorance, 106, 120; oppression, of adoptees, 94, 95, 97–98, 100–101, 106–107, 120, 177n9; racism, 107, 108, 110
parents, biological: adoption, and, 88, 97, 100, 116–117; children, protecting, 151, 152, 154, 156, 161, 162; loss of, 93–94
Pari (Rachlin's sister), 128, 136, 137–141, 142, 143
Park, Pauline, 101
Park Nelson, Kim, 102, 116, 121, 179n18
patriarchy: adoption, 94, 100, 113, 119; oppression, 12, 13, 20, 119, 133–134, 139, 144; religion, 41, 123, 126; rights, of women, 28–29, 70, 130–131, 132–134, 140–141, 142, 143, 181n12; violence, against women, 38–39, 138, 164, 181n12. *See also under* hierarchy
Paul, Heike, 14, 15
Pearson, Carmen, 165
Perrault, Jeanne, 129
Perreira, Krista, 65
Persepolis (Satrapi), 145
Persia, 129–130
Persia Is My Heart (Najafi), 180n3
Persian Girls: A Memoir (Rachlin): adoption, 130; collective memoir, 28, 32, 125, 128–129, 136, 143; epistolary, 140; oppression, gender, 134–135; reviews of, 125, 127
personal name. *See* name
Pessar, Patricia, 165, 171n6
Philomela, 136–137, 181n9
photos, use of. *See* images, use of
physical appearance, 40–41
physical violence, 111, 112, 138
pictures, use of. *See* images, use of
place of birth. *See* country, of birth
Poetics of Women's Autobiography, A (Smith), 10
political: life writing as, 13, 24, 26, 28, 57, 132–133, 154, 172n8; transnational adoption as, 89, 90
postpartum depression. *See under* depression
post-traumatic stress disorder (PTSD), 88, 112, 162
Potochnick, Stephanie, 65
poverty: gender, and, 38, 118–119; immigration, and, 43, 46, 48, 53
power: lack of, 25–26, 118–119, 133–134; political, 9, 19; symbolic, 9; white system of, 40, 94–95. *See also under* hierarchy

Procne, 136, 181n9
Promised Land, The (Antin), 6, 166

race: identity marker, 12; migration experience, 8, 14; oppression, 9, 44, 61, 68; social construct, 61, 101–102, 122
Rachlin, Nahid, 28, 32, 125–146, 180n1
racial hierarchy. *See under* hierarchy
racialization, 67, 101, 102–103, 175n4
racism: colorblindness, 101–102; effects of, 73, 74, 107; experiences of, 55–56, 82–83, 106–107, 108, 155–156. *See also under* mental illness
Rak, Julie, 17, 18, 27–28
Ramos, Blanca, 72
rape. *See* assault, sexual
readers: appeal to, 21, 46, 48–49, 50–55, 127–128, 159–160, 166, 180n4; ethical, 22, 23, 127; life writing effect on, 4, 23, 37, 154, 156; perceptions of the, 19, 25, 26, 28, 44–45, 57; witnesses, as, 82, 107–108, 112, 151, 169
reading: healing aspect of, 76, 77, 135
Reading Adoption (Novy), 179n20
Reading Autobiography (Smith and Watson), 14
Reading Lolita in Tehran (Nafisi), 127, 133, 145, 180n2, 181n12
Rees, Matt, 125, 127
Refugee Relief Act (1953), 172n14
refugees: camps, 5, 153, 154; children, 151–152, 153, 162, 176n5; conditions faced by, 152–153, 158, 160–161, 162–163; global, 33; life writing, 33, 147, 149, 150; men, 148–149; mental illness, 153, 162; qualifications, not recognized, 156; sponsors, 154, 155; stories about, 148; Syrian, 33, 56, 150, 153, 158, 161, 163, 182n5; Trump administration, 4–5, 164, 182n2; Vietnamese, 33, 150, 151, 157; women, 147, 148, 152, 156–157. *See also under* immigrants, undocumented; Other; stereotypes; United States
relational self. *See under* self
relativism, cultural, 22, 63, 83, 101, 107
religion, 8, 41, 54, 96, 134, 154
reproductive justice, 117–118. *See* justice, reproductive
rescue narrative. *See under* adoption
Resilience (Chu), 179n23
Reyes, Kathryn Blackmer, 174n8
"rhetorical sovereignty," 91
rights: children's, 98; religious, 154; women's, 21, 28–29, 117–118, 132, 133, 143. *See also* human rights
Robinson, Katy, 120–121
Rodríguez, Julia E. Curry, 174n8
Rodriguez, Richard, 174n12
roles, gender. *See under* gender
Roosevelt, Theodore, 166
Rosay, Rosalina, 14, 29, 30, 35–58, 130, 173n4, 174n17
Rubin, Gayle, 98, 100

Sa'adi, 1–2
Sabreen (Yemeni refugee), 153
Said, Edward, 99
Saldívar-Hull, Sonia, 36, 41
Salter, Andrea, 138
Samuels, Gina, 102
sanitorium. *See* institution, mental
Satrapi, Marjane, 145
Saunders, Max, 181n8
Saussure, Ferdinand de, 114–115
Savelyev, Artyom, 178n14
Scattered Hegemonies (Grewal and Kaplan), 7–8

Schachter, Ariela, 56
Schaffer, Kay, 2–3, 23, 25
Search for Anna Fisher, The (Fisher), 104
Seasonal Affective Disorder (SAD). *See under* depression
Seethaler, Ina, 8, 174n11, 182n3
self: communal, 10–11, 12, 21, 23; double, 32, 91, 94, 106, 114, 125, 137, 139, 140, 143; relational, 1, 10–13, 20–21, 23, 104, 125–126; sense of, 3, 27, 30–31, 74–75, 103, 113–114; transnational, 1, 2, 3, 17, 115–116, 121. *See also* identity
Self Impression (Saunders), 181n8
semiotic systems, 114–115
sensitivity, cultural, 65, 83
September 11, 2001, 18, 126–127
sexism, 22, 38–39, 42
sexual abuse. *See under* abuse
sexual assault. *See* assault, sexual
Shah, 131–133, 135, 180n3, 181n13
Shakir, Evelyn, 132
Shire, Warsan, 151, 154
silenced. *See under* voices
Single Parent Family Support Act, 89
Single Square Picture, A (Robinson), 120–121
Singley, Carol J., 90
skin tone. *See* appearance, physical
Slaughter, Joseph, 24–25
Smith, Jeanne, 45
Smith, Sidonie, 2–3, 10, 12, 14, 23, 25, 37, 90, 150
Smolin, David, 178n13
social: justice, 2–4, 21–25, 42, 135; perceptions, 2; status, 40. *See also* invisibility, social
social construct: culture, 122; disability, 69–70, 76; documenation status, 56; race, 61, 101–102, 122
social hierarchy. *See under* hierarchy
social justice. *See under* social
social media. *See* media, social
social network theory, 167
Soeting, Monica, 148, 149
Soft Weapons (Whitlock), 147
Soleimani, Mrs. (Rachlin's teacher), 132, 133
Songs my Mother Sang to Me (Martin), 173n2
SooHoo, Jill Kim, 102–103
Sotelo, Pierrette Hondagneu, 173n5
South Korea: adoption, 31, 88–89, 99, 120–121, 176n7; birthmothers, 92, 94, 118–119; terminology, 175n1 (chap. 3)
sponsors. *See under* refugees
Stanley, Liz, 138, 139
Stanton, Domna, 10
Steinberg, Gail, 95
stereotypes: African, 64–65, 66–67, 68; Asian, 15, 99, 107, 109, 111, 113, 179n22; Black woman, 68, 70–71, 73, 74, 79; disabilities, women with, 73; immigrants, 5, 20, 45, 46, 56, 66, 168; Iranian, 32, 129–130, 132, 145; Latin American, 42, 43, 47, 56; mental illness, 63, 73, 78–79, 80, 81; Mexican, 55–56; Middle Eastern, 145; Muslim women, 132–133; refugees, 148, 153–154, 155, 162; Syrian, 56, 160; women, 15, 42, 47, 71
storytelling, 131. *See also* history, oral
Strangers and Kin (Melosh), 88
strength, of women. *See under* women
structuralism, 114–115
style, writing. *See* genre
Subjectivity, Identity, and the Body (Smith), 12, 37, 90
Sucking Salt (Gadsby), 15
suicide, 67, 139, 142–143, 179n16
survivor discourse, 77

survivors: abuse, 71, 72; trauma, 60
Syria, 158, 160, 162–163
Syrian refugees. *See under* refugees
Syrian Women Refugees (Ezer), 182n5
systems, semiotic, 114–115

Taheri (Pari's husband), 138, 141, 142
tainted witness. *See* witness, tainted
Tainted Witness (Gilmore), 18, 44–45, 80, 149
Take My Word (Goldman), 12
Tereus, 181n9
testimonio. *See under* genre
"*Testimonio:* Origins, Terms, and Resources" (Reyes and Rodríguez), 174n8
The Age of Migration (Castles and Miller), 183n1
The Best We Could Do (Bui), 182n6
threats, death, 164
Tradition of Women's Autobiography, The (Jelinek), 10
traditions: cultural, 22, 63
transnational: analysis, of life writing, 7–8; meaning of, 3
transnational adoption. *See under* adoptees; adoption
transnational adoption industrial complex (TAIC), 31, 89, 90
transnational identity. *See under* identity
transnationalism, 123
transnational self. *See under* self
transracial adoption. *See under* adoptees; adoption
trauma: children, 72, 153, 162; family, 11, 81, 119; mental illness, and, 112; refugees, 152, 153. *See also under* adoption
Trenka, Jane Jeong, 19, 30–31, 32, 87–124, 175n2 (chap. 3), 176n7, 177n8, 177n10, 179n16
trickster text. *See under* genre

Trump, Donald, 2, 56
Trump administration: adoptees, 177n10; border wall, 29; immigrant rights, multilayered attack on, 4–5, 166, 174n15; immigration policies, 53, 55–56, 57; "Muslim travel ban," 32, 125, 155; refugees, 164, 182n2
truth, 92, 105, 122
Truth and Reconciliation for the Adoption Community of Korea (TRACK), 118
Twice Born: Memoirs of an Adopted Daughter (Lifton), 105
Twinkie, 102, 116, 179n19
Twitter. *See* social media
two-worldliness. *See under* immigration

Umma (Trenka's mother), 100, 118–119, 122
Underground American Dream, My (Arce), 173n3
undocumented immigrants. *See* immigrants, undocumented
Undocumented Migrants in the United States (Batzke), 174n14
United Nations International Migration Report, 5
United States: adoption, 31, 88–89, 96–97, 100–101, 123, 176n3, 176n5, 178n14; deportation, 53, 177n10; destination, for migrants, 3; immigration policies, 3, 47, 166; impact of immigrant women on, 15, 172n8; Iran, and, 32; Mexico, and, 5, 29, 43, 45, 51–52, 54, 56, 173n1, 176n5; myth, the, 14, 45, 46, 104; refugees, 54, 56, 148, 153, 155, 164, 176n5; statistics, immigration, 4–5, 30–31, 32, 61, 175n2. *See also* American
Universal Declaration of Human Rights (UN), 28, 50

Unruly Bodies (Mintz), 69–70

Vélez, Julia Yslas, 173n2
victimization: life writing and, 23
victims: adoptees as, 94; refugees as, 148, 159; women as, 13, 24, 40, 64, 133, 145, 156
Vietnam, 157
Vietnamese refugees. *See under* refugees
violence: domestic, 36, 38–39, 119, 138, 181n12; emotional, 110, 111, 138; physical, 72, 111, 112, 138, 156, 182n1
voices: adoptees, 31, 89, 92, 97, 101; birthmothers, 32, 92, 117, 121; immigrant women, 13, 15, 20, 22–23, 43. 50, 62, 127; silenced, 28, 37, 92, 101, 126, 136–137, 138, 148, 165
Voices of the Heart (Ling), 15
von Welser, Maria, 152
vote, right to, 132

wall. *See* border wall
Watson, Julia, 3, 10, 14
We Are Displaced (Yousafzai), 153, 182n4
Wedding Song (Goldin), 180n3
wellness, 66
Wendell, Susan, 70
West, the: civilized, as, 98–99; immigrants, view of, 17, 19, 146; superior, as, 127, 132–133
West African Guinea, 82
When Borders Don't Divide (Pessar), 165, 171n6
whiteness, 40, 77–78, 102, 110, 166
white privilege, 87, 94–95, 107, 117, 178n11
Whitlock, Gillian, 2, 3, 13–14, 19, 21, 44, 147

Why Be Happy When You Can Be Normal? (Winterson), 105
willow tree, 79, 80
Willow Weep for Me (Danquah): dehumanization, 74, 76; depression, 30, 59, 65, 70, 77, 80, 84, 172n13; genre, 30, 60, 76, 78–79; intersectionality, 63; social invisibility, 30, 62, 72
"Willow Weep for Me" (Holiday), 79
"Wind-up Doll, A" (Farrukhzad), 140
Winterson, Jeanette, 105
witness, tainted, 44–45, 80
witnessing, ethical, 21, 22, 44, 107
Woman Warrior, The (Kingston), 106
women: -centered writing, 26, 28; life writing, 10–13; rights of, 21, 22, 28–29, 117, 130–131, 133; social invisibility, 30; strength of, 24, 42, 68, 70, 119–120, 126, 144. *See also under* stereotypes
women, immigrant: assimilation, 16–17; impact on United States, 15, 172n8; intersectionality, 8, 26, 27, 50, 136, 144, 169; life writing, 2, 3, 7, 20, 49, 51, 167–168; mental health, 63, 64; portrayal of, 3, 5, 6, 20; power, lack of, 25–26, 27, 39, 141; risks, immigration, 6, 182n1; statistics, immigration, 5, 171n5. *See also under* stereotypes
Wong, Sau-Ling Cynthia, 14
Woolley, Agnes, 148, 149
Wounded Storyteller, The (Frank), 60, 105
writing: healing aspect of, 76–77, 166; life (*see* life writing); power of, 131, 135; style (*see* genre)

xenophobia: Blackness, and, 61, 62; experiences of, 47, 55–56, 65–66,

107, 108, 154–155; life writing and, 46. *See also under* mental illness

Yamamoto, Traise, 16, 20

Yang, Philip, 167
Yazbek, Samar, 182n5
Yousafzai, Malala, 149, 158, 161, 182n4

www.ingramcontent.com/pod-product-compliance
Lightning Source LLC
Chambersburg PA
CBHW030649230426
43665CB00011B/1021